282541

CHIPPERFIELD'S CIRCUS
An Illustrated History

By David Jamieson • Foreword by Dicky Chipperfield

AARDVARK PUBLISHING

CHIPPERFIELD'S CIRCUS
An Illustrated History
By David Jamieson • Foreword by Dicky Chipperfield

DEDICATION
In memory of Dick, Jimmy, Marjorie and John Chipperfield

Also by David Jamieson
Mary Chipperfield's Circus Book (Jarrold, 1979 and 1989)
The Love of the Circus (with Sandy Davidson) (Octopus UK, 1980)
The Colorful World of the Circus (with Sandy Davidson) (Octopus USA, 1980)
La Passion du Cirque (with Sandy Davidson) (Gründ, 1980)
Introducing the Circus (Aardvark, 1981 and 1990)

Acknowledgements
Many of the illustrations in this book are from the personal collections of Dicky Chipperfield, James Clubb, Anne Tunnicliffe, Mary and Roger Cawley, Jimmy Stockley, the Archives of the Circus Friends' Association of Great Britain, Sally Clubb, Rosie Chipperfield and her sister Grace, Carol Coates, Maryann Shapter, Wynne Shearme, Elaine Yelding, Ivor Rosaire, Karl Kossmayer, Alfie Gunner, Yuri Gridneff, Sandy Davidson, David Harris, Alan Southwood, the late Eric Nugus, Hal Fisher, Ken Wise, Derrick Londrigan, Richard McMinn, John Exton, George Testo, Nick Barnett, Carl Moore, Malcolm Slater and Corgi Classics.
Other illustrations are from the author's own collection.

The photographs on pages 35 (centre), 175 and 182 are from the George Tucker Collection in the National Fairground Archive at the University of Sheffield and are reproduced with their permission.

We are grateful to Ringling Brothers Circus for the photos on pages 146 and 147 (above, left)

The author and publisher would like to thank everyone who provided memories, photographs and other material for this book - see the Postscript on page 184.

Page 2. Top: huge crowds greeted Chipperfield's Sunday parades in the early 1950s. Below: aerial view of the circus in 1952. Page 3. Top: Chipperfield's Circus in 1951. Below: part of the elephant herd in the late 1940s. Contents page: Chipperfield's elephant parade in Dundalk, Ireland. Page 192. Top row: in the early 1960s - Harry the hippo with Dicky Chipperfield at the farm; Hubert plus a llama, with ringmaster Dennis Rosaire on the right. 2nd row: Land's End, 1961; clowns' pantechnicon. 3rd row: Carl Moore's model of Chipperfield's Circus in 1953.

© David Jamieson 1997
The right of David Jamieson to be identified as the Author of the Work has been asserted by him in accordance with the Copyright, Designs and Patent Act 1988.

All rights reserved. No part of this book may be reproduced, stored or transmitted in any form or by any means, electronic, mechanical, photocopying, recording or otherwise without the prior written permission of the publishers.

First published 1997 by Aardvark Publishing

LIMITED EDITIONS

Aardvark edition	Corgi Autograph edition
ISBN 1 872904 09 2	ISBN 1 872904 10 6
1st printing of 2000 copies	Printing of 1000 copies

AARDVARK PUBLISHING
Fir Tree Cottage, Little Hormead, Buntingford, Herts. SG9 0LU.

Printed in Great Britain by Ebenezer Baylis and Son Ltd., Worcester.

Contents

	Foreword by Dicky Chipperfield	page 7
	A Chipperfield Family Tree	page 8
Chapter 1	Charles II to Queen Victoria	page 10
Chapter 2	The Early Years of the Twentieth Century	page 15
Chapter 3	The 1930s and War Years	page 23
Chapter 4	1946 and after	page 41
Chapter 5	The Big Show	page 68
Chapter 6	1956-1964	page 82
Chapter 7	On tour in South Africa	page 101
Chapter 8	Back to Britain and into the 1970s	page 110
Chapter 9	Hong Kong to New Zealand - World Tours in the 1980s	page 128
Chapter 10	In the 1990s	page 140
Chapter 11	The Rising Young Stars... of Ringlings & Europe's finest circuses	page 144
Appendix 1	Chipperfield Collectables - Books, Programmes, Videos, Posters - Chipperfield Corgi Models	page 150 page 170
Appendix 2	Chipperfield Transport	page 176
Appendix 3	The Build Up	page 180
Appendix 4	Chipperfield Showfronts	page 182
Appendix 5	Carl Moore's Chipperfield Model	page 183
Postscript		page 184
Index		page 187

Foreword

The history of the Chipperfields is a long and intriguing saga of success and failure, of hard work mixed with euphoria and tragedy, in our endeavours to provide exciting popular entertainment.

Our family stories tell of our ancestors coming over the Pyrenees and roasting an ox on the frozen River Thames during the Great Frost in the days of Charles II. A William Chipperfield is said to have attended street fairs in the West Country during the eighteenth century.

James William Chipperfield (1824-1913) was an enterprising showman who promoted exhibitions such as "The Living Skeleton" and "The Vanishing Lady." His circus was seen by Queen Victoria and Prince Albert at Buckingham Palace, with his daughter, Sophia, as "The Child of Promise" on the tightrope.

His son, James William Francis Chipperfield, toured Britain with his own shows and his nine children, and boasted of being able to train any animal from a rabbit to an elephant. One of his sons, Richard, born in 1875, was my grandfather. He, too, set up on his own with his wife and family, with a bioscope cinema and a small circus.

With Richard's family circus joining forces with Purchase's Menagerie, the outfit began to grow in the 1930s, and my father, Dick, and his brothers Jimmy and John and sister Marjorie, were able to take advantage of the post-war boom for live entertainment. Their drive and ambition made Chipperfield's Circus the largest in Europe and a household name.

The day that I was born, a tigress gave birth to a litter of cubs. As Clem Merk, the lion trainer, said, "Well, that's his future sorted out," and I have indeed followed in my father's footsteps by working with wild animals. My parents kept to family tradition too by calling me Richard. If they'd listened to Clem Merk, to encourage me to train lions, I'd have been called Lionel!

With its people and the animals, the circus forms a unique community in many ways. In any one season, our own family was joined by artistes from Germany, France, Spain, Italy and Hungary, as well as the staff of men and women who worked on publicity, administration, maintenance, transport and looking after the collection of animals.

I am delighted that the shows, the people and the animals of Chipperfield's Circus, and the logistical and technical side, our big tops and transport fleets, have been recorded in this Illustrated History. Reading the text and looking through the photographs and posters has brought back the memories and reminded us of many incidents which had almost been forgotten.

I hope that our loyal circus audiences around the world, and the growing number of collectors of Chipperfield memorabilia, from posters and programmes to Corgi models, will find it equally fascinating.

Dicky Chipperfield

Opposite page: *press advertisements herald the excitement of Chipperfield's Circus in 1953.*

A Chipperfield Family Tree

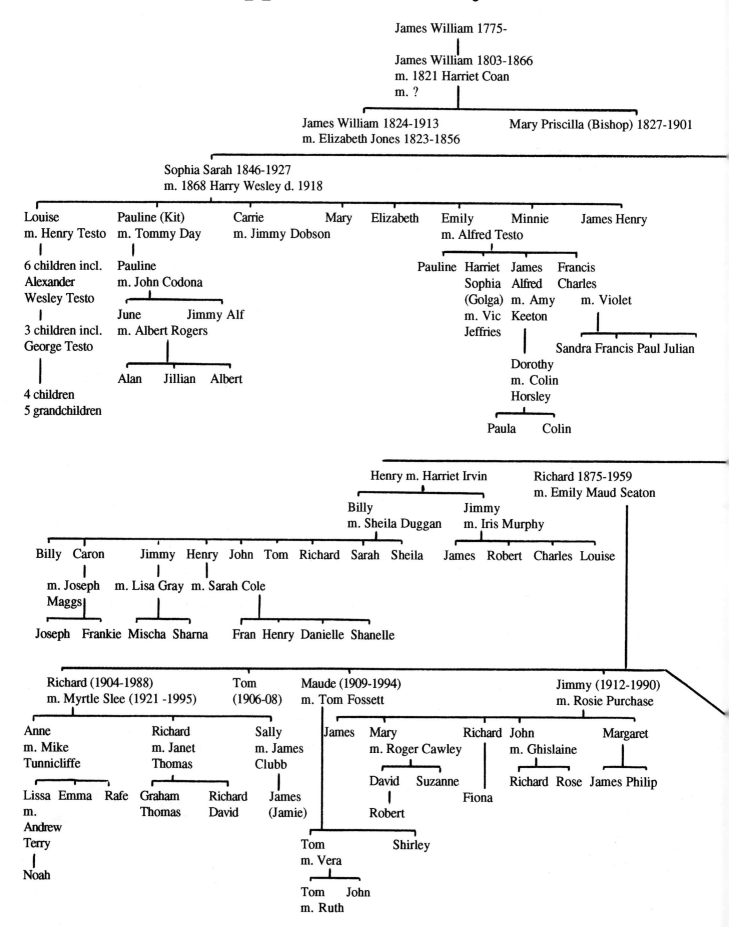

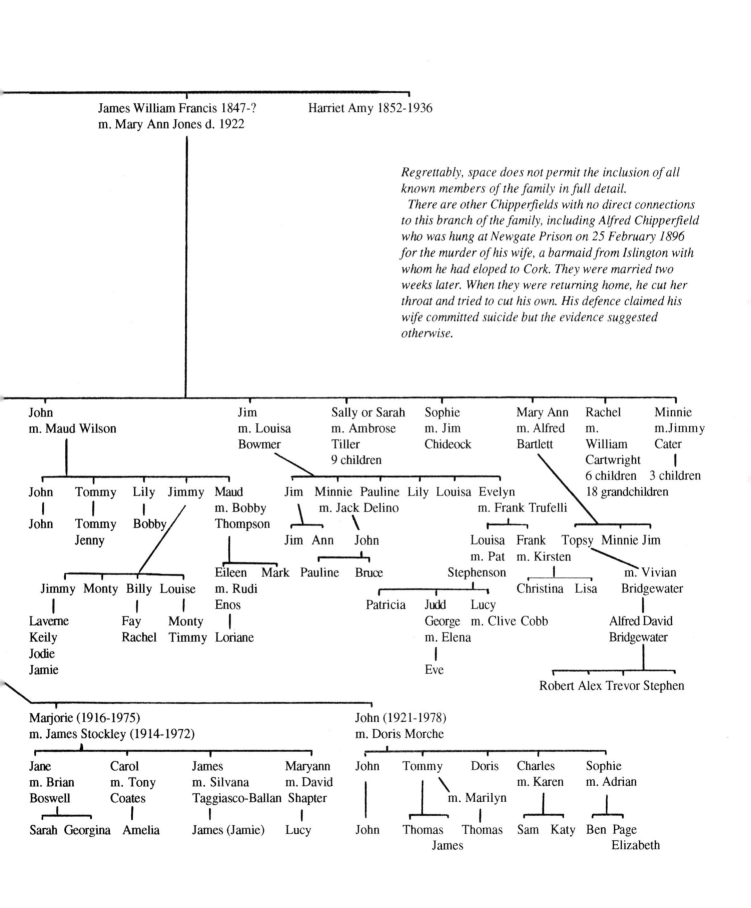

Chapter 1
Charles II to Queen Victoria

"Welcome to Circus Time! It is our great pleasure to introduce Britain's oldest established circus, which is also Europe's largest and has the largest collection of wild animals which has toured Britain for many years. It is a far cry from the days of Charles II, when the Chipperfields used to travel the fairs of Merrie England with puppets, monkeys and bears..."

This was the introduction to the circus programme for many years and, as "Britain's Oldest Showpeople," Chipperfields have always made a great deal of their roots and how they "were entertaining the British public when Charles II was King." The story has been passed on orally from generation to generation and it has, no doubt, sometimes been embellished and, perhaps, details lost with re-telling. As described by Dick and Jimmy Chipperfield, the first Chipperfield is said to have originated from the Pyrenees with a performing bear. In 1683, so the story goes, a Chipperfield set up a booth on the frozen surface of the River Thames during the Great Frost. He roasted an ox on the thick ice, selling portions of meat to the crowds of Londoners who ventured out into the cold for the amusements of the Frost Fair. It's also said that a Chipperfield took a performing bear onto the ice during this event. On 5 October 1983, a special commemorative envelope was issued, marking the "300 years since the first Chipperfield's performance at the Frost Fair on the Thames," to tie in with the launch by the Post Office of four British postage stamps, celebrating in pictures various outdoor entertainments.

Frost Fair on the Thames

According to the family tree in the Chipperfield programme in Christmas 1958, a William Chipperfield attended street fairs in the West Country, with a folding booth carried on his back like a rucksack, during the eighteenth century, and James Chipperfield, born in 1775, became a leading public figure in Falmouth and was a well known attender of the fairs in the south and west of England. His son, James William Chipperfield, had a bootmakers and costumier business in Drury Lane, London, and, during the summer, toured the fairs with a small show. His wife carried a 'back slang' on her back, a small box with a peephole through which the public could see scenic views, while Mrs Chipperfield manipulated various strings. They also had an animal show, with bears, monkeys and pigs, and they travelled from town to town using a small cart drawn by two mastiff dogs. He was said to be over 80 when he died.

James William Chipperfield was born on 30 August 1803. As a small boy, he assisted the conjurer, Hamlin, who gave his shows in inns. He married Harriet Amy Coan at Bury St Edmunds, Suffolk, on 5 November 1821 and they toured with their own conjuring show in a horse drawn wagon that he'd made himself. This happy marriage came to an end when Harriet died of pneumonia in Falmouth and James William subsequently married less happily, to "a red-headed old pig of a woman." He retired and died at the age of 63 in Cheltenham on 26 August 1866. His son, also named James William Chipperfield, was born on 2 April 1824, and his daughter Mary Priscilla, who later married a Mr Bishop, was born in Ossett on 11 June 1827 and died in Norwich on 24 January 1901.

This James William was said to have fought William Sanger for the hand of his bride. Sanger lost and James married the lady, "Miss Bright." William Sanger was one of the Sanger brothers but his waxworks exhibition did not do well in comparison to the highly successful circuses run by the more illustrious 'Lord' George and 'Lord' John Sanger. Material in the Testo family states that James William married Elizabeth Jones, born in June 1823, and that the wedding took place in 1846 when he was 22. Elizabeth's father, Henry Jones, was born in 1799. He was a musician who left the family home in Batheaston, near Bath, but he died at the age of 37 in 1836 when he fell from the shafts of his horse drawn caravan, his injuries proving fatal. His widow married a man called Bright and certainly Henry's son, William, took the name of his stepfather, and this explains why some accounts suggest that James William fought William Sanger for the hand of Miss Bright.

Above left: *James William Chipperfield, born in 1803.* **Above right:** *his son, James William Chipperfield (1824-1913) and his wife Elizabeth (née Jones). Her death at the age of 33 left him with three young children to bring up.*

James William and Elizabeth had three children. Sophia Sarah was born on 13 December 1846 and she was almost certainly the "Child of Promise... Now about ten years of age" who was described as performing on the tight rope in Chipperfield's Caffer Circus in the 1850s or 60s. James William Francis was born on either 6 June or 4 October 1847 in Tottenham Court Road, London, and Harriet Amy on 16 August 1852.

Charles Keith was a circus performer and proprietor who has left a detailed record of his profession at the time in the book, *Circus Life and Amusements in All Nations*, published in 1879. In his early days, having become an itinerant acrobat, he spent the summer of 1856 "with Chipperfield's and Manley's circuses - small concerns attending fairs and small towns. With them I travelled the best part of England, and returned to London as usual for the winter."

Elizabeth Chipperfield died on 9 October 1856 at Hull Fair when she was only 33. It is possible that her death was due to heavy drinking. She was buried in the cemetery across the road from the fairground. Her death meant that James William was left with three young children aged between ten and four. According to written material left by James William Chipperfield, his son James died on 26 August 1866 when he was 19, but he was in fact disowned and disinherited by his father because of his insistence on marrying Mary Ann Jones, who was possibly his cousin and who was deemed to be unacceptable as a daughter-in-law because James William believed all the Jones family to have a fondness for strong drink.

We know more about James William Chipperfield than other Chipperfields of this era from an article in the World's Fair newspaper on 8 June 1912 which summarises the life of England's oldest showman. "The old gentleman was born in a caravan in St Martin-at-Oak on April 22nd, 1824, his father being a showman of credit and renown. During his long career he has been working in the showbusiness all the time, excepting in the winter months. Born and bred a showman, he was 'clowning' for his father as a lad, being then engaged in the 'Lilliputian Circus,' as it was called. One of his early reminiscences is going into a den of animals at Wombwell's menagerie, when he was only fourteen years of age. His first venture 'on his own' was in connection with the 'Lillputian Circus,' where he had an 'educated pony,' and his daughter appeared as the youngest tightrope dancer in the country. At his show Chipperfield introduced Zulus and Kaffirs, and the Aztecs from Mexico; and he also entered into the marionette business, and showed his ingenuity by presenting a 'moving figures' exhibition, in which all the figures were made by himself, and were made to walk in life-like style.

"Then he brought out the 'Living Skeleton,' which was one of the most successful hits, and was more than once a feature of Tombland Fair (in Norwich). His versatility was also revealed in the production of 'The Ombras,' or shadow-work exhibition, and the 'Ghost Show,' with its strange illusions. This show, by the way, was burned down in Lincolnshire, and involved the showman in considerable loss. He was not down-hearted, however, and was soon at work again in the conjuring business - at which he was very clever. Then he scored a success with the 'Vanishing Lady,' which attracted much attention at the Fairs; and Mr Chipperfield gradually worked his way to the front again with a small travelling menagerie, in which 'Vixen,' a well known lioness, was one of the leading features, together with performing hyenas and wolves. His last appearance at Norwich Fair was about sixteen years ago, and at the present time the veteran is travelling towards Scotland with his menagerie. Needless to say that Mr Chipperfield is a man of much ingenuity and resource, and he still occupies his spare time in making mechanical figures. He has been an intimate friend of the late Lord George Sanger for many years, and he has a large circle of Norwich friends who all wish him well on his travels." James William had property in Norwich, including a public house which, according to his own papers, he sold on Saturday 25 September (year unknown) "for 825 pounds." He also owned houses in Short Street and Shadwell Street in the Newmarket Road end of Norwich, although, when he died, he was living in Leeds.

The Caffers and Zulus mentioned in the article on James William Chipperfield are also in the poster for Chipperfield's Caffer Circus which is one of the earliest documents in the family's possession, probably dating from the 1850s or 60s. This bears a royal coat of arms and the words "Patronised by the Queen and Prince Albert and Royal Family at Buckingham Palace." The features presented by J. Chipperfield include "The Celebrated Performing Pony," "The Child of Promise," aged about ten, on the tight rope, the Zulu Caffers "who are accompanied by an interpreter," and the show concluded "with the Flying Lady."

Chipperfield had entered into an "expensive engagement with Mr Caldecot's Zulu Caffers," who had been seen by the Queen and Prince Albert at Buckingham Palace. In London, the poster stated, the admission for the Zulus alone was two shillings and one shilling, whereas Chipperfield's show, "illuminated with portable gas," was priced at 6d for front seats and 3d for gallery.

Left: *Robert Tipney, "The Living Skeleton."* **Right:** *James William Francis Chipperfield.*

"The Living Skeleton" was advertised in the Western Morning News in Plymouth on 4 May 1867. A small boxed paragraph in the amusements section stated, "Chipperfield's wonderful Living Skeleton exhibition will open in the Union Dock, Martin St., Saturday May 11th, and every evening from six to ten p.m. Go and see him." Two further boxed advertisements read, "Go and see the Lillputes or twin sisters from the City of London. They are inches shorter and pounds lighter than Tom Thumb. Go and see them at Chipperfield's No. 2 Exhibition" and "Go and hear the monster Big Ben drum - the largest drum in the world, nearly eight feet high and 23 feet in circumference. Played on the outside in conjunction with Chipperfield's band." Tom Thumb, the American dwarf who was 25 inches high, had been brought to London by Phineas T. Barnum in 1844. He had audiences with Queen Victoria and became a great favourite of hers, returning to London with his bride in 1864. His name had passed into public awareness to such an extent that James William Chipperfield referred to him in his advertising.

Another small advert on 18 May went into more detail about Chipperfield's main attraction. "Mr Chipperfield begs to inform the public of Plymouth and the surrounding district that he is now exhibiting on the Union Dock, Martin Street, Plymouth, the Living Skeleton, Mr Tipney, who is 26 years of age and weighs only 49lbs. He is a native of March, in Cambridgeshire. His dimensions are seven inches round the thigh, five inches round the calf of the leg, four and a half inches round the arm, a trifle larger round the wrist than a shilling, and five feet high. Open every evening this week from 6 to 10 p.m. Admission 3d." Robert Tipney really was extremely thin. He had virtually no lips or flesh on his nose and needed a cushion to sit down. In his home village, he was the object of jokes but with Chipperfields he received a good salary. During the exhibition, he would come out of a coffin bathed in blue light. The more macabre the show in those days, the better it did with the general public. When he was examined by doctors in Oxford, no major physical problems were discovered. He and his family later left Chipperfields to work on their own but they could not manage the business side of the exhibition and they returned home where sadly Robert died in the workhouse at a comparatively young age. The workhouse authorities let Chipperfields know and they paid for his funeral expenses. Otherwise he would have been buried in a pauper's grave. Jimmy Stockley remembers his mother, Marjorie (née Chipperfield), telling him that she went to Guys Hospital in London to try to find Tipney's medical records but it seems that they were lost in the blitz.

According to the Testo family, Harry Wesley, nicknamed Jimmy, came to work with James William Chipperfield around this time, probably in an administrative capacity. He was an educated man from Bridgwater, Somerset, and he was a musician. He and Sophia Chipperfield wanted to get married but, since they would inherit the business on James William's death, and it therefore might not bear the name Chipperfield, James William only agreed to the marriage on condition that Wesley changed his name to Chipperfield. They were married in 1868 and had seven daughters and one son. They were Louise (1869), Mary (1872), Elizabeth (1875), Pauline sometimes called Kit (1877), Emily (1879), Minnie who died in her teens in 1895, Catherine or Carrie (1883) and James Henry (1887).

As they grew older, most performed with the animals in the family's menagerie, for example, Carrie with snakes, Jimmy with the lions and Emily with wolves and hyenas and sometimes the lions. Louise married Henry Testo, and Emily married his brother Alfred. Pauline married Tommy Day, known professionally as Captain Bartlett the lion tamer. Day's Menagerie always featured male lions called Wallace and presented Spitfire in the bouncing lioness routine. Their version had an impressive end as the trainer would leave the door open and the lioness, having bounded round the small cage, would stand at the open door, roaring. Carrie became the wife of Jimmy Dobson, and Elizabeth and Mary did not marry.

James William's disinherited son, James William Francis Chipperfield, and his wife Mary Ann, founded their own business, and James became an animal trainer. "I can train anything from a rabbit to an elephant" was one of his favourite expressions, and he used to declare that he knew every village in Great Britain. He and his wife produced a family of nine children. The 1891 Census for Crediton in Devon lists James Chipperfield, showman, aged 42, born in London, as the head of the family, one of four families living in caravans in the town, the other three family's occupation being hawkers. James Chipperfield's wife Mary, aged 44, born Poole, Dorset, is followed by their children, Sophie (aged 23, born in Hampshire), Leah (aged 22, born in Staffordshire), James (aged 19, musician, born in Chester), John (aged 17, musician, born in Pembrokeshire), Richard (aged 14, acrobat, born in Leicestershire), Mary (aged 11, scholar, born in Norfolk), Henry (aged ten, scholar, born in Middlesex), Rachel (aged seven, scholar, born in Dorset) and Minnie (aged two, born in Wiltshire).

The places of birth indicate the family's travelling life style and it is the children of Richard Chipperfield, aged 14 in 1891, who grew Chipperfield's Circus to the heights it achieved more than half a century later.

Below: *a family photo, believed to be of Chipperfield's during the horse drawn era*

Chapter 2
The Early Years of the Twentieth Century

Above: *Chipperfield's Electric Theatre with the Burrell engine, Queen of the Midlands.*

At the turn of the century, there were at least two branches of the family in operation. James William Chipperfield, and his son-in-law Henry Wesley, were running their menagerie, as well as James William Francis Chipperfield operating his shows.

In 1902, with the cinema in its early days, Chipperfields were one of a number of fairground operators who added moving pictures to their attractions. According to a World's Fair article (8.1.1938), Richard, James William Francis Chipperfield's son, took a cinema camera to Stratford-upon-Avon and obtained pictures of the Shakespeare Birthday Procession as well as of Marie Corelli riding in a carriage in the parade. He was one of the first to show moving pictures in Manchester and Birmingham and he holds the record of being No. 2 "to exhibit the biograph in London." The pictures were 40 feet long and six were exhibited in six minutes, including the disaster to the Albion on the River Thames, and a bull fight.

In the World's Fair, probably half a century later (30.9.1950), the writer Southdown says that he saw Chipperfields touring the fairs with a one pole tent, showing pictures of the Boer War (1899-1902). He adds that this tent had dark blue canvas to keep out the light for the bioscope part of the performance. There was also the live re-enactment of a scene from the Boer War. A khaki clad rider came into the ring and was shot. Falling from his horse, he was attended by a red cross nurse who rendered first aid to the head wound and, in so doing, quickly put a red stained bandage round the forehead. While this was being done, another shot rang out across the ring and the horse fell to the ground but after the horse's foreleg had been bandaged (again with red paint stained material) it got up. When it left the ring, it did so on three legs, with its rider holding its rein with one hand and supporting himself with the other resting on the nurse's shoulder.

A rare catalogue of "Chipperfield's French Menagerie," printed by Willsons in Leicester, dates from around this time. I think that this was operated by James William and Henry Wesley Chipperfield. The catalogue commences, "Visitors are kindly requested to notice the splendid condition of these animals. We are rightly and most justly called the Wandering Teachers of Natural History. These Animals have been brought over thousands of miles of land and sea, regardless of expense, as it were to your very own door step."

Right: *A photographic portrait of James William Chipperfield by Marr & Co., Norwich. He wrote on the back: "Taken April 22, 1910. My age is 86 years old. For my dear daughter Harriet. Hope to give another next year." He died three years later.*

Below: *Chipperfield's Menagerie at Hull Fair in 1905. This was probably the menagerie owned and run by James William Chipperfield and his son-in-law Harry Wesley.*

Left: *Banging the drum for Chipperfield's Circus and Cinematograph at Stratford Mop Fair in 1903.* **Right:** *Peter the camel in James William Chipperfield's menagerie.*

There are 19 exhibits described. They include: a golden pheasant; a pelican; a striped or Bengal hyena; Russian bear; Persian cat ("the winner of seven prizes"); "Hicknemans, or mongoose"; lemur; various species of monkeys; racoon; green St Jague monkey ("presented to this Menagerie at Ayr, on Sept. 9th, 1903"); a group of wolves which was presented by Mdlle. Aymie; Brutus the "untameable lion" imported by Cross, the animal dealers, of Liverpool in 1899 and that "caused the death of his tamer, on Sept. 12th, 1903"; the "notorious lioness, Vixen, the man-eater"; the lioness Princess; a pair of lionesses (Norma and Jula) presented by Prince Lowdtano "who enters their den and puts them through a daring and pleasing performance"; a vulture; the "hybrid, or part horse and part camel"; a lemon crested cockatoo "over 45 years old, and the only one ever taught to dance"; and pythons - "Mdlle. Olga will perform with these venomous monsters, and will terminate her performance by placing the head of one of the reptiles within her own mouth." Of course, pythons are not "venomous" but constrict their prey, killing by crushing or strangulation.

The 1912 World's Fair article about James William says that his menagerie was then on its way to Scotland and a subsequent report (20.7.1912) of the Glasgow Fair mentions a large number of attractions, including cinematographs, and states that "besides the varied collection of animals (owned by Chipperfields) there is the horse with six feet, and a horse like unto one Gulliver must have seen on his travels in the land of Lilliput." The importance of cinematographs, or travelling cinemas, in those days may be seen from the inclusion of a full page of Cinematograph Notes in each weekly issue of the World's Fair newspaper.

James William Chipperfield died on Sunday 23 February 1913, at his home in Schwanfelder Street, Beeston, Leeds. He was buried in Beeston and the funeral was, at his specific request, a quiet affair. The principal mourners in the first coach were Mr and Mrs Harry Wesley Chipperfield (daughter and son-in-law), Mr and Mrs James Chipperfield (son and daughter-in-law), and James Henry Wesley Chipperfield (grandson). In the second coach there were Misses Elizabeth, Pauline and Catherine Wesley Chipperfield (granddaughters) and Mr and Mrs Alf Testo (grandson-in-law and granddaughter). In the third coach were Mr Horatio Ashington, Mr John Hancock, Mr Harry Ashington and Mr Ryan. Wreaths included one from James and L. Chipperfield and family (grandson and great grandchildren). Because of the presence of Mr and Mrs James Chipperfield, son and daughter-in-law, at the funeral, it is logical to believe that James William Francis Chipperfield had wanted to pay his respects to his father, even though he had been disowned by him over 40 years before.

Above: *Louise Chipperfield married the showman Henry Testo. She is seen here in the living wagon built by Howcroft's of Hartlepool circa 1910 with Marilouise (Bisey) on the step, Henry Jnr. sitting on the water butt and Alfie on it, holding Henry's hand.* **Below left:** *James Henry Chipperfield as Captain Pezario the lion tamer in 1905.*

Henry Wesley Chipperfield passed on just a few years later at Wishaw, Scotland, on 9 November 1918 at 4 p.m. Described in the World's Fair as the proprietor of Chipperfield's Menagerie, Harry Wesley was buried in a coffin of polished oak born by Harry Dawson, Eddie Pinder, William Cockburn and William Hiscoe. The principal mourners were: first coach, Mrs Sophia Wesley, widow, and Elizabeth, Pauline and James Henry, daughters and son; second coach, Emily and another daughter (the reference is blurred), Mrs James Hancock, James Dobson and Frank Montano; third coach, Mr Sam ? (the reference is unclear), Mr Ralph Sylvester Snr., Mr William Cockburn, and Mr H. Knowles. Others attending were Sam Evans, Tom Paulo, Eddie Pinder, Joseph Smith, Harry Dawson and William Hiscoe. Wreaths were from the widow; Elizabeth, Pauline, Carrie and Jimmy, daughters and son; Emily and Alf Testo, daughter and son-in-law; Harriet Chipperfield, sister-in-law; Pauline and Daisy,

granddaughters; Pauline, Golga, Jimmy and Francis Testo, grandchildren; Mr and Mrs William Testo; John Evans; William Cockburn; and James ? (the reference is unclear).

Frank Montano, a mourner in the second coach, was a lion trainer in the menagerie, according to a letter published in the World's Fair nearly 20 years later (11.9.1937) from James Henry Chipperfield. Montano was mauled at one time by a lioness called Vixen, a frequently used name. Chipperfield wrote that Montano was in the Hartwood Home for the Aged, near Shotts, Scotland. James Henry Chipperfield himself worked the lions as Captain Pezario.

One source (Southdown in the World's Fair, 30.9.1950) suggests that the menagerie had not toured much after 1914. He also makes reference to the fine big cinematograph show operated by the late Mr J. H. Chipperfield, known as Chipperfield's Electrograph, with an organ and two wagons forming the front. He saw another big Chipperfield show, at

Welshpool. This was Chipperfield's Palace of Light, a sister show to that of the late Mrs A. Holland which was also known as the Palace of Light. None of these references are dated. There is a fine 98-key showman's organ in the Thursford Collection near Fakenham, Norfolk. This was built in 1911 in Paris by Charles Marenghi and Company, apparently for a branch of the Chipperfield family.

The death of Mrs Mary Ann Chipperfield on Wednesday 15 February 1922 at the age of 76 at the Fair Ground, Troedyrhiw, near Merthyr, south Wales, was reported on the front page of the World's Fair (25.2.1922). She was the wife of James William Francis Chipperfield. Their nine children - Sophie, Leah or Sally, Jim, John, Richard, Mary Ann, Henry, Rachel and Minnie - all worked in one form of showbusiness or another.

Eldest son Jim and his wife Louisa had six children - Jim, Minnie, Pauline, Lilly, Louisa and Evelyn. Richard McMinn wrote in the magazine Circus, published by the Circus Association of Ireland, that they went to Northern Ireland from Bristol in 1912 with Chadwick Brothers' Circus. Jim bought a lorry to transport their belongings. This still had the name of the previous owner - Barry - painted on it. Minnie, born in 1900, said later, "Money was short and we saw no point paying to have our name put on, so we just used Barry," while Pauline claims that their father was simply tired of people mispronouncing "Chipperfield." (There's been occasional confusion in the 1990s when the Chippendales male dancers have been described as the Chipperfields!)

After 1914, they started their own show, commencing in halls and then in a tent with a ring and a stage. This show, described as a Hippodrome, was a mix of circus and variety. It included an acrobatic act by the five girls. This featured a somersault by Minnie from her sister Evelyn's shoulders as she was playing the violin. She commented, "Father used to get them cheap - a shilling each at the pawn shop," and they managed to smash quite a few of them while practising. They also performed on the trapeze and the wire and helped run the show. Silent films were shown as part of the entertainment. In the 20s, Jim Barry Jnr. and his sister Pauline developed a motor cycle wall of death show and the circus was expanded to include outside acts and travelled with other fairground rides.

Jack Delino joined the show and he married Minnie, then aged 26, and they had their own "drunk on the wire" routine. There were seasons of Barry's Circus in the Rotunda Gardens, Dublin, which included many top artistes of the day, such as Zachini's human cannonball act, Carré's horses and the Fratellini clowns.

The Barrys toured the Royal Italian Circus in Ireland in 1927 and 1928, providing the tent and transport, and the owners, G.F. Trufelli and W.H. Treherne, received a percentage of the box office takings. This celebrated show had been seen all over the world and featured performing animals, notably trick ponies, two elephants, and animal pantomimes with monkeys and dogs enacting various scenes.

In 1928, Jack Delino persuaded his friend, the Great Carmo, to go into partnership with the Barrys to promote one of the biggest circuses to tour Ireland. Carmo had made his name as an illusionist on the music halls and his circus was a good one. The Carmo Circus only visited large cities, such as Belfast and Dublin, and Mrs Barry and her daughters Minnie and Pauline supervised the tour, and Evelyn managed the Royal Italian Circus in association with Treherne and Trufelli, concentrating on smaller towns. The following year, Carmo toured England with Bertram Mills with a strong programme including Togare with the lions, Captain Ankner with a large group of horses, and Baby June the cycling elephant. At the end of the season, Mills and Carmo parted company, Mills subsequently setting up his own highly successful touring circus which went out in 1930. Carmo continued his tour but the weather was against him and his show was twice wrecked, once by snow and then by fire.

Frank Trufelli of the Royal Italian Circus married Evelyn. They established Barry's Amusements in Portrush, later managed by their son, Frank, and their daughter, Louisa, married Pat "Packet" Stephenson, from another well known circus family, noted for its riding, dogs and wire acts. The family ran an amusement arcade in Bangor which Minnie and Jack managed, while sister Pauline ran her own amusements at Bellevue Zoo, Belfast, and then at Shane's Castle, County Antrim. When Barry's Amusements in Bangor closed, Minnie operated an ice cream concession at Crowfordsburn Country Park, near Bangor, and at the annual Ideal Home Exhibition in Belfast. Here the family's living wagon, built for them in the 1920s by Spence and Johnston of Donegall Road, Belfast, was on display, with its mahogany wood panelling, bevelled mirrors, initialled windows and a pure onyx wash basin. Minnie died in 1987.

James William Francis Chipperfield's second son, John, married Maud Wilson in 1905 and they established the West Midlands fairground side of the family. They had five children - John, Tommy, Lily, Jimmy and Maud. Maud Chipperfield married Bobby Thompson, general manager of Chipperfield's Circus for many years, and their two children, Eileen and Mark, have also worked in circus, Eileen in an administrative capacity before marrying Rudi Enos and setting up their own tent hire and manufacturing companies, and Mark with dogs and ponies.

Richard Chipperfield as a boy clown (**left**)*; and as a young man* (**centre**) *and clown* (**right**)*.

The third son, Richard, was born in Sileby, Leicestershire, and he first performed in public at the age of five. He developed his own entertainment enterprises, as well as siring the generation of Chipperfields who, after the Second World War, were to take the story to new heights. In 1901, Richard married Emily Seaton, the daughter of George and Ellen Seaton. George was a famous horse trainer and fairground operator, his stated occupation on Emily's birth certificate being swing boat operator. Ellen was a member of the Clarke family, also well known on the fairgrounds. Richard and Emily had six children, Richard, born in 1904; Tom, born in 1906, who died in infancy in 1908; Maude, born in 1909; James, born in 1912; Marjorie, 1916; and John, 1921. Emily is given a second name, Maud, on Marjorie's birth certificate, and indeed she was usually known in the family as Maud.

James William Francis Chipperfield's daughter, Mary Ann, was born in 1880, and married into the Bartlett family in Fordingbridge. Alex, the daughter of her grandson, Alfred David Bridgewater, joined the current Clubb-Chipperfield company and has presented Sally Chipperfield's beautiful Samoyed dogs in circuses and pantomimes in the 1980s and 90s.

Fourth son Henry had two sons, Jimmy and Billy. They opened their amusement park in Weymouth in 1953 and ran it until the early 1980s, as well as opening a supermarket at the front of their premises in Amesbury in 1956. They operated Coventry Zoo from 1969, later adding a Dolphinarium, and Billy, his wife Sheila and family now tour with their amusements.

As it was Richard's family that developed the household-name circus, it is on his activities that the story now concentrates. Richard was an accomplished painter, working on the dramatic scenes that adorned show fronts in the fairgrounds, and he experimented with other novelties, including selling goldfish when they were a great rarity and a Teddy Bear pit with some young cubs. He formed a variety show, which performed in a square canvas booth with a small stage, with a parading stage at the front to attract the patrons to the show which contained singers, dancers, comedians and jugglers. Richard himself then started in the travelling cinema business, firstly with his brother-in-law and then on his own. In 1911, he bought a complete cinema outfit, which included a steam-driven traction engine and a large mahogany living wagon. He built and painted an enormous wooden front for Chipperfield's Electrograph, and variety acts and Richard's wife, Maud, singing the songs of the day, would augment the films. It was also known as an Electric Palace, the name given in an advert in 1912 by Mrs James Chittock when trying to sell ("cheap") a well carved band carriage and first class harmonium (also "cheap"), her full address being the Fairground, c/o Chipperfield's Electric Palace, Charlbury, Oxfordshire.

With the outbreak of the First World War in 1914, Richard and family settled in Amesbury, establishing a permanent cinema there which initially did well because of the troops stationed in nearby Burford until they all departed because of the Irish rebellion. The Chipperfields remained in Amesbury after the war, sustained by Richard's painting ability as much as by the takings from the cinema, until Richard Jnr., then 19, persuaded his parents that they should get back on the road, travelling from fair to fair by traction engine, earning their living with their dart boards and hoop-la stall, and in due course with a circus which gradually expanded from its small beginnings.

The comedy illusionists Jack Desmonde and Elsie Moncaster had a long career in showbusiness. In The World's Fair (3.8.1963), Jack told of his first time working on a fairground: "I worked for Chipperfield's Side Show and my assistants were Jimmy Chipperfield; his sister Maude; and three more girls who used to dance and parade on the front. The ground was the 'Silver King's,' and he, at the start, handed me 7/6. He put Chipperfield's on his ground and his son, Tom Norman, was also on the ground with his big show and Alf Steward with his boxing booth; there were no microphones - just an organ - and one of the Normans also helped on the front. Admission was 2d and 4d, and Mrs Chipperfield was on the front looking after the takings. I received 12/6 a week, with food and sleeping arrangements included. I was the 'Big Chief' something or other (the title changed at times), and I used to put Jimmy and one of the girls in a box illusion; Maude worked three snakes."

Chipperfield's Circus was at Barnstaple Fair in September 1929. World's Fair writer Pegasus noted that Harry Paulo's circus was so packed with visitors that he was unable to get his usual chat with its proprietor, adding "the same inability was experienced at Chipperfield's."

Chas. Hughes gave a good description of Chipperfield's Circus when it augmented Pat Collins' fun fair at Dudley in December 1929 (reported in the World's Fair, 4.1.1930). Referring to himself as an "old timer," Mr Hughes greatly enjoyed the "recollection of the past" afforded by the company's outside parade of artistes and ponies, accompanied by "its splendid orchestrion and clown with drum," drawing patrons to its "cosy and comfortable booth." The "clean and clever performance in the ring" was provided entirely by the proprietor, Mr Richard Chipperfield, and members of his family. The show comprised: Mr Jimmy Chipperfield on the slack wire; ponies presented by Mr Richard Chipperfield Jnr., who was also ringmaster and provided a "novel balancing act"; Miss Margery (Marjorie) Chipperfield, "a surprisingly lithsome and graceful contortionist" who performed "Japanese evolutions on the perpendicular ladder"; Miss Maude Chipperfield as an Eastern snake charmer with "some fine specimens of the large reptile kind"; a "talking horse" which was a handsome black cob; "a sagacious and

Left: *Maude Chipperfield and her snakes appeared as a sideshow attraction in the funfair at Bertram Mills Circus in Olympia, London, in the winter of 1927-28, returning there in 1931-32. Maude married Tom Fossett in 1928 and they developed a first rate aerial act which later included their children, Tom and Shirley. They were regularly featured with Chipperfield's Circus in later years, after the war.*

bucking mule"; and "some capital clowning and entrées" by Messrs. Richard and Jimmy Chipperfield. Mr Hughes remarked that the horses and ponies were "all in splendid condition, and enter into their work with evident spirit and enjoyment." One afternoon, Chipperfield's company went from Dudley to Birmingham to give a special matinée at the Palais-de-Danse to a "large and appreciative audience," with the ponies being carried in motor wagons.

In his autobiography *My Wild Life* (published in 1975), Jimmy Chipperfield wrote, "I put the traditional Chipperfield sense of balance to good use by learning to walk the wire. No one could really teach me this; it was just a question of practice and patience, and it needed a terrible amount of both. I had no pole, but merely used to extend my arms, and at first I fell off continuously... The wire we used was a semi-slack wire, about five feet off the ground, and in order to balance on it you have to move your feet as the wire gives (the technique for a tight wire is quite different, but we did not have the equipment for that). I found that if I kept my eyes on the same line, looking at a fixed point at the end of the wire, it was much easier, and at last I was able to stay upright for a few seconds at a time. In the end I found it was like riding a bicycle: once you have mastered the trick of it, you can always do it, and it is no harder to lie down on the wire, or to juggle with balls and hoops, than it is to stand up."

It seems likely that the "talking horse" mentioned was Black Spangle. Jimmy Chipperfield refers to his acquisition as marking the beginnings of their "return to a proper circus" and he was trained to do the fortune-telling routine, full of audience participation with the ringmaster asking the horse when a pretty girl in the audience would get married or how many children she'd have. The horse was trained to start counting with his front foot, or to nod or shake his head, and the cues were almost imperceptible so the audience thought they were seeing a genuine "Talking Horse". Jimmy's uncle John, who was very good with animals, had been the one to suggest they train the routine.

The snakes used to shed their skin and the family would cut the discarded skin into pieces and sell it in small envelopes as "lucky snakeskin." Dick Chipperfield used to relate how they purchased Black Spangle after sales had gone particularly well. His father was not so happy, complaining of the cost of feeding him, especially when he was being trained and not earning his keep, until he became the talk of the fair, attracting large audiences, the first day they showed him. Then his father told Dick, "Make sure there's a rug on that horse, won't you."

Chapter 3
The 1930s and War Years

Above: *"The show with the live baby elephant" on the fairgrounds - with the ponies, organ and drums on the stage of the "walk-up front." Dick "spiels" to get the public to "walk up" and come into Richard Chipperfield & Sons' Big Show. On the right, his father Richard.*

Chipperfield's Circus was a regular attender at the major fairs, for example at Coventry Carnival Fair in 1930, where, in showland vernacular, they "had a fiddle," to quote H. M. Jay in the World's Fair (5.7.1930), or did good business, in comparison to some other side shows which were well below the previous year. They were at the Great Fair of Barnstaple later on when that Fair celebrated being 1000 years old. Pegasus wrote in the World's Fair (27.9.1930): "Chipperfield's Circus! What memories does this conjure up of the old days when the name of Chipperfield ranked with those of Manders and Day! What has become of their old menagerie, I wonder? Anyway, their name brought back the time when the circus tent was as popular as the movie show is today. Days that are gone, I fear, for the public taste is no longer equine. Horses (save in the racing calendar) have lost their appeal and given place to the motor maniacs who rush up and down our highways, and even our byeways, like imps possessed."

Johnny Quinn wrote in his Irish Notes in the World's Fair (21.3.1931) that "there is a very clever little stage circus working in London this week, with a lot of nice ponies, performing elephant, also performing donkey. The show is that of Mr Richard Chipperfield, and the programme is run by his own clever family. Richard Jnr. is the manager and ring director. The clowns are Funny Jim and Slim Sim." The elephant that Chipperfields had acquired was called Rosie and she was bought from Chapmans the animal dealers in Tottenham Court Road for £400. She proved to be a great attraction for a small circus but she caused her share of headaches. To quote Jimmy Chipperfield, "Although she was never positively malicious, her tendency to bolt caused us endless anxiety, and many a stable up and down the country was left perforated by her dainty silhouette." They eventually sold her to a zoo, along with Black Spangle, as the two had become great friends.

Dick Chipperfield had great ambitions to work with wild animals but his father, Richard, had missed out on the traditional Chipperfield interest and flair for animals, so he was not able to pass on any knowledge in the usual way. Dick had nonetheless gained some experience by hanging around menageries in his youth, and it was in the autumn of 1931, when Chipperfields joined forces with the Purchases, that he got his chance.

Left: *Rosie Purchase, left, with Marjorie Chipperfield. Rosie remembers the dress, pink with a dark blue underskirt, as the one she wore when dancing in the lions' cage.* **Right:** *Andrew Purchase with three lion cubs.*

The Purchases had been in the menagerie business for several generations and the combination created a more sizeable show to attract the public. The families had become acquainted with each other at the fairs they attended and Jimmy Chipperfield had first met Rosie Purchase, his bride to be, at Mitcham Fair when he was 16 - "I plucked up the courage to ask her out - correctly addressing my invitation to her father. There was no question of my taking her out alone - the social rules of the day precluded that absolutely - but fortunately I had my sister Maude to act as chaperone." On that first date, they went for a five shilling trip in an aeroplane at Croydon aerodrome, marking the start not only of Jimmy and Rosie's courtship but also of Jimmy's active interest in flying. They eventually eloped and got married in July 1934, at the age of 22, rather than face Jimmy's father, who strongly approved of Rosie but didn't think his "layabout second son" (to quote Jimmy) was good enough for her.

John Turner's detailed book, *Victorian Arena - The Performers, a Dictionary of British Circus Biography* (Lingdales Press, 1995), gives this information. Andrew Purchase was born in Puddleton, Dorset, in 1802. As a boy, he worked on a farm and then went to sea for several years, becoming a fairground showman in 1825. From running a waxworks, he went on to become a menagerie proprietor, dying on 28 December 1879 at the age of 78. He was the father of Andrew, James, Mark and Luke. Andrew Jnr. was born in 1837.

Mr Robert Fossett's Circus at the World's Fair in the Royal Agricultural Hall, Islington, London, included a lion trainer called Beaumont who was attacked at the opening performance on Christmas Eve 1895, the lion inflicting injuries which proved fatal. The programme featured Captain Ricardo in the den with four lions; a performance with wolves by Captain Ricardo; and an "exciting performance with three full grown lions, Brutus, Caesar and Hannibal by the

African lion king." Another source (quoted in the World's Fair, 28.3.1925) states that Alexander William Beaumont, "the African Lion King," was killed in 1896 and Andrew Purchase Jnr. (presumably Andrew Purchase III) took the Beaumont name and worked the lions as Captain Paul Beaumont. He was noted with Purchase's "Royal Menagerie" in 1910. It is not known whether the original Beaumont had any connections with the Purchase family. There is another interesting link with the future as Dick Chipperfield would use the name Ricardo in later years.

In 1899 the Purchases had a good collection of animals, with five or six cages, and with three wagons of waxworks. In 1908, the coloured lion tamer Marco was attacked at Purchase's Menagerie and a report (World's Fair, 15.2.1908) mentions that the lion, Wallace, had attacked the son of the "veteran proprietor" on several occasions and that the "skirt dance" by a young lady, Miss Laurence, had been temporarily abandoned owing to the lion's "recent bad temper." Andrew Purchase II was a partner in Purchase Brothers' Circus and Menagerie which, with 20 wagons in total, travelled in 14 countries for eight years. He died on 11 August 1909 aged 74.

His son Andrew (i.e. Andrew III) had been in partnership with his father and continued the menagerie. He had four brothers, Tommy, James, John and William and one sister, Jeanie. A 1912 reference to Purchase Bros. Circus and Menagerie states that there were five cages of animals and that it was the only circus staging a wild west show at the time. With the exception of Sanger's, it was claimed to be the only combined circus and menagerie in tour in Britain. John Purchase was with the Purchase Brothers show, then joined Thomas Ord Pinder's circus in 1913, and the following year went to South Africa with Bostock's Royal Italian Circus, staying three and a half years. He joined His Majesty's Forces in Singapore but was invalided out with malaria. He was with Frank Bostock for three seasons, including one in France and was noted as the manager of Pat Collins' lion show in the 1920s. John joined G.B. Chapman's Zoo Circus as general manager for the 1928-29 season but was at liberty in February 1929. William was noted training animals in America in 1916. Tommy was born in 1877. He lost a leg as a boy but always carried on with his work on the show as if nothing untoward had happened to him. He ran a snake show on the fairgrounds in the 1920s, then a lion show, as well as doing a cowboy act with his wife. Their children were Rosie (born in 1912), Grace, born two years later, and Tommy. Rosie as a teenager added to the show's appeal by dancing in the lions' den.

They would set out with the menagerie as early as February as the show was not as subject to the weather as a circus big top would be. The wagons would be arranged in a square, with a ridge pole down the middle and a canvas cover over the top. The public came into the square area and the trainers showed the lions and tigers in the wagons they lived in. This compact unit could be part of the big fairs in the cities or visit villages and towns in its own right.

Rosie Chipperfield recalls the menagerie which included monkeys, a raccoon, a giant rat, a lemur that lived in the wagon with her, and the snakes which Rosie used to display in the snake pit. When the pythons shed their skin, they too cut it up into small pieces and put each bit into an envelope which they sold to the public as 'lucky snakeskin'.

The Chipperfield and Purchase shows were pitched alongside each other at Oxford Fair and then at Stratford, Barnstaple and other fairs they travelled together. Reporting on Barnstaple Great Fair (World's Fair, 26.9.1931), Pegasus wrote, "I looked for Chipperfield's, and found them - in the same old spot, but augmented on this occasion by Purchase's renowned lion show, with its lady performer whose dance in the lion's cage proved a splendid draw. The proprietor of the circus is a shy individual, and I was unable to corral him for a chat... so I was content to admire the programme which the above combination was this year putting forth, and involuntarily found my thumbs pointing upwards to the sky. One word adequately describes it, and that one word is 'Good'." The Barnstaple Fair was a large one, with many riding machines and gallopers, McKeowen's boxing booth, John Lock's animal curiosities, Mons. Ugo's spider illusion and 13 clairvoyantes.

Above: *the front of the Chipperfield/Purchase show with Rosie and Grace Purchase dancing.*

The following spring, the show went to Manchester for the Easter fair and tragically they learnt how dangerous wild animals could be when Tommy Purchase was badly mauled by a lion on Good Friday, 25 March 1932, at Queens Road, Manchester. He was rescued by Dick Chipperfield Jnr., who saved his life at the time, but the lion had punctured Tommy's lungs. He developed gangrene and septic pneumonia, dying from his wounds on 13 April.

Rosie Chipperfield recalls that they had acquired a second male lion from G.B. Chapman, the animal dealers in Tottenham Court Road, and, even though he had attacked someone before, Tommy Purchase had successfully put him into the act. The original lion, which was very good, had come from Day's Menagerie. Rosie had just been dancing in the cage when the attack occurred. Her father had backed into the new lion inadvertently and it bit his artificial leg. Dick Chipperfield told how the Chapman lion seemed to realise that it was biting into wood and metal, as its jaws moved up the false leg, before pulling him to the floor, ripping his ears, biting him in the neck and driving its claws through his back into his lungs. The tragedy created considerable interest from the newspapers. The front cover of the Police Gazette for Thursday 31 March 1932 had portraits of Captain Purchase, Miss Purchase and Richard Chipperfield, as well as two larger drawings, with the captions 'Miss Purchase danced in the lions cage' and 'The lion attacked him. Mr Chipperfield to the rescue'.

Rosie Chipperfield recalls that, years later, her mother was in hospital in Southampton and was thought to be having 'funny turns' by the woman in the next bed because she talked about her husband having been killed by a lion. The attack was written about in a children's reading book. Rosie's daughter, Mary, was given the book when she was in school in Germany in the 1950s and she was not believed when she said that the story was about her grandfather until her father, Jimmy Chipperfield, was asked about it and confirmed that it was true.

Tommy Purchase had also worked Vic, or Vixen, the 'untameable lioness', in a separate display, which looked, and was, very dangerous. Vic would be shown in part of the wagon cage, only eight feet by six feet six inches and eight feet high. With Vic manoeuvred to one end, the trainer would enter by the door at the other end, the door would bang shut, the lioness would charge and hurtle round the edge of the area for several circuits, with the man side stepping her by moving from the edge of the cage to the middle, before emerging to greet a terrified audience. The 'bouncing' lion was an exciting finish to the show and, in spite of the risk, Dick Chipperfield was keen to take her over. Tommy's elder brother, Andrew, was around 70 at this time and had been retired from presenting the lions for many years. He taught Dick Chipperfield a great deal about working wild animals.

Above: *the crowds walk up the steps and cross the stage to pay 6d for the show at Oxford St Giles Fair. Notice Marjorie the contortionist, the pelican and Richard under the large 'finger.'*

Although Vic put on a great show of roaring and attacking before the general public, she had a good rapport with Andrew and, when no one was around, would roll over on her back and let him stroke her stomach through the bars. Several days after Tommy Purchase's death, Andrew went into Vic's cage to sweep it out, slowly and quietly talking to her all the time. This having been successfully done, he got Dick Chipperfield to do the same and two days later he took over the display and worked Vic for several years and kept her until she died from old age.

Life continued for the families and Kingsley wrote in the World's Fair (20.8.1932) that Mitcham Fair was "more brilliant than ever... Chipperfield's Lion Show, a very fine show, was doing good business, and finely put over. One might here make a criticism in a friendly way. The neighbouring shows found it difficult to work by reason of what might be termed over-exhuberance on the part of the lion show in the matter of noise. The show undoubtedly spoke for itself without the aid of drums, organ, loud speakers, revolvers and what not. This criticism is offered in the best interest of everyone concerned and not as a sort of spoilsport. Of Miss Rosie Purchase, the brilliant dancer in the lion's den, one cannot speak too highly."

They were at Oxford St Giles Fair and then at Bridgwater St Matthews Fair. Adagio enthused (World's Fair, 8.10.1932), "Then there was Chipperfield's wild beast show, which did very well. They give a fine outside show, having dancers, benders, a rolling ball walker, and animals and birds. While they have both an organ and a radiophone to attract the crowds. Inside, Miss Rosie Purchase (daughter of the late Capt. Purchase, the famous lion tamer) dances in the lion's den, as well as doing a snake charming act. The trainer also makes a big Bengal tiger perform, and makes a short and sweet entry into the den of 'the most ferocious and untameable lioness in captivity.' This finishes up a very good show." Presumably the "radiophone" was a record player, like a radiogram or phonograph, rather than an early radio operated telephone! During October, they were also noted at the Fairs in Salisbury and Devizes.

They were on the road early in 1933, visiting Lambourn Valley, and a report in the World's Fair (25.2.1933) by "Line Up" under the heading Chipperfield's Circus states, "Compared with other shows, Chipperfield's is small, but you get your money's worth all the time, for every item is really good." There were the "well trained" animals shown by Dick and James - the lions, the tiger, and "the polar bear, like the tiger a fine specimen, was a wee bit sullen at first, but soon reacted to the coaxing of the trainer, and rolled a barrel and manipulated a see-saw." Dick Chipperfield recalled that the polar bear also came from Chapmans. Originally there were two and they had sat at each end of a see saw, with Dick balancing it by standing in the middle. One of the bears was responsible for Dick's first and probably worst accident when it attacked him, picking him up by the ankle and dragging him along the floor of the cage. Dick remembered his nose going ping - ping - ping along the bars.

Top left: *Dick with young lions in the wagon cage in the 1930s.* **Right:** *Dick about to 'get in' with Old Vic.* **Below left:** *Chipperfields later revived the "bouncing" lionesses as "The Original Wild Animal Presentation." This 1965 photo shows Dick's son in South Africa.*

There were two pelicans, one of which had been with Chipperfields for 40 years. Richard Chipperfield announced that after every inducement they had still not laid an egg. Their names were Jonathan and Abinadab. There was a boxing kangaroo and Vixen the "untamed lioness." Tom Purchase, aged 16, gave a "splendid exhibition of rope spinning that brought down the house" (following in his parents' footsteps with a cowboy act) and Marjorie performed on the crystal globe and as a contortionist. But, says the writer, "the titbit of the whole show was Rosie. When she fearlessly stepped into the cage inhabited by Pasha a splendid specimen of a male lion, rising five years, one could have heard a pin drop. Not a sound broke the silence, as she gaily danced and pirouetted, and wound up by patting him and twisting his tail. But when she had finished her turn, the applause showed how highly the audience appreciated her pluck and loyalty." He goes on to describe her as "the epitome of delicious English womanhood... a dainty little lady with a lissom body, surmounted by a really charming face in which glowed eyes of surpassing beauty." Rosie also displayed the "sacred python."

The company, now described as Mr R. Chipperfield's Lion Show, had a successful tour of North Wales, according to a later report (World's Fair, 29.4.1933) - "The show is not a large one, but the performances with lions, tigers, bears, kangaroos, and the latest addition, two man apes, are splendid. Messrs. R. Chipperfield, junr., and J. Chipperfield are two young and live British trainers." Richard Chipperfield Senior was described as "a fine spokesman, and his 'gift of the gab' is an acquisition to the show." Will Newth's report (World's Fair, 17.6.1933) stated, "R. Chipperfield's Wild Beast Show visited Camborne during the fair last weekend and proved a great attraction... When I visited them on Saturday evening, the parade was in full swing... the front is most attractive with organ, drums and bells, not forgetting the trombone, Miss Marjorie proving herself a real expert on the rolling globe. The outside show attracted a large crowd and there was no difficulty in getting them inside, all being eager to see young Dick Chipperfield enter the den of the untameable lioness, this act later on being the talk of the town." The show comprised Rosie with the "man monkeys," also the reptiles and her "dainty dance in the lions' cage," Dick with four young lions, Jimmy with the Bengal tiger, the bear, the boxing kangaroo, and "the proprietor, Mr Richard Chipperfield, senr, described the various animals and acts and kept the audience laughing with his witty remarks. Those cranks who are so fond of denouncing animal acts should pay a visit to this exhibition and see the splendid condition of all the animals; it would help them to change their views on the subject."

At Mitcham Fair in August 1933, Chipperfield's Wild Beast Show was seen as well as Kayes Bros. Circus, Shufflebottom's Texas Show, Tom Norman's Silver King Circus and Sedgwick's Menagerie. Sedgwick's was another old established menagerie family and their show, with a "very smart walk-up front," featured Frank Sedgwick working as Lorenzo with lions, and "Miss Chipperfield," no doubt Maude, putting "a healthy looking big cat through a snappy routine." Albert Anthony, in his Circusdom column (World's Fair, 19.8.1933), writes of the "outside parade which was an entertainment in itself" while, inside, the public got "so much excellent fare in return for very little outlay." This comprised three items - Rosie with two pythons, and with one chimpanzee (presumably one of the "man apes") in a "specially constructed chimpanzee compartment" and then Dick with rousing display with four lions. Albert Anthony comments on the "perfect diction" of Rosie's lecture on the snakes, adding, "With her personality, speech and appearance, I'll warrant she would cause a stir at Elstree, but that would mean losing her, so let's hope the 'flicker' people don't come across her." Dick spoke "also in perfect English let it be noted" about the chimp when Rosie presented this display. Although advertised as chimps, the family says that they were probably baboons.

J.S. Fisher wrote about Richard Chipperfield whom he met at Taunton Fair (World's Fair, 30.9.1933) as "a hard bitten man of the world... his beast show ranks with the best travelling." A dog was acting as mother to three lion cubs born at Glastonbury Fair and a good way had been found to boost interest in the show. On the Thursday evening, usually the flattest for business at the fair, Dick Chipperfield took a Taunton lady into the cage for ten minutes. This provided a "good draw," to the extent that the rest of the fairground was quite deserted and "it took 15 minutes to empty the show... the field had all been drawn into Chipperfield's show." "Flattie Hurd" (World's Fair, 7.10.1933) noted that "Chipperfield's Circus was looking spick and span, beautifully lighted and decorated as only a true showman knows how. They played to capacity, and Mrs Chipperfield was kept busy in the pay-box, while Mr Chipperfield, Snr., was amusing the crowds with his pair of pelicans. Two local ladies were due to enter the lions' cage and the proprietor got good publicity over this stunt in the press."

Right: *Marjorie on the rolling globe, with her brother Dick spieling behind her.*

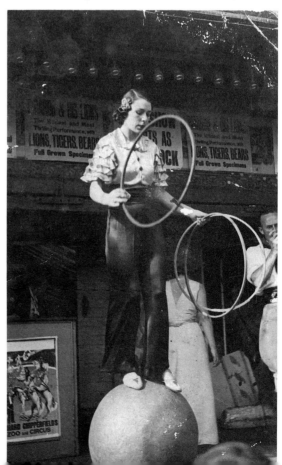

Chipperfield's Wild Beast Show spent a successful resident season at Paignton Pier in the summer of 1934, after which it reverted to travelling, including the regular visit to Barnstaple Fair. Rosie (by then Mrs Jimmy Chipperfield) received praise for luring back a monkey which had escaped onto the roof of a house. During this time it had attacked Albert Proctor. That November and December, the show was run as a circus in Spooners big department store in Plymouth, and Albert and young Tommy Purchase clowned as Sausage and Tomato. Also feature were ponies and a donkey, Dick with the untameable lioness and Rosie with her snake in "an amazingly smart and clever Christmas show."

Richard Chipperfield's
BIG NEW SHOW!
60th BRITISH TOUR.

Owing to the Fine Show of

RICARDO AND HIS LIONS

We are retaining this Show for ONE MORE WEEK,
COMMENCING FEBRUARY 25th, 1935.

As an added Attraction RICARDO has promised to enter the cage with

TWO FULLY GROWN
ROYAL BENGAL TIGERS

which he is just starting to train.

This will provide you with a real good thrill, as these are considered the most dangerous of all wild animals, and this will be the first time these two have appeared before any audience. One night during the week he has promised to take

A LOCAL YOUNG LADY INTO THE CAGE,

so the ladies who would like to enter on
FRIDAY NIGHT, MARCH 1st, please
hand in their names to the Management.

ON SATURDAY, MARCH 2nd,
ELSWIN DAVIS, OF CAERNARVON,
is going into the Lion's Cage, and will draw a sketch of the Lions as they appear.

MOODY BROS., LTD., 34, Livery Street, Birmingham.

In the spring of 1935, they went out as Ricardo Bros. Circus, in a beautiful new two pole big top with blue and white stripes, made by Penrose of Truro. This was said to seat 3000 (probably an overestimate) by Pegasus (World's Fair, 18.5.1935) who disliked the change in name - "The adoption of a foreign circus title by well-known circus families is, to my view, deplorable; but circus folk tell me the public is to blame. The latest to adopt this re-christening business are the Chipperfields, who this season have discarded their centuries-old appellation and taken that of Ricardo" - though he accepted that Ricardo was a form of the name Richard, and there were at least two people of that name on the show. The "Circus-Zoo" included no riding acts but there was the see-sawing pony and a "Jerusalem moke," as well as the five lionesses, Marjorie on the globe, Jimmy and Tommy as "excellent clowns" and the Cycling Duffys, whose act "sets the audience in a roar." The circus accompanied Anderton and Rowland's Great Jubilee Fair for at least part of the season.

Above: *"Chipperfield's The Great Outdoor Concessionaires." - "Chipperfield's Great 1937 Enterprise." Grace worked on the trapeze rigged in the centre; Richard Snr. is on the right.*

In *My Friends the Animals* (published in 1963), Dick Chipperfield wrote that, to move closer to their ambition of running a large circus, the lions and tigers needed to be presented in the big cage, a large steel arena built up in the circus big top, not in their wagons. He says that the Czech trainer Harry Kovar, who had worked for G.B. Chapman's Circus, joined Chipperfields and a big cage was made and Kovar got the lions working in it and presented them in theatres too, bringing in money which was used to develop the show.

Ken Wise, a keen circus fan from Southampton, paid his initial visit to Chipperfield's Circus over 60 years ago. He writes, "I first saw the show at Christmas 1935 when they staged a circus at Edwin Jones department store in Southampton. It was on the top floor and everything, including the animals, had to be taken up in the service lift." They had a zoo in Beales department store in Bournemouth one Christmas.

The late Hal Thomas was a great circus enthusiast who kept a marvellous collection of note books on his visits. A school teacher by profession, he not only saw Chipperfields but travelled and performed with them for a few days, leaving us with a unique detailed description of the show at the time. He wrote, "Coming into the Haywards Heath area of Sussex on my motor bike on Sunday 22 March 1936, I encountered a circus name new to me - Chipperfield's Zoo-Circus - which was on the move. First, Jimmy Chipperfield and Frank Carlos with their Foden steam wagon and trailer, and further back, trying to negotiate a couple of awkward bends in the town, Dick Chipperfield with his petrol lorry and trailer and the paternal two wheel caravan. On Monday evening, the 23rd, I attended the performance at Cowfold, or Crowborough, and helped in the pull down.

"I joined Chipperfield's Circus at the Portsdown Hill Fair, outside Portsmouth, Saturday 11th April. On Monday 13th April, Bank Holiday, circus performances from 11 a.m. almost continuously till after 11 at night. I clowned, juggled and contributed some acrobatics. Tuesday 14 April, pulled down and loaded. Hans Brick did a scarper. Wed. 15 April, Hans Brick re-appeared with a car and small cage to remove his lion, Bebe, having arranged to join Sedgwick's fairground menagerie. Mr Chipperfield senior cursed him fluently. Sat. 18 April, Winchester Fair, performances all day. Su. 19 April. Moved to Ludgershall. Heavy rain during build up. Monday, two performances. Tues., on to Burbage. In bitingly cold weather, I got hopelessly lost somewhere on Salisbury Plain for many hours and was frozen with cold. A heavy fall of snow, so no performances. Wed. 22 April. On to Marlborough, pitching on the Downs, above the town."

Hans Brick was a versatile circus artiste, at once stage having partnered the great musical clown Grock. Brick was a trainer of ability with a unique 'feel' for animals. He trained his male lion, Habibi (presumably the Bebe mentioned by Hal Thomas), to do an act involving the lion firing darts and retrieving them. Brick worked for a variety of British and continental circuses and his memoirs were published under the title *Jungle Be Gentle* (Peter Davies, 1960).

The programme described by Hal Thomas was: "Overture - panatrope; two skewbald mares, Spangles and Starlight, liberty and pedestal horses, presented by Miss Marjorie Chipperfield; Henry the donkey, chasing the clowns round the ring; Bess, the little black 'Don't Jump' pony; the clowns with the omelette entrée, Jimmy Chipperfield and me, 'How to Make an Omelette', much egg smashing, dove pan production of a pigeon; Marjorie Chipperfield, contortionist; clowns tumbling, Jimmy Chipperfield, Hans Brick, Tommy Purchase and me; The Pagoda Trick, building up a pagoda on chin using bamboo sticks, Mr Chipperfield senior, or sometimes Dick Junior; the pelican, brought into the ring, fed with fish, and Mr Chipperfield recited 'A wonderful bird is the pelican, His beak can hold more than his belly can'; Bruni the wrestling bear, a large Russian bear wrestling with Frank Carlos inside the ring cage, Jimmy Chipperfield as MC; wire act (sometimes) by Jimmy Chipperfield, walk, juggle three balls, sit gingerly on chair; Dick Chipperfield entered the cage of the untameable lioness Lena or Spitfire, £1000 challenge, Lena was housed in one narrow section of the beast wagon which was sited at one end of the tent; one tiger, presented by Jimmy Chipperfield as 'Jack Kohler', leap through flaming hoops, sit up on pedestal; rolling globe by Marjorie Chipperfield, in and out of flower baskets, up and over the seesaw, played seesaw with Tommy Purchase at the other end of the board; clown entrée, Jimmy Chipperfield and me with ringmaster Mr Chipperfield in 'Buzzing Bee' entrée with much expulsion of mouthfuls of water; clown entrée, the dove pan illusion, Jimmy Chipperfield; Dick Chipperfield with his five forest bred lionesses presented *en ferocité*, a fast exciting act trained the previous year by Sidney Howes ('You have all seen the film of Lady Eleanor Smith's Red Wagon, well I can now reveal to you that the lady trainer in that film was not the famous film star... but it was our trainer!'- a nice piece of misdirection)."

A few words of comment and explanation can usefully accompany Hal's notes. 'Panatrope' is the circus word for a glorified record player, presumably using 78 rpm records in those days. The pagoda trick was a Chipperfield speciality, utilising the family's excellent sense of balance, and this has been mastered by representatives of succeeding generations, including Maude's son Tommy Fossett and his son Tom, who both performed it while riding a unicycle. The omelette entrée, with plenty of egg smashing, was also a family tradition, later seen to great effect when performed by Tommy Fossett in the guise of clown Grimble. The 'Buzzing Bee' entrée is one of the standard clown routines. It is still popular and has been seen on Germany's cult Circus Roncalli and on British circuses in recent years. It involves the clowns impersonating bees, collecting honey in the form of water, and giving the honey to each other by spitting it at each other! Sidney Howes was a British lion trainer who was active from the 1920s to his retirement in 1979, working for three employers, Chapman, Robert Bros. and Cottle & Austen. He specialised in an exciting and lively display of lions and lionesses, designed to show their speed and ferocity. It is possible that Chipperfields bought a group of lionesses trained by Sidney Howes, from Chapmans, as Sid was experienced in working lions in a big cage, but it seems unlikely that he worked on Chipperfields, although, as recalled by Dick Chipperfield, Harry Kovar, who was a colleague of Sid Howes on Chapmans, did.

Hal's notes continue, "The steel cage was erected beyond one of the king poles and stayed up throughout the stand. Beyond that was the beast wagon, in the end compartment of which was the 'untameable' lioness Spitfire. The rest of this wagon was the home of the other five lionesses, so they were present in the tent throughout. Under the beast wagon crouched Grace Purchase, Rosie Chipperfield's sister, operating the panatrope. There were no ring curtains. The ponies were tethered outside and some inside the wallings. Seating was high and low gallery. A new front door canopy arrived when we were at Winchester. On the fairgrounds, a walk up front was used on which the artistes paraded, and when competition from a neighbouring show (Len Smith's booth circus) was becoming intolerable, the liberty horses were also paraded at the front.

"The tent was a two pole, low pitch, green, 60 foot diameter with a 30 foot ring. The transport. 1. Foden steam wagon with trailer carrying most of the circus and equipment (Jimmy Chipperfield and Frank Carlos). 2. A Tillings-Stevens motor bus (Dick and Johnny slept in the front part of it), pulling the wild beast wagon and the two wheel caravan trailer of Mr and Mrs Chipperfield and Marjorie (an Eccles?). 3. Rose Purchase driving a very open touring car, minus hood and most of the usual attachments, in the back of which the donkey Henry stood and also the stakes were carried. It pulled Jimmy and Rosie's ten foot, box shaped, rear-door plywood trailer. 4. Mr Chipperfield senior driving an ex-baker's van carrying the harness.

"The personnel comprised: Mr and Mrs Richard Chipperfield senior; Dick Chipperfield junior, aged 30 or 31; Jimmy Chipperfield, aged 23, and his wife Rose Purchase; Marjorie Chipperfield, aged about 17; Johnny Chipperfield, aged 14. First season on the road; Auntie; Tommy Purchase, aged 16. Rose's brother; Grace Purchase, his older sister, i/c panatrope; Frank Carlos, beast man and bear wrestler, formerly with G.B. Chapman; Hans Brick; and Napoleon, the one-eyed tentman."

Hal writes that this was "the show's second season as a circus, previously it was a small menagerie. In 1935, it toured the valleys of Glamorgan and reported a tough time. It visited Tregaron. Had an engaged act, trick cyclist Will Duffy. Noticed on the show a cloth banner with the words Ricardo Bros. Circus." Presumably Tregaron was Hal Thomas's home town.

The recitation of the pelican rhyme by Richard Chipperfield is a reminder of the importance of witty sayings, poems and comments in the smaller circuses and fairground shows. Many of these were passed from generation to generation. Jimmy Stockley recalls that, according to his mother Marjorie (née Chipperfield), her father, Richard, was very fond of reciting in the ring as a clown a piece called "The Ragged Jacket" -

>I'm only but a simple clown
>And live by honest labour -
>Of fortune's share, I have little to spare
>To help a needing neighbour.
>Content and health is a poor man's wealth,
>With honesty to back it.
>My meaning's pure, that I am poor,
>I respect a ragged jacket.
>
>If health were a thing that money could buy,
>How the rich would live and the poor they would die!
>But God in His mercy has made it so,
>That the rich and the poor to the grave must go.
>And - when I'm dead and gone, and there's a hundred years to back it -
>Who will say whose were the bones that wore the ragged jacket?
>
>So here's success to the circus man -
>May his tirence wear no frown!
>May his beef and beer increase each year!
>May his wages never go down!
>May his dear little wife be the joy of his life
>And never once kick up a racket.
>But do all she can to please the old man
>And mend up his old ragged jacket!

The Chipperfields did not only enjoy traditional poems and rhymes. A liking of the works of Kipling, notably the poem, "If," is described as "almost obligatory" by Jimmy Stockley.

Ken Wise writes, "For Christmas 1936, Chipperfields were at the Edwin Jones store in Southampton again, but this time they were outside in the car park under the big top. Both in 1937 and 1938, Chipperfield's attended the Easter Bank Holiday fair on Southampton Common. It was a lovely, clean, compact little show, with a walk-up front, two pole green and white top, and a neat little zoo. The big cage was built up alongside the back door, and the music was by panatrope.

"The transport, painted red and well lettered, comprised eight main loads - three Leyland box lorries (one with a beast wagon body), and a Sentinel super-six steam wagon (making Chipperfield's the last circus to use a steam vehicle). The four trailers consisted of two beast wagons, front wagon and big top wagon with the king poles packed on the sides, plus of course artistes' cars and trailers (caravans). I remember waiting on the edge of Southampton Common early on Easter Sunday morning in 1937 for the loads to come down the Avenue. They came in a close convoy, the Sentinel steam wagon leading, with Chipperfield's Circus on its tram-like front. I watched them pull onto the Common and followed them through the fairground to their pitch at the end of the fair. Hal Thomas told me that the cab on the Sentinel was a nice warm place to dry clothes after a wet build-up or pull-down! I knew Mr and Mrs Richard Chipperfield, parents of Dick, Maude, Jimmy, Marjorie and John, and later I got to know other members of the family. The animals on the show at this time comprised lions, tigers, bears, horses and ponies." The Sentinel DG6P wagon was a six-wheeler, fitted with pneumatic tyres and carried the registration number MW 9709.

Andrew Purchase, Rosie, Tommy and Grace's uncle, had celebrated his 70th birthday on Thursday 11 March 1937 but he was no longer travelling, having settled down to live with his son, John.

In 1937, the Bronnetts started their own circus in Sweden. They were a family of German clowns who had made a considerable reputation, appearing at Bertram Mills Circus at Olympia and other plum dates. They booked most of the Chipperfield acts for the season while Richard Snr. remained in England for the summer and hired the big top and their regular fairground sites (which are hard to obtain) to a boxing promoter, one of whose protegées was a future star boxer, Freddie Mills. For Dick, Jimmy, John and Marjorie, the work abroad was excellent experience of a different culture and different audiences, as they presented their horses, lions, bears and Marjorie's rolling globe act to the Scandinavian public. The Bronnetts thought that the Swedes would be more supportive of a British show than a German one and they also booked a troupe of Scottish girl pipers. The Bronnetts called the show Circus Scott, and staged a parade in Stockholm with the pipers and all the artistes dressed in kilts. One of the girls, Dot, had married clown Eddy Orry on Chipperfield's. Dot later re-married, her new husband being Tom Ayers, and they were on Chipperfield's Circus in the 1970s, where Tom was a mechanic.

Circus Scott was not Chipperfield's only step into the big time as, just before the Swedish contract, they had been approached to present Bruni their wrestling bear in a Hungarian gypsy scene in a show at the prestigious London Palladium with the top comedians of the day, the Crazy Gang. As pre-arranged, Jimmy returned from Sweden mid-season and wrestled with Bruni in the shows from July to December, during which time Jimmy and Rosie had their caravan in Kentish Town, where their daughter Mary was born on 27 November 1937, a sister for their son, also called Jimmy, born in 1935. Jimmy the father was taken ill in December as a result of a rough wrestling bout with Bruni, and his left kidney was crushed and removed by surgeons on New Year's Eve. While he was out of action, Frank Carlos presented Bruni.

The following year, Chipperfield's ventured into Cornwall and the writer Spotted Dog (World's Fair, 14.5.1938) mentioned the large group of lions shown by Richard Jnr. and the growing number of horses. The writer says it was remarkable for those days that there were no horse drawn vehicles, all the horses and ponies going from place to place "with no work to do" - "it clearly shows the changing times." Richard Chipperfield Snr. was ringmaster. The only criticism Spotted Dog voices is that the amplified music was "altogether too strong."

Right: *Jimmy in action with Bruni.*

J. S. Fisher wrote in the World's Fair (21.5.1938) of Chipperfield's Circus at Hatch Beauchamp, a large village on the Taunton-Chard road. He met "young Richard" who had just returned from Sweden. He spoke enthusiastically of "the patronage the Swedish people give to a circus." Mr Fisher paints this vivid picture in words of the scene he saw, "Pitched in a green meadow, the two pole tent looked so new it might have been its first day out. Paint and varnish shone on caravans and beast wagons as they lay around the sides and in rear of the tent. It looked the perfect circus of the romantic story books. The beast wagons looked particularly bright and clean in scarlet paint, with the title 'Chipperfield's Circus" on their sides, and the bears and lionesses were in fine condition. Miniature ponies contentedly cropped the grass in their freedom of the meadow, and under the canvas the liberty horses (tethered) munched Somerset hay just as contentedly. Walking quickly through the tent it struck me that all seating and wallings were new. Their bandbox appearance, as of everything, was very noticeable... The high tone and good quality of everything has pleased Somerset folk."

Right: *this photo was taken in 1938 on Southampton Common by the late G. A. Tucker of Portsmouth. Ken Wise purchased the photo, and was amazed to find that he was in it! To the left of the picture, is a trio of teenagers. Ken is the one on the left; he was 16 at the time.*

Right: *this photo of Chipperfield's Circus and Zoo also probably dates from around 1938 as it mentions the "Wrestling Bear." It shows the two pole big top and fairground-style walk-up front.*

An advert in July sought winter engagements for the circus and zoo, giving the address 8 Queen Anne Terrace, Plymouth. Their "Thrilling and Pleasing Christmas Attractions" included The Children's Dream, The Three Bears (with "Big Father Bear, standing seven feet high (from the Crazy Show at the London Palladium)", lions, tigers, leopards, "horses any size and colour," and they promised "All enquiries answered by return."

The show was engaged for the Royal Hippodrome, Eastbourne, with performances at 2.30 and 8 p.m. during Christmas week. The Eastbourne Gazette (28.12.1938) spoke in glowing terms - "No trouble has been spared to make this stage circus a pictorial and interesting entertainment, and the management are to be congratulated on compressing so much variety and genuine amusement into so small a space so neatly and effectively." With the scarlet-coated orchestra directed by Mr Willoughby, the programme of 16 items included: trick and comedy riders Johnny and Anita on piebald and skewbald horses; Miss Marjorie on a large golden ball; clowns Sausage and Tomato - can you make a Chinese omelette; the Girl on the Flying Trapeze; the dogs - "they seem to enjoy the fun as much as the audience" - with their master, Mr Kelly; Joey the Shetland pony with the clowns; Henry the donkey; Bruni the wrestling bear; a troupe of "pretty ponies"; Sausage and Tomato on a shopping expedition; fun with Min and Bill; the liberty horses presented by Marita; Miss Anita (who later went to Bertram Mills' Circus), aerial act on the rope; "the climax of the evening... with the wonderful bear and lion turns" - "Rosa and her Grislies" and the lions presented by Ricardo. The "Grislies" were brown bears shown by Rosie and Dick Chipperfield in the big cage. They were dangerous to work and one part of the act involved them sitting down to be given a bottle of milk each which they held in their fore paws to drink. Rather than hand them the bottles, the presenters would throw them to the bears. On one occasion, the bear didn't catch the bottle, which broke on the floor, resulting in an annoyed bear chasing Dick Chipperfield round the cage. He recalled this when his son-in-law Jim Clubb encountered a similar situation with his bear act in the 1970s.

To see how Chipperfields figured in the circus scene at this time, it is interesting to look at the review of 1938, as written by the World's Fair circus correspondent Albert Anthony, the *nom de plume* of Edward Graves. He wrote that the circus business "marches on as sturdily as at any time since given a new lease of life in the period immediately following the dark days of 1914-18." Bertram Mills Circus was "still unchallenged as our mightiest tenting circus of present times" and it continued under the direction of the brothers Cyril and Bernard Mills after the death of its founder, Bertram Mills, at Easter. The other touring circuses mentioned were those of Lord John Sanger, G.B. Chapman, Bob Fossett, Rosaire, Pinder, Fossett & Ginnett, Paulo's (changing its name to Frisco Frank's mid-season), Chipperfields, Dicky Kayes and John Scott, and Miss Ada Chapman's Royal Bengal Circus. Permanent summer circuses were headed by Blackpool Tower and the Great Yarmouth Hippodrome, as well as those at Skegness Winter Gardens, Chessington Zoo and the Coliseum theatre in London. Christmas was a time for major circus shows in exhibition halls, Bertram Mills at Olympia, the Royal Agricultural Hall in Islington, Belle Vue in Manchester, Liverpool Stadium, Bingley Hall in Birmingham, Bristol, Wolverhampton, Kelvin Hall in Glasgow and Waverley Market in Edinburgh, with circuses on the theatre stage presented by Lord John Sanger, G.B. Chapman, Chipperfields and Arthur Joel.

In 1939, Dick Chipperfield got married, at the age of 36, to Myrtle Slee, the sister of Fearnley Slee, the vet in Plymouth who Chipperfields consulted. They were to have three children, Anne born in 1941, Dicky born in 1943 and Sally born in 1949. Although she was to play an important role in the running of Chipperfield's Circus, Myrtle only appeared in the show for a short time. She was an accomplished accordionist and she played "Lady of Spain" alongside her sister-in-law Marjorie when she presented the bulls, two Devon shorthorn reds, bought by Myrtle's father, Mr Slee. She also trained to do a trapeze act during the first part of the war, but the arrival of her children meant that she never actually presented it in the show.

Ken Wise writes, "In 1939, I saw the show at West End, a village just outside Southampton, and also at Eastleigh, where I helped pull down. Richard Chipperfield Snr. was not with the show that year owing to ill health. A new front, folding out from a lorry, replaced the old walk-up front, and the Sentinel steam wagon had gone. The Balmoral Kilty Lassies were with the show at this time. Never in my wildest dreams did I imagine that delightful little circus of my youth would become the big show of the 1950s!"

War was declared in September 1939 and Chipperfields returned from Norfolk to the winter quarters in Stockbridge. However, some circuses did continue. The annual Christmas circuses in the King's Hall at Belle Vue, Manchester, had begun in 1929. Belle Vue was a large entertainment complex which included a major zoological gardens, permanent funfair and speedway track. The circus was always well supported and it ranked as one of Britain's most important winter circuses for over 50 years. It usually included a range of acts and animals from the continent but the war meant that the promoters had to look almost exclusively to British talent for its programme. This resulted in Chipperfields providing several of the displays in 1939-40, including Grace Purchase, voltige riding, with a male clown in pink Colombine dress and with Richard Chipperfield Jnr. in tails as ringmaster, 'keeping up' the horse; Marjorie Chipperfield with two bulls; Field & Chase (Jimmy Chipperfield and Tommy Purchase) in a comedy routine with a man and 'woman' in a small buggy drawn by a prop horse; Richard Chipperfield's rousing five lion act; Bruni the wrestling bear; and Marjorie Chipperfield's horses and cream pony. Chipperfield's Circus would provide acts in three further shows at Belle Vue. It closed in 1982.

With the uncertain future, the directors of G.B. Chapman's Circus decided to hold a sale of its animals and equipment at Tanfield Stud on 12 March 1940 with many circus and fairground people present. The 115 lots did not attract keen bidding and the prices were generally considered poor. Richard Chipperfield Snr. and sons successfully bid for one tiger (£20), two tigresses (£50) and three performing black bears (£20). Chessington Zoo acquired Locus the High School horse for 70 guineas, six kangaroos for £24 and a leopard for £9. Miss Ada Mary Chapman, who was running her own circus and who was the sister of the late G.B. Chapman, bought two large performing elephants for £150 and one small one for £145. Beast wagons were sold for £15 each and a ring cage and tunnel for £18, while a complete big top with poles went to a dealer for £115 in spite of strong bidding from Billy Smart, then a fairground operator. (Smart's entry into the circus business came in 1946 and, like the Chipperfields, his show grew rapidly in size and importance in those post-war years.)

Chipperfield's opening stand of the 1940 tour was recorded in the World's Fair (25.5.1940): "It takes more than petrol and meat rationing and the rigid blackout laws (which necessitate showing in day-light only) to deter Richard Chipperfield and his circus company, who began what promises to be a most successful tenting season at Andover on May 13th. During the winter at Stockbridge, Richard has been working on the three Chapman tigers he bought at the sale and also on three Himalayan 'Teddy' bears to add to his large and amusing show. Mr Chipperfield, senior, is not tenting this season, having decided to take it easy at Amesbury, but his son Richard is piloting the two pole, one ringer with inherited success." Mrs Richard Chipperfield was cashier and James Chipperfield supervised the billing. The programme was: Grace (Purchase), equestrian act; John Chipperfield burlesquing the first act; Marita (Marjorie Chipperfield) on the rolling ball; Miss Ruby Vinning's French poodle act; clown interlude, "making a Chinese omelette," James Chipperfield; Frank Saxona with Bruni, the wrestling bear; the Vinning ponies, a duo act; "backing up horse" presented by Marjorie Chipperfield; clowns with a stubborn pony; "Min and Bill go to market" comedy turn; Majorie Chipperfield's waltzing horses; the bucking mule and the clowns; Rosie Purchase and her three Himalayan bears; ten Vinning ponies; three Russian bears presented by Richard Chipperfield, who also showed the three tigers and finally the four lions. They toured until the autumn and were noted back in winter quarters at Chattis Hill, Stockbridge, in October.

With Richard Chipperfield Snr. and his wife ensconced at Wishford, Dick joined the Home Guard, having been declared unfit for military service. The family encountered difficulties in obtaining food for the animals and tragically some had to be put down. Petrol was rationed and much of the transport and equipment was requisitioned. Nevertheless, they attempted to retain some components of the circus and subsequently worked for some of those shows which did manage to keep going, bringing much needed entertainment to the public. Among the numerous restrictions was the Control of Paper Order, which came into effect in November 1941, limiting the number of pieces of paper that could be used to advertise any show to ten.

Jimmy Chipperfield was initially found unfit for service, as a result of losing a kidney, but he persisted and went on to have a distinguished career as a pilot in the Royal Air Force but only after he had overcome the lack of the mathematics education he had missed as a boy. He went to Stockbridge village school at the age of 27 and passed his exams with flying colours. His determination inspired the artist Edward Seago to write a book about Jimmy's war-time experiences under the title *High Endeavour*, published in 1943, which was reprinted several times during the war. In June 1941, Jimmy and Rosie's third child, Richard, was born, but, that November, their six year old son, Jimmy, fell and broke his arm which tragically resulted in tetanus from which he died.

In January 1942, Marjorie Chipperfield was pictured in the World's Fair with two of her horses, about to join a stage circus, and in April she went with her globe act and the liberty horses to perform under the big top at the new Reco Brothers' Circus, operated by Herbert Wroe (famous for his comedy wire act as Reco) and Harry Paulo. From October 1942, she was with Harry Benet's circus, on the stage of various theatres, with six liberty horses.

Ken Wise writes, "The Chipperfield circus was off the road during most of the war but, in 1942, while I was on leave from the RAF, I found Dick and Myrtle presenting a small show of tiger cubs at a Holidays at Home fair on Southampton Common and I spent a very pleasant time with them. Also during the war, while stationed in the West Country, I visited Bob Fossett's circus at Salisbury. Mr and Mrs Chipperfield were guests on the show, and I travelled back with them on the train. They proudly showed me photos of Jimmy in his RAF uniform in a cage with his tigers." It's interesting to note the family's very early breeding success with tigers as well as with lions. It was generally believed in the zoo world at that stage that tigers were very difficult to breed. Frank Carlos also showed the three tigers in stage circuses. Pilot Officer Jimmy Chipperfield, with the Night Fighter Squadron, was pictured in the World's Fair in 1943 and, when on leave, he went to Circus Proprietors Association meetings with Dick.

Circus Pie was the name of the entertainment presented under a big top in New Street in the centre of Birmingham in the summer of 1943. The promoter, Harry Dare, had made an application for the show to include lions, tigers and bears and, in an effort to receive permission for these wild animals to appear in a city striken by air raids, the Birmingham Evening Despatch quoted Mr Chipperfield as saying, "that the animals concerned had been exhibited ever since they were born - in fact, though they did not want to say so in public - they were domesticated." The Watch Committee of the city didn't give their permission until the afternoon of the opening day and various conditions were made, including the need to remove the animals from the city before the evening blackout, so the show was able to include Chipperfield's lions and a group of bears, both acts being presented by Clem Merk. Myrtle Chipperfield also recalled having a lioness with its cubs on display in Birmingham around this time.

Commencing on 20 December 1943, Harry Benet presented his Royal Britannic Circus at Her Majesty's Theatre, Aberdeen, with the bill headed by the lions with Richard Chipperfield and also Marjorie and her horses, including two thoroughbreds, and the Gridneffs, billed as "Our Russian Allies," with their unsupported ladder act. Harry Benet, who had made a name for himself in presenting pantomime, musical comedy and revue, had another stage circus at the Theatre Royal, Glasgow, at the same time, with liberty horses and a group of lions and tigers from Bertram Mills' Circus.

Right: *Marjorie Chipperfield married James Stockley on 15 December 1945.*

In 1944, Chipperfields supplied a number of acts to Cody's Circus, operated by Harry Coady, who had been a clown with Mills and a singer in variety. The acts were Marjorie with her rolling globe routine and presenting the horses (Rosetta the coloured pony, her thoroughbred horses and the liberty troupe), and Frank Carlos with a mixed group of lions and tigers. Cody's was featured in the Hull Holidays at Home season that summer. There the programme augmented by Mr Barrett with his ponies and dogs who joined "after being bombed out of London." This was George Barrett, father of Blackpool ringmaster Norman Barrett.

That same year, Captain Ricardo's lions and tigers and Chipperfield's bears were noted with Poole's Circus, operated by Dick Sandow and family. Dick Chipperfield was presenting his six lions at Harry Benet's Royal Majestic Circus which returned to the Theatre Royal, Glasgow, in December 1944. Around this time, Dick Chipperfield also trained Gena Lipkowska to show the lions and tigers. There were two tigers and a lion and lioness in this group, which originally included two leopards at the farm but they never worked, as they didn't like going into the metal tunnel leading to the big cage. Gena was the wife of the celebrated horse trainer, Czeslaw Mroczkowski, who produced marvellous liberty acts for Bertram Mills Circus before the war. After it, they spent many years showing horses with Ringlings in America.

In March 1945, Harry Benet's Circus was on stage at the Hippodrome Coventry, and Chipperfield's lions were presented by the well known trainer of the time, Jan Doksansky, in the final spot on the programme. Poole's Caucasian Circus and Menagerie opened its tour on Easter Monday in Stafford and the full programme of this big circus included Richard Chipperfield and his lions, Chipperfield's bears, Marjorie Chipperfield with her coloured liberty ponies and Captain Frank Carlos with Bengal tigers. The bill also included the Gridneff family and horse trainer Joe Barry, all of whom would feature in post war Chipperfield shows.

In 1945-46, Chipperfield acts headed north to Scotland for the annual circus and carnival at Kelvin Hall, Glasgow. The bears were shown in the circus ring while Dick Chipperfield's lions were a special attraction in the menagerie outside the circus, with performances twice daily.

But, with a hard-won peace and when those members of the family who'd been in the forces had been demobbed, the Chipperfields could return to the circus they'd worked so hard to develop in the 1930s. There was a key addition to the team as Marjorie married Jimmy Stockley on 15 December 1945. Jimmy was born in Stoke on Trent in 1914, the son of a potter's jiggerer, and he had been in the motor trade there before the war. He became a navigator in the RAF and flew with Jimmy Chipperfield and through him met Marjorie. The marriage certificate shows that James Stockley, aged 31 and a Warrant Officer in the RAF, married Marjorie Suzanne Phyllis Chipperfield, 29, "circus artist," at Blaby Register Office, Leicestershire. James Stockley was then living in nearby Oadby and the witnesses were Don Ross and Maureen Van Der Gray. Don Ross was a well known stage circus producer.

 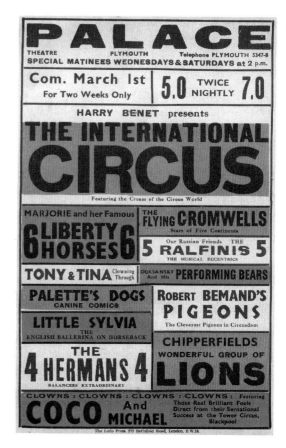

Above left: *Jimmy Stockley (top) and Jimmy Chipperfield (sitting) with their wives, Marjorie (left) and Rosie (right).* **Above right:** *Marjorie showed the horses and Chipperfield's lions were probably presented by Jan Doksansky on this Harry Benet stage circus.*

In May 1945, Jimmy Stockley was decorated with the DFM (Distinguished Flying Medal) for his service to his country. Flight Sergeant James Stockley, Navigator/Radio with 100 Group, Bomber Command, 85 Squadron, had clocked up 187 hours in 37 sorties. In his recommendation, the Air Vice-Marshal, Air Officer Commanding 100 Group, wrote -

"On the night of 20th March, 1945, Flight Sergeant Stockley, in his capacity as Navigator/Radio, assisted his pilot (Flight Lieutenant Chapman) in the destruction of two enemy aircraft whilst engaged on an offensive sortie in support of the Bomber Command attack on Bohlen. Near Kassel a ME.110 was destroyed, and shortly afterwards a rocket-assisted HE.219 was encountered in the act of firing a salvo of rocket projectiles into the main bomber stream. By expert manipulation of his apparatus, Flight Sergeant Stockley brought his pilot into favourable position and the enemy aircraft was destroyed.

"On their previous sortie, this same crew had damaged a JU.88 in the Wurzburg area.

"Flight Sergeant Stockley joined No. 85 Squadron in January, 1944, and transferred from defensive night-fighting to a Bomber Support role when the Squadron came into No. 100 Group in May, 1944. Since that date, he has taken part in 37 sorties in support of the Main Force Bombers, and throughout his tour he has shown the greatest keenness and determination as a Navigator/Radio.

"In addition, during July and August 1944, he took part in 16 patrols against flying bombs and assisted in the destruction of one. In recognition of his outstanding devotion to duty and the inspiring example which he has set to fellow aircrew, I recommend Flight Sergeant Stockley for an immediate award of the Distinguished Flying Medal."

Jimmy Stockley's forte was transport and his mechanical ability was superb. His presence was to prove a vital ingredient in keeping the post war show on the road as the fleet became larger and larger. Indeed, the choice of ex-Army Four Wheel Drive vehicles (FWDs), available relatively cheaply after the war, and the smart and distinctive colour scheme of red and blue and white walled tyres played no small part in establishing the unique atmosphere of the post-war Chipperfield's Circus.

Chapter 4
1946 and after

Left: *the opening stand in Southampton, Easter 1946.* **Right:** *clown Mickey Cavanagh.*

"Circus comes back from war" was the headline for a Daily Mirror article (22.4.1946) about the opening of Chipperfield's Circus on Southampton Common that Easter. Hal Thomas's notebook reveals that they did tremendous business for two days, and that "they had to give five performances."

Ken Wise writes, "In 1946, I was still in the RAF but I managed to get leave so that I could see Chipperfield's first post-war circus at the Easter Fair on Southampton Common. It was great to see the show again. I remember chatting to John who had just been demobbed from the RAF Regiment."

A large green and white striped two pole big top, 100 foot round, had been ordered and just received new from Penrose, the tent manufacturers in Truro. They had to get a special licence from the Board of Trade as canvas was still rationed and Jimmy recalled that the cost - £3000 - to them was "staggering" but they paid the deposit and the rest came from the takings during the season. Hal Thomas writes of the red and white ring fence; a circular red ring carpet with a large gold star in the centre; the king poles, queen poles and seating painted in a pastel shade of blue; low seating extending around three quarters of the ring and the remaining quarter having continental style boxes. Four flood lights were placed around the ring with two batteries of lights high on the two king poles. The red wagons were lettered in blue. The zoo contained nine adult lions, several cubs, three tigers, two bears, one kangaroo, monkeys, two bulls ("domestic type"), two llamas, horses and ponies.

As listed by Hal Thomas in his notebook, the 17 acts in the programme were: Overture - La petite Eva, fast riding act by Eva Gridneff - Mickey Cavanagh, the famous clown - Jax and Max, comedy bar act by the Gridneffs - Mickey Cavanagh - Sequin the High School horse, "a beautiful three year old thoroughbred mare... she will march, dance the Polka, the Fox-trot, and the Rumba" - more clowning - Marsaline, the lady wire walker (Bertha from the Gridneff family), assisted by Roxana (Marjorie Chipperfield) - clowns Field and Chase (Jimmy Chipperfield and Tommy Purchase), comedy conjuring and the egg entrée - Chipperfield's performing bears, two youngsters about 18 months old whose first appearance Hal Thomas describes as "unruly" - Spangle, the "horse with a human brain," to quote the printed programme - Field and Chase with a clever pony - two performing bulls - Marjorie's horses:

Above: *post-war excitement for four children - Chipperfield's Circus has arrived!*

two waltzing horses and then four skewbalds in a liberty routine joined by a white Shetland pony for pedestal work - "Our Russian allies - the Amazing Gridneffs," unsupported ladder act - three young tigers presented by Dick Chipperfield, with pyramids, leaps through hoops and a tiger walking along a thick rope on a pole- one lion and four fast lionesses presented by Dick Chipperfield. This list corresponds with that in the small printed programme.

A key member of the team joined a few weeks after the start of the tour. Bobby Thompson was born in 1920 and he had known the Chipperfields well from his childhood, as well as being first cousin to Dick, Maude, Jimmy, Marjorie and John. His father, Robert Thompson, who was not from a showbusiness family, met and married Maud Seaton, sister of Emily Maud Seaton, the wife of Richard Chipperfield, in Amesbury where the families settled during the First World War. Christened Robert Richard Seaton Thompson, he went to school in Amesbury and, during each holiday, went with the small Chipperfield family circus to the fairgrounds. He also knew his future wife from childhood for she was also a member of the family, namely Maud, the daughter of John Chipperfield, Richard's brother.

Bobby Thompson gained a scholarship from the LCC (London County Council) to go to University College School in Hampstead. He left there in 1937 and went to work for Tasker's Trailers in Andover, becoming a welder. When war came, he could have remained there as it was a "deferred industry" but he cancelled his deferrment and went into the RAF in 1941. Bobby says he "worshipped" Jimmy Chipperfield, his cousin, and he recalls how the family fought to get him into the RAF as he was rejected initially on the grounds that he had a kidney missing. They eventually won and Jimmy became a pilot but Bobby's eyesight was not good enough for any role as aircrew - "so I became a radar operator and was stationed everywhere. I always say that I had the most wonderful free tour you could have - Italy, Egypt - at one stage I went to the Rome Opera House every four weeks, I visited Pisa and Florence, and saw Cairo and the Pyramids in Egypt... all this in days long before package tours, when travelling to such places was very rare," he says. When he was demobbed, he went to see Chipperfield's Circus and asked Dick and Jimmy, "What's the position?" He says they pointed to a 15-foot trailer, which was 12 to 15 inches deep in letters and papers as nobody had done any correspondence for weeks, and said, "You're running the show." He was appointed General Secretary.

Top: *building up the two pole big top.* **Above:** *an idyllic scene - Chipperfield's in 1946.*

Edward Graves visited the show in June in Torquay, on the eve of Victory Day, and enthused about its "good honest" qualities in his World's Fair Motley column (15.6.1946). Referring to some unscrupulous circuses that advertised acts that they did not have in their shows, Mr Graves comments, "Here is a circus which really has lions and tigers; a show advertising only what it is going to present to the public. To emphasise that fact, the double crowns incorporated photographs of the animal groups and other acts. To all the claims made on the billing the show lived up." He notes the presence of a live drummer alongside the recorded music from the panatrope, and that Johnny Chipperfield was doing a comedy ride, as the traditional ballerina Madam Spangaletti, following Eva Gridneff's voltige riding. It was Dick Chipperfield who rode High School on Sequin and who presented the bears, and the bulls - "Dick has not had these uncommon performers for very long and wisely confines his calls upon them to simple tricks." Perhaps because of the people in the area understanding the difficulties of handling bulls more than some townsfolk would, "This contribution received an ovation which must have pleased Dick well; good reward for his patience and skill as a trainer of animals of diversified types." Of the Gridneffs, he says, "A p.a. (public address system) announcement introducing them as 'our Russian allies' produced a good hand but this was dwarfed into insignificance by the ovation given these six artistes at the end for the sheer merit of their performance." The tigers now numbered six and had been presented by Jimmy Chipperfield, billed with his RAF rank of Flying Officer, but here in Torquay they were shown by Frank (Frank Carlos) with a routine of pedestal ensembles, pole walking and a "cleanly executed globe walk." On the day of Mr Graves's visit, Jimmy had taken four of the cubs (from a total of 17 lions on the circus) on board HMS Implacable in Portsmouth harbour and the captain had christened one of them Imp. The Chipperfields being proud of their own war service record, they invited 100 naval ratings to be their guests at Devonport as one of their contributions to the Victory Week celebrations.

Above: *"Our Russian Allies" - the Gridneff family - Kenya and Eva on the ladder, Rosa and Bertha with hoops, Dimitri and Mischa with their hands raised and Igor at the rear.*

A fine spread on Chipperfields appeared in Picture Post for 27 July, with six photos of the build-up, backstage and the acts, and an inspiring article about life on the road. The feature, in one of the most popular magazines of the time, contributed to the growing national reputation that Chipperfield's Circus enjoyed.

All shows had to pay Entertainment Tax and many proprietors, including Richard Chipperfield, complained bitterly that it was "crippling the business," just as VAT has its effect today. Among Mary Chipperfield's earliest circus memories are having to stick the Entertainment Tax stamps onto the tickets in the living wagon every evening.

The children's novel, *Wagons and Horses* (Collins), by Olivia Fitzroy was actually published in 1955 but the circus that is the background for the fictional story is Chipperfield's around 1946-1948. Olivia Fitzroy was a great friend of the family, spending three years with the show, and her intimate knowledge and affection for the people, animals and the travelling community shine through in this memorable juvenile novel.

"The Circus Comes to Town" was the circus revue staged and produced by Louis Barber in the winter of 1946, playing Brighton Hippodrome and then Birmingham Hippodrome for the week of 4 November. The Chipperfield contributions in the printed programme were the riding acts, with La Petite Anna in place of Eva and with the comedy of Madam Spangaletti, Flying Officer Jimmy Chipperfield with the bears Bruin and Bonzo, Marjorie with the horses and pony Vido, Johnnie with two bulls, Johnnie riding High School on Sequin, and Jimmy with the tigers. This was the top of the bill act, which closed the show and was presented in a colourful setting, with the dancers opening the act with tom toms and an Eastern dance. Chipperfields used the specially written overture for "The Circus Comes to Town" for many years.

It will be noticed that Dick Chipperfield was not listed and the reason was an important one in the development of the show towards the Big Time, for he left England in December for Ceylon (now Sri Lanka) to purchase elephants. This was a massive step for the family and one that required substantial funds. A limited company - Chipperfield's Elephants Limited - was formed, with the young generation of the family as directors. Dick purchased eight elephants, a sizeable herd indeed when you consider that the largest circus in Britain, Bertram Mills, had a troupe of six and those of the other shows that had any at all had one or two. Dick made contact with the Kamala circus in Ratnapura and, with the proprietor's help, acquired his first elephant, which he named Kamala in his honour, and then Mary and Dahlia and another five, including a small one he called Sally (after his aunt Sally) with a large bump on her forehead. This bump was said to be lucky and Dick was advised against selling her, as this would bring bad luck, but to keep her and enjoy good fortune. The eldest elephant was 12 years old and the youngest five. All had worked in Ceylon and understood basic Singhalese commands such as hedda (lie down), dit (go back), and belah (foot up). Right through to the late 1970s, three of these original elephants, Mary, Lelia and Sally, were members of the Chipperfield herd, part of the family for over 30 years until their deaths from old age.

A documentary film, Mary Chipperfield's Trunk Call to Sri Lanka, was made by Ian Christie for BBC Scotland and screened throughout the UK in 1983. Speaking from Colombo, Mary recalled the family's long association with the country - "My uncle was here in 1947 for the first time - he came twice - and then my mother was out here two years later and altogether they brought back 25 elephants... I think the first one they bought was from a lawyer, about 60 miles from Colombo, and by the time they'd been to one farmer and another farmer, they collected them all up together in a place called Ratnapura and then there was no transport, so they used to walk them in the evening - it was too hot in the day - and they used to walk about 15 miles a night. And then they arrived in Colombo and found there was no pier so they had to take them all over individually to the boat on a little raft and they said that was quite a sight." On the first trip, there were two other elephants, one of whom was Big Charlie, destined for Harry Coady's Circus in England. J.H. Williams later wrote about the tusker in *Big Charlie* (1959).

Below: *Dick Chipperfield paid Mackinnon Mackenzie & Co. 5333.33 rupees for the transport of the first eight elephants and 1579.41 rupees for the "passage of self and mahout," Soyza.*
Below right: *the receipt for the first elephant.*

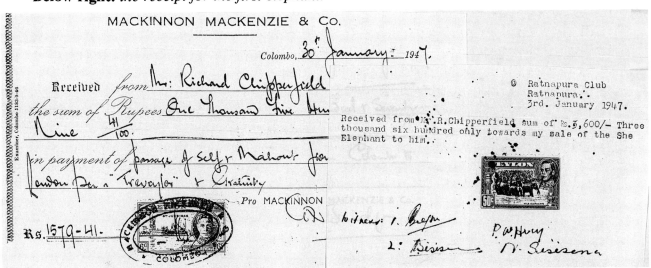

Above: *each of the four wheel drive (FWD) tractors pulled three trailers.*

Bobby Thompson recalls that the purchase of the elephants typified their determination to have "the biggest show - we were Chipperfields and we were going to do it. At the time, there was really only us and Bertram Mills and whatever they had, we'd beat it. They had six elephants so we got eight. If they had a 150 feet round tent, we had to have one measuring 165 feet. The Chipperfields formed a determined composite family unit, each with their own responsibility, Jimmy looking after the publicity, and the administration with me, Marjorie the costumes, Myrtle and Rosie the box office, Jimmy Stockley the transport, Dicky the elephants and wild animals, and John the hay eaters."

When it came to pulling down the circus and moving on to the next ground, each of the men drove a tractor with three trailers. Bobby Thompson remembers being stopped at Ollerton roundabout by the police who measured his load which was 119 feet long. That of the tentmaster behind him was 122 feet. The FWD SU-COEs and Macks were classed as heavy locomotives and so they were allowed to do this. "The left hand side of the windscreen was so full of discs, that you could hardly see out of it," jokes Bobby.

Below left: *one of the newly arrived elephants from a later shipment greets trainer Wenzel Kossmayer on board ship at the docks. On the left, Jimmy Stockley. On the right, with glasses, Bobby Thompson.* **Right:** *walking a baby to the elephant trailer.*

With the arrival by ship of Dick and the elephants, one of the leading continental trainers, Wenzel Kossmayer, was engaged to train them. Dicky Chipperfield notes that Kossmayer was to be a "great guiding force" for the flourishing British circus, bringing a continental influence which manifested itself in many ways, from the animals' routines to the discipline of the staff and the adoption of European style stable tents for the elephants, horses and other hoofed stock. Ken Wise writes, "In 1947, the circus was on Southampton Common, again at the Easter Fair, this time with their first group of elephants, eight of them. They travelled in two large box wagons, four in each, with Dick and Myrtle's living trailer behind, towed by an FWD tractor. It was a very wet weekend and the ground was so muddy that all the loads had to be winched off." The elephant herd was the main new feature of Chipperfield's show that year. Other newcomers were clown Fiery Jack plus partner with his comedy car, in place of Mickey Cavanagh, and two girls, Joyce and Daphne, as the Astrals ring and trapeze act (a name given them by Chipperfields). The troupe of dogs was presented by Johnny Chipperfield, who rode High School on Susan. On the transport front, there were six new tractors, FWDs, and, at the winter quarters farm near Stockbridge, each had been given the uniform streamlined body that was to become a Chipperfield trademark. Reports during the summer indicate the progress made by the elephants. From a brief parade round the ring in April, they were providing two displays by the July stand in Derby. Wenzel Kosmayer showed five baby elephants and Dick Chipperfield presented three larger ones with girl riders in the Elephantasia routine that was to feature for many years. Kossmayer took senior elephant Mary to Denham Studios to take part in the film "Vice Versa" with Roger Livesey. The season ended in September in Croydon. One report lists Jimmy as showing the lions at this time as Dick Chipperfield had returned to Ceylon in August to purchase another dozen elephants, for they had been booked to provide an unprecedented herd of 20 for the first Christmas circus at Harringay Arena in north London which Tom Arnold was presenting in competition with the well established Bertram Mills Circus at Olympia. In spite of floods caused by the monsoon, Dick found his 12 elephants, although one, an orphaned baby of only six months, sadly died on the first day out at sea.

The Louis Barber stage circus returned that autumn, with Jimmy Chipperfield showing his tigers and also three of the elephants as the main attractions. Johnny showed his dogs and monkey, and the horses. The riding, High School and bear acts were also included, as was clown Fiery Jack. They played the Brighton and Birmingham Hippodromes again as well as Liverpool and Sheffield Empire, where midget clown Albert Horton had the misfortune to loose an arm when he bent down to pick up some props by the tigers' cage and was mauled by Rajah. While in Birmingham, eight year old elephant Kitty walked up the stairs to the third floor children's department of Lewis's department store where she was on display for two hours each day.

The "Mammoth Circus" in Harringay, produced and directed by Clem Butson for Tom Arnold, created quite a stir. The vast rectangular building could seat 7000 people. It had the circus ring in the centre, flanked by a stage on either side, and with the space between these performing areas and the seating used for parades. Clem Butson wrote later in *Golden Years of Circus* (Circus Friends Association, 1982), "Our main worry was providing a show big enough to fill the arena and, surprising though it may sound, the production budget was always fairly vague. However, when opening the first season, we already had a £100,000-worth of advance bookings, a staggering amount when one recalls that admission prices were from 3/6 (17.5p) to 15/- (75p) for adults."

The programme of 18 displays included Albert Schumann's liberty and High School horses from Copenhagen, clowns Polo Rivels, Comotti and Paul, three cowboy acts performed simultaneously, three juggling acts, Alberti on a 45 foot swaying pole, the Geraldos brilliant double trapeze act, and the six Zemgannos on the flying trapeze. Chipperfield's provided their bulls and bears, the tigers presented by Frank Carlos (programmed as Frank Carless) and the lions with Dick Chipperfield, as well as the main feature - "Elephantasia - Chipperfield's

Above: *the elephants with their mahout Soyza, Wenzel Kossmayer and his brother Karl.* **Right:** *Marjorie Stockley, with Soyza and Amos.* **Below right:** *Karl Kossmayer with Mary, Anna and Monica in the Carré building in Amsterdam early in 1949. Wynne Shearme, the middle rider, recalls: "We sat in this little trailer of Marjorie Stockley's at night, stitching sequins on these covers and on costumes."* **Below:** *Dicky Chipperfield.*

Elephant Parade presented by Wenzel Kossmayer - For the first time in any circus ring - The Ultimate in Animal Training falls to the famous British circus family, the Chipperfields, who proudly introduce to the circus fans their 20 Indian elephants."

The elephants made "a grand picture," to quote Edward Graves of the World's Fair, as they paraded round the arena, with Wenzel Kossmayer mounted on a horse at their head. Three of the elephants with their girl riders then performed their routine in the ring itself. This display closed the first half and towards the end of the show Kossmayer returned with seven baby elephants for another routine. The Times reviewer (24.12.1947) was impressed with the elephants but concerned that some of the show was lost: "In the large oval of Harringay arena, the circus ring looks anything but mammoth. The space between it and the audience is sometimes useful, as when 19 elephants use it to make a parade of splendour, and sometimes an embarassingly empty place, to be filled as far as possible with such innovations in the circus as chorus girls and female clowns. But, allowing for the encircling gulfs, the circus has the makings of a spectacular show." The circuses at Harringay were indeed spectacular. They were presented for a total of 11 winters and Chipperfield animals were featured in five of them. Writing in King Pole (published by the Circus Friends Association), the doyen of circus fans, Harry Nutkins, considered the Harringay shows to be "the finest production of circus the world has ever seen - and that's saying something! But the vastness of the building and its shape prevented the attainment of that atmosphere which is so necessary to a circus."

Above: *Frank Carlos with the globe walking tiger from the Chipperfield group at Harringay.*

Having wintered at Wethersfield, near Braintree, Essex, Chipperfield's Circus took to the roads again in 1948 with a programme similar to that of the previous year. The three Austins - brothers Len (Spider) and Alby Austin and Billy Merchant - were added to the clown roster and Rudi Blumenfeld, who had helped the young John Chipperfield with his riding back in 1937 in Sweden, was added to the key staff as equestrian director. He had the distinction of presenting the two bulls and also the dog act. Wenzel Kossmayer's brother, Karl, was also with him on the show, helping with the elephants.

The two up and coming circuses, Chipperfields and Billy Smart's, came very close to each other when they played Portsmouth and Southsea. Billy Smart was still travelling his funfair alongside his ever growing circus. Chipperfield's 'nightwatchmen,' a goose called Horace and Danny the dog, who lived by Marjorie Stockley's wagon, were alert to any possible trouble.

Left: *from top to bottom, clowns Len Spider and Alby Austin, white face clown Jackie Sloan, Little Billy Merchant were on Chipperfield's in 1948.* **Right:** *Little Billy Merchant.*

Edward Graves in the World's Fair (1.5.1948) made note of the excellent poster coverage during his visit to the show in Swindon. The new facility of being able to book seats by telephone, available on week stands, was quite an innovation at the time The two pole green and white big top made an attractive picture, flanked as it was by nine streamlined FWD tractors - "painted red with the title emblazoned thereon in blue, they contributed to an ensemble one is not likely to forget in a hurry." In the elephant tent, he saw a staggering total of 23 elephants, including one very small one indeed. Reflecting on whether the show should be dubbed the Elephant Circus, Mr Graves suggests, "At first, that sounds like making sense, but to reflect is to realise how far short of the truth it falls. This mighty aggregation of elephants form but part of a show which is now one of the very best in Britain." He concludes, "Unstinted praise is due to Dick, Jimmy, Marjorie and Johnny, and all in any way associated with them. Their aims are high, and not mere talk, as results are proving."

Wynne Hayes (later Wynne Shearme) had joined Chipperfield's early in 1948 when she saw an advert in The Performer variety magazine for "ballet dancers wanted to work with elephants." She had previously been in Kirby's Flying Ballet and came from a showbusiness family, her father being a comedian. She went for an interview, saw the 23 elephants and rode Mary, the leader and the largest one, always at the front. When Dick Chipperfield asked her what it was like, she said, "They smell a bit but I could get used to it." He later told her that they interviewed lots of dancers for the job but they all talked about what riding the elephants would do to them, such as the bristly hairs on the elephants' backs scratching their legs or the girls being afraid of heights, and Wynne, who modestly reckons she was the least glamorous of those girls seen, was the only one who didn't react in this way. Dick Chipperfield told her later, "You stood there and were not afraid of them and when you said you could get used to anything, I knew you would do what you were told." They took her under their wing and she loved being with the circus.

Top: *Marjorie with the horses and pony in 1946.* **Centre:** *Johnny Chipperfield as comic rider Madam Spangletti with straight man Wenzel Kossmayer in 1947.* **Right:** *Johnny with the two bulls, Pablo and Pedro, in a practice ring at the winter quarters.*

Wynne recalls the winter quarters at Wethersfield as being "miles from anywhere but there was a post office and a pub in the village. The family were great people in the winter for wanting to go to the pictures. I remember 'The Jolson Story' being the rage and when we went out on tour for the big elephant act we had all Jolson music on the panatrope - 'Rosie,' 'Mammy,' 'Robert E. Lee.' They would have a great admiration for whoever the hero was at that moment. You think back at how wondeful life was then but at the time it was probably quite horrendous to me, all these people trying to get me to do things, like not fall off a horse, put my head in the elephant's mouth and be carried round until I thought my neck would break. All these things you did because you had great respect for the trainer and you accepted the discipline because you learnt if you didn't do it their way you'd have an accident."

When Wynne was with the circus initially, she rode a horse from town to town, leading a couple more. In 1949, it was her photo in the programme with Hilda the hippo and from 1950 she did a voltige ride with Johnny Chipperfield. One day when it was raining hard and she led her ring horse to the ring. Dick Chipperfield told her to take her dressing gown off and put it over the horse - "You don't have an act without the horse. That's what makes a circus artiste. We can't be doing with jossers," a josser being anyone from outside the business. After her years with Chipps, she went to Bertram Mills where she met her husband, John Shearme.

Out of their herd of 23, Chipperfield's provided elephants for two leading continental circuses in 1948, one group presented by Karl Strassburger with Circus Strassburger in Holland, and the other to Circus Schumann in Denmark where Wenzel Kossmayer showed them. Wynne Shearme remembers being one of the girl riders and dancers with the three elephants, Mary, Anna and Kamala, in Holland. Chipps was a popular show to be with, and artistes like the Baker Boys riders would finish the season with Mills and come on holiday for a few weeks, and Stafford Bullen from Bullen's Circus in Australia stayed for a while and did some riding.

By the end of the 1948 season, business had continued to be so encouraging for Chipperfields to be thinking of a much larger big top for the following year. The John Scott family with their riding act had also joined, following a disastrous fire on their own show. Chipperfields had further extended their animal collection, with a new group of nine young lions performing in the show and, in the zoo, the young hippopotamus named Hilda, with accommodation including her own tank, a troupe of zebras, and ten new black bears. The bears were trained initially to work on lunges, not in the big cage, and there were two groups of three. Horse expert Joe Barry trained a group of zebras and showed them and one trio of bears on the stage that autumn, for a Louis Barber show where Chipperfields also provided lions, horses and dogs. When the tenting show closed in Chesterfield in October, the tigers and older bears were already included in a stage circus presented by Tom Arnold. This was where Doreen Duggan, then a dancer from the Kay Kirk School of Dancing in Coventry, met Johnny and in due course the Duggan sisters and brothers joined the circus.

At the second Harringay Christmas show, Chipperfield's elephants returned, this time a group of ten, again presented by Wenzel Kossmayer. Dick Chipperfield was back with his new act of nine young lions, and the opening parade included the ten zebras and Wenzel Kossmayer leading the hippo round the ring fence. They also had acts at other winter circuses in December 1948 - elephants, horses, dogs and monkeys in Leicester; and Ivor Rosaire with four small elephants at the Stanley V. Parkin circus at Bingley Hall, Birmingham. In Kelvin Hall, Glasgow, Marjorie Chipperfield showed "with complete assurance" three elephants, each with a girl rider, providing "a strong finish to a powerful programme," to quote the World's Fair, and Tommy Purchase presented the tigers twice daily in the fun fair. They were then using the old RAF Station at Lasham, near Basingstoke, as its winter quarters. Ivor Rosaire took five elephants Banda, Shandra, Blackie (all bulls), May and Jane to Sweden that summer, working with the Mijares-Schreiber Amerikansk Jätte-Circus. Ivor was an experienced trainer from a celebrated circus family and he showed the "Band of Five" (with another bull, Jimmy, replacing Jane) in Germany, Holland and Belgium over the next two years.

Above: *Ivor Rosaire in Sweden in 1949 with the "Band of Five" elephants.*

The 1949 touring season began in Croydon on 28 March with the first use of the promised new big top, a two poler made by Penrose of Truro. It was white with red faced edgings. It was a 150 foot round top, 60 feet high, with a 50 foot centre. It had 44 queen poles, each 38 foot long, and could accommodate 3500 seating and another 500 standing. As the World's Fair headline put it, "Chipperfield's now de luxe." Edward Graves waxed lyrical of the magnificent tent and quoted Mrs Chipperfield Snr. as saying of her children, "I am proud of them tonight. They've worked hard for it." Ken Wise writes, "In 1949 I was at Croydon to see their first stand in the 'big time'. The big two pole white top and menagerie, enclosed by fencing, reminded me of Bertram Mills Circus" - considerable praise indeed!

At the opening Croydon stand, the high wire act was not able to work so Reco and May were substituted with their star comedy on the wire routine. Reco also did some voltige at the start. Joe Barry trained and presented the eight zebras, wearing numbered red harnesses, and rode double High School with John Chipperfield on Susan and Sidi. These acts and the contributions of the Gridneffs, the Austins and Fiery Jack, combined with Chipperfield's lions, tigers, baby bears, horses, dogs, bulls and two elephant presentations, were accompanied by a major innovation, a band instead of recorded music, conducted by Ambrose Tiller, who was an established circus bandmaster. He was also a cousin to the Chipperfields as he was the son of Aunt Sally who had married into the Tiller family, famous for their Tiller's Marionettes show, based in Long Sutton, Lincolnshire. Sally the elephant was named by Dick Chipperfield after his aunt. Ambrose Tiller was a useful person, helping to build the front and bandstand, but his stay was relatively short. There was some conflict when members of the band joined the Musicians' Union. Ambrose departed and James Beale took over. With all these innovations, it was small wonder that Dick's wife Myrtle, returning to the show in March from hospital with their newly born daughter, Sally, was staggered by the way the show had changed almost overnight into a big circus.

For the third winter season at Harringay, in 1949-50, Chipperfield's ten elephants with Wenzel Kossmayer were judged "a performance easily registering as 22 carat" by Edward Graves in the World's Fair and he was impressed too with 'Paul's Peerless Poodles' presented by Johnny Chipperfield, and the liberty group of seven zebras shown by their trainer, Joe Barry. The Times reviewer gave "the prize to the zebras 'in free liberty'... these sleek little creatures, mysteriously perfect." In the King's Hall, Belfast, John Pearson's Mammoth Circus was in opposition to G.L.Birch's tenth annual show at the Hippodrome, with Chipperfield's five elephants, Cavalcade of Horses, the Percherons and High School with Ivor Rosaire.

Above: *Chipperfield's Circus layout, with the two pole tent, zoo and stables in Perth.*

The cage act at Prince's Circus, Pavilion, Rhyl, was Chipperfield's tigers. Harder Jonsson was presenting the eight lionesses with Pete Collins's "Jungle Fantasy," on tour in the theatres.

Looking at the cuttings for the 1950 tour, you are constantly struck by the excellent crowds the show was drawing - "resounding success," "truly enormous business" and "played to capacity" - as it visited Grimsby, Hull, York, Nottingham, Birmingham and the West Midlands, Bristol, and later Hove, Southampton and Aldershot, among other towns. The transport fleet included an aeroplane for Jimmy who was dubbed the "Flying Circusman" by one newspaper as he frequently piloted himself and his brother around Europe on business. Wynne Shearme recalls how, when the show used the old RAF station at Lasham as its winter quarters, Jimmy in his plane would 'buzz' anyone who was on the ground. Having been in the war, the Chipperfield brothers were fired with the spirit of adventure and a taste for danger!

Advance manager John Hinde made a black and white film of the show for publicity purposes. It shows the first stand after leaving the winter quarters, with the transport going through the streets of Andover to the ground, the build up of the two pole tent and the acts in the show. The polar and black bears were very young and shown by Dick Chipperfield, who also presented the elephant herd, with Joe Barry assisting. Joe showed four zebras and Trevor Bale was seen with the tigers and as a mounted cowboy with the horses and two bulls in the round-up. John Chipperfield rode High School and presented the four Percherons and the troupe of palominos.

The 1950 printed programme running-order listed these attractions: Overture under the direction of J. Beale - Winnie and Johnnie, skill and comedy in a whirlwind riding act - the Bradfort Troupe, springboard act - the Royal Percheron cart horses - Oodles of Poodles - Fiery Jack and Co., comedy car - Chipperfield's liberty horses: two beautifully matched creams, spotted jumping horse and the Golden Palominos, presented by J. Chipperfield - Elephantasia, girls and elephants - the High School riding act - Jackie Sloan on the high stilts - Cubano acrobats loose - the zebras presented by J. Barry - Our Grand Cowboy Round-Up, riders, cowgirls, wild horses and bulls - the Caesars, double perch act - Chipperfield's mighty group of elephants - the Four Dresslers, high wire act - Chipperfield's group of black grizzly and polar bears - the Royal Bengal tigers - Ricardo and his African lions.

This list alone does not quite do justice to the comedy, for, as well as lanky Fiery Jack and his car, there was run-in clowning by Tommy Goodall and Merry Herbert, with carnival novelties as well as stilt walking by Jackie Sloan, and a haunted house routine by all the clowns. From Belgium, the five-strong Bradfort family provided two acrobatic routines, the first using a springboard and the other, as the Caesars, balancing on top of high perch poles. The Dresslers were another continental act, providing a thrilling aerial display on the high wire. Trevor Bale, an experienced British artiste who'd also ran his own circus, joined the show and presented the new group of bears, an enormous group of 19, with ten Canadian black bears and nine polar bears, and then donned tropical kit, complete with pith helmet, to show the tigers.

Above: *the matinée audience mingles with the queues for the evening performance on a wet and muddy day in Newcastle-upon-Tyne.* **Below:** *Chipperfield's two pole big top in 1949. Note the man fitting covers to the king poles.*

When Jimmy and Dick Chipperfield had to leave the show in Bristol in August, to fly to Madrid in connection with some of the elephants appearing in Spain, Trevor proved an able presenter of the animals usually shown by Dick, including the lions. Dick also presented the Percherons and the two elephant displays, one with three pachyderms and three girls, the other with ten elephants. Ivor Rosaire was away from the show that year, presenting another group of Chipperfield elephants in Holland. This success was highlighted in a Daily Mail article in August - "Jumbo in demand - four 'gambled' in elephants... three brothers and their sister have captured for England one of the world's most unusual heavy industries - the export of performing elephants to the continent. Before the war the continentals, particularly Germans, had almost a monopoly of the export of performing animals to other countries." The Spanish booking was with Circo Price where Harder Jonsson (Trevor Bale's brother) presented the "Big Three" elephants, ridden by Maureen and Elaine Duggan and a girl called Christine.

The troupe of Golden Palominos created considerable interest. The programme stated that they had been allowed to import them with the permission of the British and Canadian governments and that they represented Europe's only stud of "thoroughbred Palomino horses from Canada." It certainly seems that there were relatively few horses of this colour in Britain at the time compared to today. They had arrived from Canada in the summer of 1949 in Bristol docks, and, when the group of eight was shown by John Chipperfield in the circus, these beautiful horses impressed audiences with their attractive colour, set off by pale blue harness, as well as by the routine they performed. In the choice of these horses, Chipperfields struck a new note, rather than following the traditional choice of Arabs, much favoured by Bertram Mills at the time. This was yet another example of their determination to make their show different and distinctive to the general public. It was also unusual in that there were ten mares and two stallions, with the ambition of setting up a breeding group, whereas most circus liberty acts today comprise only stallions as they are considered more showy. Mary Chipperfield remembers the horses well. They were all named after places in Canada - Hamilton, Toronto, Quebec, Montreal and so on. The five horses in the cowboy troupe shown by John Chipperfield were matched skewbald mares Linda and Bella, the darker ones, and Lindy and Jassy, the lighter ones named after characters in the Margaret Lockwood film, "The Wicked Lady," and the spotted jumping horse was Stella. The transport fleet had grown inevitably, there now being 12 streamlined tractors plus equipment vehicles, elephant wagon, office, mobile snack bar, generating plant (with four generators), blue living trailers of the artistes, and the family's chocolate coloured living wagons, built by Bidiscombes near Andover.

Below left: *the jockey dogs - Wynne Shearme keeps an eye on poodles Carmen and Carlo.*
Below right: *part of the "Elephantasia" routine with three elephants and three girls.*

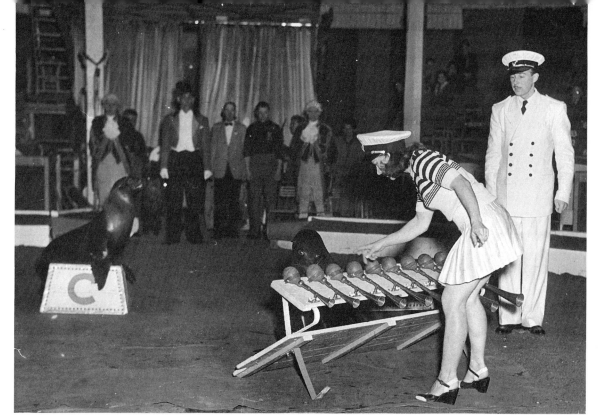

Above: *Captain Miaz presents Chipperfield's new sealions at the Southend Kursaal circus.*

In December 1950, John and Jimmy Chipperfield took a collection of animals to the Christmas circus at the Theatre Royal, Dublin, including Royal cream ponies and Spot the jumping horse, the High School horse, wild horses in the pinto round-up, the elephants, the Percherons and the tigers. In spite of the strong programme, the show did not do well, probably due to a lack of publicity. In Belfast, Dick led the Chipperfield contingent at the King's Hall, with his lions, Susan the High School horse, the palominos, five baby elephants and the mixed group of polar and black bears, shown by Serge Kuhne. At the Southend Kursaal, the circus included Captain Miaz with Chipperfield's three new sealions as well as Miaz showing the zebras and helping his wife, as Madam Alva, present the poodles. Chipperfield's brown bears were at the Waverley Market circus in Edinburgh. All the acts for these four shows were booked by Jimmy Quinn, a very active agent at the time and a great friend of the family. Ivor Rosaire presented ten Chipperfield elephants, each with a girl rider, at Tom Arnold's fourth Harringay circus, having been booked by R.G. Blackie Ltd. of Shaftesbury Avenue, London. These appearances were highlighted in Chipperfield's full page advert on the front of the variety magazine, The Performer. The Harringay show concluded with Roman Glory, a spectacular scene featuring chariot racing from Circus Williams in Germany. During the dress rehearsal, Harry Williams was thrown from his chariot and suffered injuries from which he died - a reminder of the potential danger which is always present in many circus displays.

The main change in 1951 was the arrival of a new big top, with four king poles in a square, made again by Penrose of Truro, and a massive new front, to which fountains were added. This was one of the first four pole tents to be toured in Britain. Previously, Carmo had a Penrose-made square four poler for his tour in the winter of 1929 and spring of 1930. W.H. Wilkie's Circus had a four poler for its resident summer season of circus in New Brighton in 1950. Bertram Mills Circus travelled one in 1952 and Sir Robert Fossett's Circus toured with one in 1954. Circuses on the continent had used four pole big tops before and they were more stable in high winds but erecting four king poles took longer than two. They also made it easier to rig more complex aerial equipment and more substantial lighting. The new showfront had been built by Lang Wheels (Manufacturing) Ltd., producers of showman's riding machines. It was freestanding, held rigid by a row of battens, and painted to show Eastern pillars and domes with circus scenes on both sides of the central entrance. It was a very heavy piece of equipment, requiring two vehicles to carry it.

Above: *an aerial view showing the restaurant tent at the top, the large front supported by wooden struts at the back, the big top, and the menagerie, with the wagons for the lions, tigers and bears nearest the big top, the elephant stable on the right, horse stables at the bottom and exotic animals and monkeys on the left. The family's wagons are top left with those of the artistes on the right.* **Below:** *the big group of polar and Canadian black bears presented by Ernesto Kuhne in 1951. Dick Chipperfield, in the uniform, is at the cage door.*

58

Above: *huge posters were displayed on permanent hoardings - Cheltenham in 1951.*

The programme was similar to that of the previous year, with the addition of the sealions, presented by C.H. Miaz, and with E. Kuhne as both master of the horse and zoo superintendent. The continental musical clown act, les French, began a long association with Chipperfields, in place of Fiery Jack's comedy car, and there were additional aerial displays from the Great Arturos, performing on an unsupported 50 foot swaying pole, and Gina Rio on the solo trapeze. An appearance by Hilda the baby hippopotamus was also promised. Run-in clowning was by the French and Jackie Sloan with carnival novelties and stilt walking, and by Merry Herbert and Hubert. Hubert in particular had a long association with Chipperfield's. The programme gave the permanent address as Down Farm, Stockbridge, Hampshire.

That summer season, Albert Jesserich presented three elephants with girl riders, Elaine Duggan among them, under Circus Mikkenie's novel big top construction in Belgium and Luxembourg. They were back in England for the winter booking at the Southend Kursaal circus which had a strong Chipperfield contingent, including John Chipperfield with liberty horses, High School and voltige and with George the giraffe in the menagerie. Harder Jonsson was ringmaster and also showed a group of lions from Robert Brothers' Circus.

Having supplied animals for John Pearson's shows in King's Hall, Belfast, for two winters, Chipperfield's Circus was presented there in 1951-52. The programme includes the groups of bears, tigers, lions, Percherons, poodles, sea lions, palominos, zebras and elephants, plus Ranée the tiger riding an elephant. The camels were introduced "for the first time" and human acts were the Cutanos in the air, Miss Taniko's slide for life, balancer Wolmini, the Carlinis clowns, the Raspinis unsupported ladder act and juggler Edoardo (Raspini). There's also a programme for "Chipperfield's National Stadium Circus" for the 51-52 season in Dublin, but the show had few Chipperfield acts (probably only the horses and ponies), although it did contain 20 items, including Bill Stephens and his lions, and musical child prodigy Baby Mistin.

With Mabel the elephant, Sheila Duggan, or sometimes her sister Elaine or Wynne Shearme, did a spectacular trick, where the elephant picked up the girl's head in its mouth and carried her around the ring. It was a clever display, indicating how the elephant could appreciate the need to apply the right amount of pressure with its mouth, enough to carry the person but not enough to crush or hurt her. When people in the boxes offered her ice cream, Sheila recalls how Mabel would stop, put her down and eat it, then pick her up again. The ice cream got Sheila's hair in a terrible state, so, since she was appearing in several acts, she used to wear a leather flying helmet for the trick.

Above: *Raluy's double human cannonball.*
Right: *the Duggan sisters, left to right, Sheila, Maureen, Doreen and Elaine on Joby.*
Below: *the 1952 World's Fair advert.*

CHIPPERFIELD'S CIRCUS THE LARGEST IN EUROPE.

1952 TENTING TOUR

Chipperfield's Circus & Zoo Ltd.
Down Farm, Stockbridge,
Hants.
Tel.: Wallop 350.

SOLE DIRECTORS:—
J. S. M. Chipperfield.
J. L. Chipperfield.
R. Chipperfield, Junr.
M. Stockley.

A.B.C.

CHIPPERFIELD'S MIGHTY ELEPHANT GROUP THE LARGEST GROUP TO BE SHOWN IN A CIRCUS RING. PRESENTED BY IVOR ROSAIRE.

RANEE THE ONLY TIGER RIDING AN ELEPHANT.

GROUP OF POLAR & BLACK GRIZZLY BEARS PRESENTED BY CLEM MERE.

GROUP OF AFRICAN LIONS

THE GOLDEN PALOMINOS HIGH SCHOOL PRESENTED BY JOHNNY CHIPPERFIELD.

GROUP OF ROYAL BENGAL TIGERS PRESENTED BY TOM PURCHASE.

PERFORMING SEA-LIONS PRESENTED BY SHEIL.

THE PEERLESS POODLES PRESENTED BY DOREEN.

ZEBRAS THE ONLY PERFORMING GROUP OF THESE EXOTIC ANIMALS IN BRITAIN.

GRAND COWBOY ROUND-UP PRESENTED BY JOHNNY CHIPPERFIELD.

ROYAL PERCHERONS AND SHETLAND PONIES.

THE GREAT ARTUROS GYMNASTICS A'TOP A 50ft. SWAYING POLE.

THE DRESSLERS FLIRTING WITH DEATH ON THE HIGH-WIRE.

LES FRENCH CONTINENTAL CLOWNS DESIGNING FOR LAUGHTER.

HUBERT & HERBERT ATOMS OF FUN.

LIAZEED ARABS

THE MARTINELLIS GRACEFULLY EXCITING AERIALISTS.

THE OHSTIANIS EUROPE'S PREMIER SPRINGBOARD ACT.

THE ORTONIS SKILL AND FUN ON THE DOUBLE BARS.

LES RALUYS DOUBLE HUMAN PROJECTILE CANNON SENSATION.

GINA RIO GRACE AND BEAUTY ON THE TRAPEZE.

JACKIE SLOAN HIGH-STILTS, BIG HEADS, CARNIVAL NOVELTIES.

Above: *Stella's jumping routine with the gates held by, left to right, Doreen Duggan, Gina Rio, Wynne Shearme, with John Chipperfield on Spangles. Note the Royal Box.*

Elaine also remembers taking part in a BBC TV programme, D for Danger, with her sister Doreen, at Earl's Court. They were interviewed by Raymond Baxter with large pythons wrapped round their necks. The crew who'd been carrying round the girls' suitcases when they arrived had quite a shock when they realised they contained the snakes.

Elaine Duggan met clown and stilt walker Jackie Sloan, a member of the famous circus clan, the Yeldings. As Elaine relates, they went out together for ten years and eventually got married - once Jackie knew her well enough! Jimmy Chipperfield taught Jackie to fly an aeroplane and there was always great competition between Jackie and Joe Barry to accompany Jimmy on his flying trips. Jackie and Elaine were with Chipperfield's until the end of the 1954 season, then they toured with Bertram Mills Circus, with Jackie as the white face clown alongside Coco, Nikki and Little Billy. In 1959, Jackie had a heart attack and retired from touring, working at the amusement park in Weymouth run by another branch of the family, Elaine's sister, Sheila, having married Billy Chipperfield. In 1963, they built Newlands Kennels in Stocking Pelham, Hertfordshire. Jackie died in 1984 and Elaine continues to run the kennels today.

The 1952 season continued the onward march of the Chipperfields. Two big new attractions were the Raluys, double human cannonball, and Ranée, the tiger riding on an elephant. Both these acts were exciting subjects for pictorial posters. James Harrison was the new musical director and Jackie Williams, a very experienced trick rider, was master of the horse.

Replacing the Bradforts were the Ohstianis springboard act from Germany and the Raluys had a second act as the Ortonis on the horizontal bars. The Ohstianis, a five-handed act, had worked extensively in German variety theatres and circuses, including Carl Althoff, Barum and Brumbach. It comprised Doris Morche, who later married John Chipperfield, her father, the troupe's leader, and sister Ursula with two other men. The act split up after the Chipperfield engagement, Mr Morche retiring. Ursula regularly visited her sister Doris on the show in later years where she met and subsequently married Sergio Biasini of the Italian cycling troupe.

As an indication of the size and importance of the show, the route was printed on post cards and despatched to a mailing list of business contacts, from suppliers and agents to journalists and friends. Each route card gave the dates and ground for half a dozen towns and the circus phone number at each site as well as the miles between each town. The cards were produced for the next two years. Among the innovations was the public restaurant in a large tent at the front of the show, this being managed by Mrs Raspini, who had retired from the family ladder act. When the weather was cool, a central heating plant blew warm air from a big tube running round the big top, and there was a new Royal Box for special visitors and VIPs.

Above: *the Dresslers high wire act.* **Below:** *Dick Chipperfield presents a lively display with a group of young lionesses in 1951. His brother John is at the cage door.*

Above: *Doreen Duggan with the zebras. The numbers on the red harness were used for a trick where they got out of order and then quickly got back in line.*

There was George, the 18 month old giraffe, from Whipsnade Zoo, with his own paddock, and covered accommodation of a suitable height was provided by a converted double decker bus, originally from Blackpool Corporation, as this was one of only a few authorities to have buses with the centre opening needed for George. There were two young black rhinoceroses on display, which Elaine Duggan remembers feeding bowls of porridge to; and a number of chimps which had been brought back from Sierra Leone by Dick the previous winter.

The Duggan family's contributions included Doreen with the dogs; and Sheila presenting the five sealions and also performing voltige riding. The sealion act was notable for the simultaneous performance of a handstand trick by both sealion and presenter, and for the presence of two macaws (one called McGregor) who perched on top of poles balanced on the sealions' noses. Three sisters, Maureen, Doreen and Sheila were seen with John Chipperfield in the cowboy round up. Ivor Rosaire presented the elephant herd, with a total of 16 filling the ring at one stage. At the start of the season, Clem Merk showed the bears, Tommy Purchase the tigers, with Merk returning to the big cage for the eight lionesses. Clem Merk handled the tiger and Ivor Rosaire looked after the elephant for their double act. Merk left early in the season to go to Duffy's Circus in Ireland, showing their lions and also a group of Chipperfield's tigers, and Harder Jonsson joined at Colchester, the second stand, to show these acts. There was controversy in Glasgow when Ranée the tiger was reported as having attacked the elephant when she tried to jump back on her for a second circuit of the ring but slipped and fell at her feet. The elephant turned and dislodged one of the sections of big cage which fell onto members of the audience. An MP asked in the House of Commons whether the display was contravening the Protection of Animals Act 1911. However, as the Lord Advocate replied, both animals had been seen by an inspector from the Society for the Prevention of Cruelty to Animals and a veterinary surgeon, both of whom reported no injury. The vet said the animals were settled and subsequently saw the act in performance and rehearsal and considered that the animals' normal relationship had not been altered in any way. Ivor Rosaire also presented the Percherons followed by eight ponies acquired from the Jeserich Circus in Ireland. At one stage, the cowboy carousel included Norman Harper, the "Singing Cowboy," but it seemed incongruous and slowed down the pace of the show so was dropped.

The Sunday street parades were the subject of almost as much talk and excitement as the show itself. "Sixteen elephants cause a standstill" was the headline in Leicester and "Sixteen elephants came to Edinburgh yesterday - and Edinburgh came out to see them," holding up the

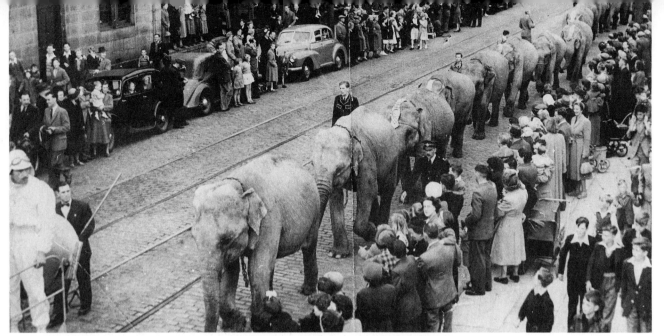

Above: *The elephants, with trainer Ivor Rosaire on the left, followed the Raluy cannon. The elephant act mainly used ten animals but at the end six more came in. They formed two groups of eight, one in the ring going clockwise, the other going anti-clockwise on the ring fence.*

tramcars for half an hour. In October, the public was urged by a press advertisement to "see history made in Birmingham" with the 16 elephants and "dozens of horses, ponies, gun carriage and tractors, etc etc" leaving New Street station for the fortnight stand at Hay Mills.

The Scottish tour had been a great success, as a result of the size and strength of the show and its publicity machine. It was helped further in no small measure by the presence of journalist and circus expert Eddie Campbell on the Daily Record, a Kemsley newspaper, which in those days was truly "Scotland's National Newspaper," as it was advertised. Eddie recalls: "I wrote stories, not just one story, but an actual series of pen pictures extending over a week or ten days. The Record circulated to every nook and corner of Scotland and Chipperfield's posters were already up in Edinburgh. The articles provided daily publicity for the show all the time it was in Glasgow and into the following week. The natives of places north were reading about the great show heading their way as bills were going up. The result was a quite extraordinary box office success in all the towns they visited." The articles, "A Critic at the Circus," included No. 1 The Human Cannonball, No. 2 Liberty Horses, No. 3 The Tiger on the Elephant, No. 4 Les French, clowns, and No. 5 The Dresslers on the high wire, with a history of the type of act and a critical assessment.

Sandy Davidson, recent president of the Circus Friends Association, has vivid memories of the show in Edinburgh - "I was a 16 year old schoolboy and had become a circus fan after seeing Mills, Barrett, Reco, Robert Bros. and Pinder in my native Scotland. I had only read of Chipperfield's Circus through magazine articles and imagined it to be a small family show. Imagine my great surprise one morning towards the end of April 1952 when I saw a van and caravan proclaiming in bold letters - 'Chipperfield's - Europe's Largest Circus.' I cycled past Murrayfield every day on my way to school and to that day only Bertram Mills Circus had used this famous Edinburgh ground. It wasn't long before Chipperfield's publicity machine went into action. A photograph in the Edinburgh Evening News showed the large four pole tent and elaborate frontage. Posters were to be seen everywhere, including hoardings, something rarely seen these days. The impact of three or four big posters of the tiger riding on the elephant's back was stunning. I could hardly wait to see this act or the double human cannonball display. For a week before the big event, the king poles were erected and I could cycle round what was to be the ring, my imagination running riot.

"On build up Sunday, 8 June, I missed breakfast and was on the ground by 7.30. I was soon surrounded by a sea of blue and red painted transport and willingly joined the army of schoolboys who helped with various chores. I was particularly fascinated by the trailers carrying animals, each one boldly lettered: Chipperfield's lions, tigers, zebras and so on.

Above: in Edinburgh in 1952. The FWD SU-Coes were built during the war in America under the lease lend arrangement so Britain did not have to pay for them until later. Although made in the USA, they were right hand drive. One disadvantage was that they were petrol driven and thus not as efficient as the Macks. **Below left:** Fiery Jack with his comedy car in the parade.
Below right: zebras crossing a zebra crossing to promote films at the Odeon, Leicester.
Bottom: the elephants' covers advertise the 1951 circus movie "The Greatest Show on Earth."

"Only the elephants were missing as the famous 16 were to arrive at Waverley Station. By lunch time, the four poler was up and the menagerie layout complete.

That afternoon, the combination of good weather and the advance publicity brought out thousands to line Princes Street and nearly everyone followed the 16 elephants, the cannon and many horses to Murrayfield and into the menagerie. Business during the fortnight was fantastic, as it had been for Mills in 1947 and 1950.

"I can't remember how many times I saw the show but I was impressed by the quality and variety of the animal acts. John Chipperfield's showing of the palominos was a liberty act of world class. Harder Jonsson worked the lions fast and furiously and the 16 elephants were the greatest animal spectacle ever seen in Edinburgh. On the human side, the Raluys were a sensation with their cannon act. I remember that after seeing the act a couple of times I was able to follow the artistes' flight without being distracted by the explosion. The nights I didn't go to the show, I would lie in bed with the window open, listening to the music and falling asleep after the explosion."

Picture Post presented a superb spread on the show on 2 August 1952, this time in colour, with 16 photos, among them backstage shots, an aerial view, the elephant parade, Harder Jonsson the ringmaster, and a novel shot from the back of the cannon just as it was fired, with a nearby attendant with his fingers in his ears.

Above: *Booking offices for Chipperfields and Bertram Mills (right) in Manchester.*

The circus came from Scotland to Newcastle and then across country to Manchester. Here they followed Bertram Mills Circus onto the council site, Platt Field. Usually, it would be considered foolhardy to come to any venue so soon after an established big show like Mills, as the public appetite for circus would be satiated, but, as Mills left, Chipperfields pulled on. It proved to be a daring indication of how well Chipperfields could create public excitement for their circus and how they could successfully challenge the Mills show. In circus business terms, Chipperfields was a force to be reckoned with. Circus enthusiast Derrick Londrigan recalls, "They did such good business that, although booked for two weeks, they stayed for three. On the arrival Sunday, half the loads were still making the journey from Newcastle so they didn't stage the full street parade, but thousands of people were there to see the herd of 16 elephants, led by Ivor Rosaire. Chipperfield's parade apparently brought more people into the centre of Manchester than a royal visit by the Queen had done."

  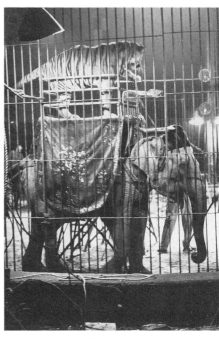

Left: *ringmaster Harder Jonsson.* **Centre:** *Mabel + Sheila Duggan.* **Right:** *Ranée + Kamala.*

"The national newspapers took up the story, with plenty of coverage the next day, but amazingly the Manchester Evening News didn't touch it," Derrick remembers.

There were five stands in the West Midlands in October-December, with reports of "crowded houses" and "standing room only," in spite of the inclement weather which included "an all-night fight" to save the big top in a storm in Perry Barr, Birmingham.

For the winter season, Chipperfield's Circus approached the impresario Jack Hylton to put the show into Earl's Court, just a short distance from Mills' circus at Olympia. In the event, there was a dispute between them, including a court hearing, and eventually Hylton went ahead on his own with two seasons of Christmas circuses, the first with Billy Smart's Circus animals, but it appears that they were not a financial success as they were not repeated.

Mr and Mrs Richard Chipperfield Senior celebrated their Golden Wedding on Thursday 1 January 1953. This was a specially happy event as their entire family was able to be present, as recorded in a photo at the time, with elephants lined up at the back, which was printed on the front page of the World's Fair (10.1.1953).

Below: *Mr and Mrs Richard Chipperfield Snr with grandchildren, from left to right, John Stuart Chipperfield, Jane Stockley, Margaret Chipperfield, and Sally Chipperfield.*

Chapter 5
The Big Show

Above: *this model of the eight pole tent was used to help in its manufacture as well as for publicity before the arrival of the real thing. The flags with CC on them and the trees have been drawn in on this photo.*

The phenomenal success of Chipperfield's Circus in the post-war years prompted the family to expand still further for the 1953 season. Previously they had been using a state-of-the-art four pole big top which seated 4,500 people. Now they were determined to go even bigger and Jimmy Chipperfield personally designed and drew the blueprints for a massive new-style canvas big top capable of holding 6,000 and with a hippodrome track outside the ring so they could present Roman chariot racing and animal spectacles.

The oval tent was 70 metres long and 52 metres across. There were 20 king poles - eight main poles, each 67 feet high, in four pairs, and 12 subsidiary ones. The circus ring fitted as usual between the four central king poles and the others at the end of the rectangle stood just outside the hippodrome track.

Stromeyer, the leading European circus tent manufacturer, was chosen to produce the new big top. A scale model was made from Jimmy Chipperfield's plans and the work undertaken at their factory in Konstanz, Germany. It was flown in two Dakota aircraft to England a few days before the opening of the season in Regent Road, Hanley, Stoke on Trent, on Monday 9 March. The press adverts boasted of a £40,000 big top with "50 tons of steel masts, 20 tons of canvas, 15 miles of ropes and rigging." The 6,000 seats weighed 75 tons and "7,000 cubic feet of hot air enter the big top each minute through great ducts, and ensure luxurious comfort even on the coldest nights."

The Roman Spectacle was the most publicised new attraction, it being made possible by the hippodrome track. It began with a grand parade of four lady riders, Elaine, Maureen, Sheila and Doreen Duggan, dressed in togas and each riding a palomino, followed by two Roman riders with pairs of horses, and four chariots. The Roman riding involved the two horsemen, Georgie Scott and Harry Stebbings, standing on the backs of their pairs of horses and chasing round the arena, after which the four charioteers - Jackie Williams, Tommy Purchase, Terry Duggan and Bob Pratt - drove their two-horse chariots round the track at high speed to provide one breathtaking climax to the show, soon followed by another, the double human cannonball presentation, Mr and Mrs Raluy being fired simultaneously from their cannon across the ring into a safety net on the other side. Sally Chipperfield recalls that, as a young child, the sound of the cannon at about 6.45 p.m., marking an end to the matinée, was the signal for her to have to go to bed.

Above: *the canvas sections arrived by aeroplane from Germany.*

The Scott and Stebbings families were members of the Dorchester riding troupe which joined the show that season. It was one of the established bareback troupes of its day, having been seen at Blackpool Tower Circus, and it was featured in the Cowboy Carousel on Chipperfield's. During this, many of the show's horses were run round the hippodrome track, led by cowgirls, Mary Chipperfield and Doreen Duggan among them, in a spectacular sequence, made more effective as they went in a different direction to the riders in the ring.

The headlines were enthusiastic - "Crowds besiege the Circus... there can be no mistake about it, it's terrific" and "Circus route crowd causes four mile jam." After Stoke on Trent, the 1953 tour included Nottingham, Worcester, Swindon, Bristol, Parkstone (Branscombe Recreation Ground), Portsmouth, Hove, Eastbourne, Hastings, Ashford, Folkestone, Margate, Gillingham, and into London, with stands on Clapham Common, Peckham Rye, Lea Bridge Road Leyton, Victoria Park and Wormwood Scrubs.

Chipperfield's became the first travelling circus in Britain to have its own newspaper, with Chipperfield's Circus News. The Gillingham edition heralded the visit to the Kent town from Monday 31 August. "After nearly 2,000 years, Roman chariot racing is still public thriller No. 1," a headline claimed, as well this advert, "Meeting a friend - waiting for the show - make your rendezvous the circus restaurant." There were articles by such notables as J. H. Williams ("Elephant Bill"), equestrian expert Brian Vesey-Fitzgerald on famous circus horses, journalist Eddie Campbell on the post-war success of the Chipperfields, and E.H. Tong, superintendent of Whipsnade Zoo, on the Bactrian camels, which came from this zoo. Lieutenant-Colonel J. H. Williams OBE had become famous for his books *Elephant Bill* (1950) and *Bandoola* (1953) about elephants in the teak forests of Burma. When he saw Chipperfield's herd of 16, he wrote, "I heard all the happy sounds I associate with elephants. Ears flapping, tails swishing, trunks swinging, fanning the dust from each handful or trunkful of hay before they passed it to their mouths... The truest fact I know of the elephant is its adaptability, its happiness in captivity." An article by ringmaster and animal trainer Harder Jonnson, entitled Life with the Lions, was accompanied by a photo of him with a cub and with Ben Lyon, star of the popular radio programme, Life with the Lyons. The "Special South London Edition" heralded the Clapham Common stand from 7 September 1953, with the 16 elephants parading from Victoria Station to the ground at 3 p.m. on Sunday the 6th.

Above: *an aerial view of the Big Show with four very long queues.* **Below:** *the seating plan.*

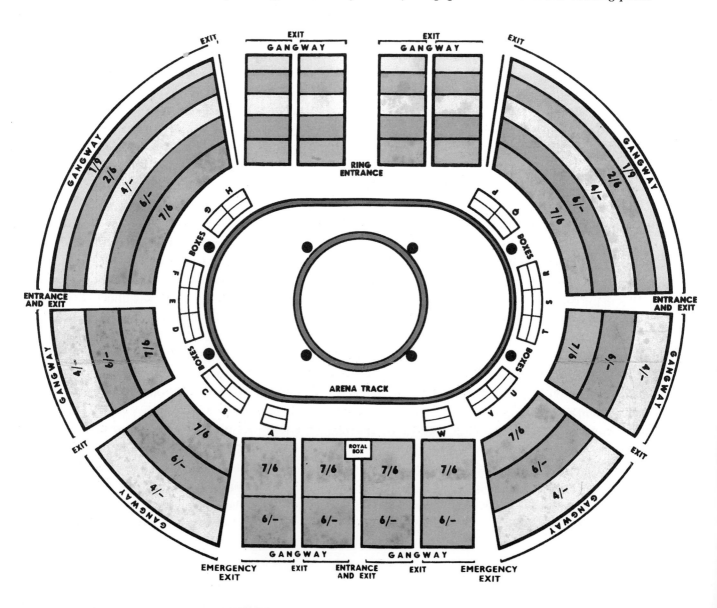

Right: *the double human cannonball act of the Raluys was a big talking point. Seen here during a street parade, the huge cannon was mounted on a specially modifed truck. With the Big Show, the cannon did not fire the humans straight across the ring from the ring doors as had happened in 1952. Instead the cannon drove round and was stationed at the widest part of the track facing the net which was rigged over the track at the other end of the arena. The two humans were therefore fired a distance of 90 feet.*

Edward Graves noted the Chipperfield Big Show publicity machine in action in Margate in August, with the Sunday parade bringing out thousands of people in the rain. "No doubt about it, when Chipperfield's play a place they 'hit' it hard and proper, the arrival parade being but a unit in the process," he wrote in the World's Fair (29.8.1953). They successfully tackled London too - "As regards the advance work, John Hinde and his team found many things very different to those experience in provincial towns; it has been their toughest assignment yet. Nevertheless, reinforced by the prodigious efforts of Lofty Dredge, the PRO, a very good job of work was done. In particular, I liked the assault on public apathy via the Press medium. On August 28 every one of the South London Group of nine weekly newspapers carried a half-page advertisement which somehow managed to convey the idea of the vigour behind the Chipperfield enterprise. It was great stuff, but lo and behold, in those papers a week later (September 4) the circus had a full page so planned as to fairly hit one in the eye and compel attention. Towards the end of last week Frank Pursell and his team arrived and put up one of the two sets of king poles and this had tongues a'wagging. Never before had the people seen such a circus tent skeleton, 'not even Barnum and Bailey' as one elderly resident of Clapham informed me in awestruck tones." The parade from the unloading railway station, Victoria, of the 16 elephants and their travelling companions, camels, horses, llamas and ponies, with an escort of tractors and Raluy's cannon, with a local marching band, was a tremendous success - "all other traffic came to a halt" with "thousands upon thousands" coming to watch, cheer and enjoy the free spectacle down Buckingham Palace Road and along the Avenue to Clapham Common itself - "never before had I seen so many people there."

Don Stacey is a circus commentator with considerable experience during the past 50 years, including three decades as chief circus correspondent for the World's Fair. He writes, "For about two or three years at this time, Chipperfield's Circus was undoubtedly one of the very best in Europe. I still recall vividly that fantastic tent, the marvellous facade, the fountains outside, and above all the huge queues to get into the show - all part of the postwar circus hysteria! The show inside was truly exciting - a tiger on an elephant, big bear act, big lion act, dogs, horses, huge elephant group, cowboy carousel, exotics, sealions, penguins, pelicans - all sorts of creatures you had not seen in a circus. There were the Domis on the wire, the Henris looping the loop, Les French clowns. It's true that there were not many human acts as opposed to animals in hindsight but it was such a big exciting show, rivalling anything in Europe at that time, even the big shows of Krone and Franz Althoff in Germany. The thrilling Roman Spectacle at the end was very exciting, though not 'for the first time in Britain' as claimed. Put it in the context of postwar Britain, it was the biggest and best show on the road for a while. It was far bigger than both Smart and Mills at the time and far more interesting to an entertainment starved audience. They splashed the towns with posters and the newspapers had huge adverts, half page usually. To a youngster, too, the vehicles looked marvellous - big living trailers, a huge number of pale blue and red wagons, and the big reception wagon which was remarkable at the time."

The 1953 programme was - Overture: orchestra under the direction of James Harrison - Polar and black grizzly bears - 3 Henris: looping the loop on the trapeze - Ricardo and his African lions - Ranée the tiger riding an elephant - The Cutanos, four girls and a man, flying trapeze - The Grand Parade, horses, clowns, elephants - Sheila and Little Hubert, skill and comedy riding act - The Domis, tight wire act - The Peerless Poodles - The Royal Percherons - The Sayers, Britain's famous clowns with their 'streamlined' automobile - John L. Chipperfield presents the Equine Cavalcade, including Zarak the wonder jumping horse, the tiger spotted stallions, the Shetlands and the Canadian golden palominos - Les French, clown entrée - High School riding display - The sailor and the penguins - The sealions - Jackie Sloan on the high stilts - The Chipperfield exotic group, including camels, zebras, llama and giraffe - Our Cowboy Carousel, including the Dorchesters riding troupe - Chipperfield's mighty elephant group - The Roman Spectacle, Roman riding and chariot racing - Raluys, double human cannonball. The opening bars of the Overture were not from a circus march, as might be expected, but were "Tantivy, Tantivy, a hunting we will go."

Harder Jonsson continued to show the bears, making this group into something special, a routine "packed with audience appeal" (World's Fair. 28.11.1953) with lots of "sociable association between trainer and animal" such as one black bear shadowing the trainer, another taking food from his mouth and off his bald pate, and another who pats the trainer's pocket, the source of the supply of titbits. Little Hubert and Herbert were established members of the company, Hubert excelling in his comedy riding as Madam Spangletti. They paraded additional animals from the zoo, among them some penguins (with the two clowns dressed as sailors), as white hunters they introduced a pelican, and as bearded Arabs they brought in a llama, each item serving to divert the audience's attention from the prop setting and also helping to give the show its unique flavour as a predominantly Animal Circus. Clown Fiery Jack joined the show in the summer and John Chipperfield was partnered by Doreen Duggan in the High School riding. A large end of season party was held in the North Pole pub at Wormwood Scrubs, with a magnificent cake, a circus ring with four chariots and bareback riders on top, and this was cut, with plenty of ceremony, by Mr and Mrs Richard Chipperfield Snr. Visitors from the circus world included Bertha Gridneff and family; Bob Fossett; agent Jimmy Quinn, his wife Doreen and daughter; sealion trainer Arthur Scott; Joe Barry just back from working in Ireland; the proprietors of Robert Brothers' Circus, Bobby and Kitty Roberts and Tommy and Marie Roberts; Jacko Fossett; Betty Fossett and her son, Reno; and long time circus fan and friend of the family, Ken Kemsley from Nottingham. At the final performance of the season, all the artistes and Mr and Mrs Chipperfield Snr. had received floral tributes from the Chipperfields.

Shortly after the end of the 1953 season, the Stockbridge winter quarters were used for filming some sequences for a movie which required the Indian elephants to be disguised as African elephants, perhaps with large false ears and tusks attached, as in some of the Tarzan films. For the 1953-54 winter season, Chipperfield's sent acts to Prince's Circus at Liverpool Stadium. Joe Barry was equestrian director and presented three elephants, ridden by Sheila, Maureen and Elaine Duggan, as well as a combined liberty act with John Scott's Shetlands followed by Chipperfield's spotted and coloured horses in a trick and jumping pot-pourri. The Dorchesters riding act, including John Scott, was featured in the show, as were Sheila Duggan with Chipperfield's six sealions and Doreen, assisted by Maureen and Elaine, with the dogs.

Above: *the chariot racing in the hippodrome track with Jackie Williams and Tommy Purchase as the charioteers seen here.* **Right:** *charioteer Terry Duggan in the zoo.* **Below:** *the show's trade advert in the World's Fair for 1953.*

Europe's Most Vigorous Circus Enterprise!

☞ *Now on its Mightiest-yet Tenting Tour of Britain* ☞

CHIPPERFIELD'S ZOO & CIRCUS
LIMITED
DOWN FARM, STOCKBRIDGE, HANTS.
Telephone: Wallop 350.

SOLE DIRECTORS:—J. S. M. Chipperfield, J. L. Chipperfield, R. Chipperfield, Jnr., M. Stockley, M. E. Chipperfield, R. F. Chipperfield, J. Stockley.

General Manager .... Robert R. S. Thompson
Programme Director .... Richard Chipperfield, Jnr.
Transport and Electrical Manager .... James Stockley
Production and Gen. Admin. ... James S. M. Chipperfield
Costume Supervision .... Mrs. M. Stockley
Equestrian Director .... John L. Chipperfield
Master of the Horse .... J. Williams
Superintendent Elephant Trainer .... I. G. Rosaire
Wild Animal Trainer and Ringmaster .... H. Jonsson
Advance Manager .... J. Hinde
Press and Public Relations .... W. Dredge
Tentmaster .... C. Waite
Chief Electrician .... A. McVicker
I/c Pole Crew .... F. Pursel
Travelling Artist .... W. H. Smee
Posters .... W. E. Berry
Consulting Veterinary Surgeons ... F. W. Slee and S. Poles

Presenting to the Public in Europe's Biggest Tent:-

Chipperfield's 17 POLAR & BLACK GRIZZLY BEARS   Chipperfield's 14 AFRICAN LIONS
presented by HARDER JONSSON

EQUINE CAVALCADE, with JOHN L. CHIPPERFIELD presenting the Chipperfield Horses, including Zarak — the wonder jumping horse, the Tiger Spotted Stallions, the Shetlands, and the Canadian Golden Palominos.

THE ROMAN SPECTACLE with high-speed Roman Riding by GEORGIE SCOTT and HARRY STEBBINGS, and Breathtaking Chariot Racing by JACKIE WILLIAMS ("The Greatest Roman of Them All"), TOMMY PURCHASE, TERRY and BOB.

COWBOY CAROUSEL with Britain's Jet-Age Bareback Riders, the FIVE FAST AND FURIOUS DORCHESTERS.

THE CHIPPERFIELD EXOTIC GROUP, camels, zebras, llamas—and a GIRAFFE—presented by MAUREEN.

Chipperfield's **SEA LIONS** presented by SHIELA.

THE CUTANOS — Grace and Daring on the Flying Trapeze.

LITTLE HUBERT and **MERRY HERBERT**.

RALUYS — 2 Human Projectiles fired from one cannon at the same time!

THE DOMIS — Artistry and Excitement on the Silver Wire.

THE 3 HENRIS — Two-way Looping the Loop in Mid-air.

JACKIE SLOAN.

RANEE, the only Tiger riding an elephant, presented by RICARDO and IVOR ROSAIRE.

SHEILA AND LITTLE HUBERT. Whirlwind and Comedy Riding.

Chipperfield's Group of 16 **ELEPHANTS** presented by IVOR ROSAIRE.

HIGH SCHOOL DISPLAY by JOHN AND DOREEN.

THE PEERLESS POODLES shown by DOREEN.

PENGUINS and PELICANS.

LES FRENCH — Clowning — Just for Fun.

HARRY, BARRIE AND POODLES — Karnival Kings of Komedy.

THE 3 SYLVANIS — Golden Plastiques.

Yes! It's Chipperfield's! *The Oldest Showpeople with the Newest Ideas*

Above: *the Domis on the wire.* **Below left:** *part of the grand parade.* **Below right:** *Elaine Duggan displaying a python.* **Bottom:** *the Dorchester riders, with John Chipperfield 'keeping up' the horse.*

Above: *Mary Chipperfield, Henry the donkey, Hubert and Herbert, and Sheila Duggan.*

An application by Chipperfields to bring their circus to the centre of Blackpool during the peak holiday period from 25 July to 7 August 1954 prompted a clash of views among members of Blackpool Town Council. Originally, the circus had offered £200 rent for the use of the Waterloo Road coach park but this had been increased to £500 and had gained the recommendation of the General Purposes Committee. The full Council thought otherwise, considering the competition it would provide to the existing entertainments in the town to be unfair. The highly popular Tower Circus, with an international reputation and limited seating capacity of around 1850, was not at risk, it was suggested, but other businesses would suffer. Councillor J.S. Richardson, using the seating capacity of 9,000 per performance (clearly an exaggeration - the advertised capacity was 6,000!), with two or three shows a day, and seat prices of four or five shillings, stated, "Over 14 days these travellers in the night could lift £50,000 in Blackpool and they do not contribute a penny piece in rates." Despite views in favour of the circus visit, Chipperfield's application to come to Blackpool was rejected.

In September 1954, two of the Big Three touring circuses clashed by appearing in the same place, Salisbury, for the same three day period, Monday to Wednesday 13-15 September. R.M. Williams, Chief Reporter of the Salisbury Times & Journal, wrote, "Bertram Mills had originally agreed with the Corporation to visit Salisbury from September 29th to October 3rd but when they heard that Chipperfields were seeking to visit the city a week prior to them Mills decided to bring their dates forward to September 13, 14 and 15th. Hearing this Chipperfields decided to come here on the same dates. It was expected that both organisations would lose heavily but the reverse was the case. The tremendous advertising arising from the dispute led to both shows being packed out at all performances and it was estimated that 58,000 visited the two circuses." Mills had the Corporation site at Hudson's Field, off the Castle Road, and Chipperfields rented Cooks Field, Wilton Road, from Mr Tom Cook.

Dicky Chipperfield recalls: "My father, uncle John and uncle Jimmy knew that Mills had the Old Sarum site in Salisbury booked. Jimmy in particular felt that the south was 'our patch', being Wiltshire/Hampshire boys, and they made the decision to make a big jump to get to Salisbury at the same time as Mills and to challenge Mills's position as No. 1. The 'circus war' made the national newspapers every day. Chipperfield's Circus parade was very big. We were billed as 'Europe's Largest' and Bertram Mills was 'The Quality Show.' Chipperfields had a

Above: *pull down - the eight king poles and their guy wires, festooned with lights.* **Below:** *the Mack crane truck, driven by Frank Purcell hoists a baled-up canvas section onto a trailer. On the right: tentmaster Cyril Waite.*

great depth of animal content and was a larger show, with the big tent and chariot racing, but Bertram Mills was undoubtedly more polished, a beautifully produced show. Both did very good business but Chipperfield's caught the public's imagination. The three Chipperfield brothers were just at the right age, hungry still, courageous - they went for it. Chipperfields had the surprise element over Mills who were caught on the hop inasmuch as their advance publicity unit had already moved onto the next town, and couldn't be brought back, when we arrived. Mills was highly respected but had perhaps become complacent without challengers for so long." Bertram Mills Circus was then a public company and there were comments in the press that week that Jimmy Chipperfield had bought shares in Mills and intended to come to the Annual General Meeting to ask questions. However, Jimmy was later reported as saying that as he bought his shares on 13 September, after the register was closed, he was not a registered shareholder and so could not attend.

Above: *the interior of the luxurious Knebworth reception wagon with Dick Chipperfield admiring an ivory rhinoceros given by Sir Garrard Tyrwhitt-Drake.* **Right:** *the exterior today.*

There was a new reception wagon, to entertain VIPs and visiting dignitaries, and this "Knebworth Hall" wagon created a lot of interest when shown on BBC television from the show in Gloucester. In interior, it followed the design of the Baronial Hall of the Hertfordshire stately home. Inside, there was a push-button system for panelling to slide back and reveal a cocktail bar, radio and television. The glass featured sand-blasted pictures of various animals. On Sunday afternoon and evening, the BBC TV programme, "Out of Doors," included various visits to the circus, showing its arrival in Gloucester, the parade, and a visit to the "Homes on Wheels," with Max Robertson commentating, plus an excerpt from the show on Tuesday.

In 1954, the programme was broadly similar to that presented the previous year. The Swiss trainer, Eugen Weidmann, who before and after this time worked for Circus Knie, latterly with a remarkable mixed wild animal group, showed the nine lionesses but he departed after a while and this role was again undertaken by Harder Jonsson. The Crystallos presented an acrobatic posing act with the artistes covered in "twinkling crystals." Pugh's Aerial Ballet was another new feature, with six girls on swinging ladders and another six at ground level holding the ropes. The girls also made appearances heading the parade; displaying four pythons; wearing carnival Big Heads alongside the Harry Sloan troupe; and in the Roman spectacle. Of the 1953 acts, only the Royal Percherons were not included. Little Herbert was no longer alongside Hubert in the show, owing to family bereavements. Elaine Duggan was now showing the poodles as well as riding one of the camels, whom she remembers as being called Achmed. John Chipperfield's horse display contained six spotted horses, followed by six small ponies and a donkey wearing L plates who baffled all attempts to get him to jump the low bar, and the 12 palominos at liberty. Dressed as a Spanish grandee, John rode High School alongside "Signorita" Doreen Duggan, or Mary Chipperfield until she left to continue her equestrian studies with the Swiss National Circus Knie along with her recently acquired Lippizaner, Maestoso. As a Knie trainee, Mary was tutored by Frédy Knie, one of the world's finest horsemen, and George Wahl, who later became the trainer of the Austrian Olympic dressage champion. Mr Wahl partnered Frédy Knie in a double High School routine at the evening performances but, for the matinées, it was Mary who had this honour.

Among the newcomers to the key posts were W.W. Dredge as Advance Manager (previously he was PRO), A. Whyatt as the new electrician, J. Rolt as house manager and Major Pat Ness as Master of Horse. They joined General Manager Bobby Thompson; Harder Jonsson, ringmaster and wild animal trainer; Ivor Rosaire, superintendent elephant trainer; Cyril Waite, tentmaster; Frank Purcell, i/c pole crew; W.H. (Bill) Smee, travelling artist; S. Poles, consultant veterinary surgeon; and F.W. Slee (Feanley Slee, brother of Myrtle, Mrs Dick Chipperfield), consulting veterinary practitioner. Following the good business in 1953, excellent houses were again encountered, notably in Plymouth and the fortnight in Cardiff.

For the 1954-55 winter season at Harringay, Ivor Rosaire presented a group of 17 elephants. Near the opening of the show, Sheila Duggan contributed a ballerina on horseback routine, and Ivor showed a "Duet in Cream" with the two pale skewbald horses. Later in the programme, Sheila presented four sealions. The Thousand and One Nights spectacle included Chipperfield's exotic group of six camels and four llamas in a liberty and pedestal routine, then joined on parade by zebras, kangaroos and George the giraffe, presented by Maureen Duggan, with sisters Elaine and Sheila on hand to assist. Chipperfield's horses were seen in the "wild horse stampede" which also featured in the Arabian production.

In 1955, it was intended that the Avantis, with their jet plane on the high wire, should replace the Cutanos and they duly arrived and took part in the opening stand in Dagenham, only to suffer a fall on the last day there, resulting in their withdrawal from the show. They were subsequently replaced by the Camilla Mayer Troupe on the high wire. The Hans Fontner Troupe provided bareback riding instead of the Dorchesters. The Cowboy Carousel and Raluy's cannon were not programmed, and three men working in gold as the Kalev Troupe performed the new acrobatic act (replacing the Crystallos). The Tarzanovas provided an aerial act on the trapeze, including a featured blindfold leap, with one man dressed as Tarzan, another in an ape suit and the girl in a leopard skin. The Domis low wire act continued to be a highlight of the show (which had no interval), with backward and forward somersaults on the wire. The forward somersault is always considered more difficult as the performer cannot see the wire as he comes out of his turn, thus making landing on the taut strand of metal even more hazardous.

The newspaper included these comments on the directors and managers in its Who's Who? "Dick Chipperfield. Eldest brother, in charge of programme and wild beasts. Uncanny knack of knowing what the public wants and proceeds to give it to them. Jim Chipperfield. Director of administration. Ex-wartime RAF pilot, still pilots one of the two planes attached to the circus, scouring the world for new attractions. Visionary with impact and practical reality. John Chipperfield. Youngest of the three brothers. Has over 70 headaches and they are all horses. In charge of horses and stables. Also ex-RAF. Marjorie Chipperfield (Mrs Stockley). Sister of

Above: *trainer Ivor Rosaire recalls bull elephant Blackie would cause an appreciative stir by looking at the audience, first to the left, then right, before performing this impressive front leg stand.* **Below:** *Maureen Duggan and the exotic act with zebras, llamas, camels and kangaroos.*

Above: *Ivor Rosaire with an elephant that seems to be push-starting an FWD during build up.*

the above, in charge of the girls' wardrobe, costumes, etc., and, of course, bringing up her own family. Jimmy Stockley, DFM. Transport Manager, ex-RAF navigator to Jimmy Chipperfield, married to Marjorie. Thinks now in terms of Mack Tractors, miles per gallon, and the shortest and flattest way between two towns. Robert R.S. Thompson. General Manager, ex-RAF. Has an overall picture of the show at his fingertips. Favourite hobby, strangely enough, is welding. W. Dredge, Manager of the Advance Admin. Unit, PRO and Editor of Circus News. Harder Jonnson. Ringmaster. Looks just as every ringmaster should. Cyril Waite. Tentmaster. Local Stockbridge boy makes good. A very "up and down" life for Mr Waite. Frank Purcell. Advance Construction Manager." Although this emphasises the leading roles played by Dick and Jimmy, it also rightly indicates an equally important reason for the show's success - the excellent team with strong and able people in key departments.

"Double Top" was the unusual name of a show televised by the BBC from the National Radio Show at Earls Court on 24 August 1955. It was "double" because of the involvement of two of the big circuses, Chipperfield and Billy Smart, with two circus rings set up in the arena. For other performances at Earls Court, there were several Chipperfield acts, including Mary Chipperfield's High School riding, but for this TV show there were aerial acts only - Camilla Mayer walking the high wire with commentator Bob Danvers-Walker outside the building, Andora's slide for life, and the Four Dernos trapeze act. Billy Smart's contributed their horses and ponies, Flying Comets, Charles Illeneb with the lions, Ifni Sahara Troupe of acrobats, the sealions with Fleming; Smart's clowns; chimpanzees; and ten elephants with Ronald Smart.

Part way through the 1955 season, Jimmy Chipperfield and family left the show. In *My Wild Life*, he wrote of his reasons, including "the realisation that there was just not going to be room in the business for all the members of our families. I and Rosie, by then, had four children; Dicky and his wife Myrtle had three, my sister Marjorie had three, and my younger brother John four. In another generation, I could see, the show would have fifty directors, and the situation would become impossible." Furthermore, Jimmy cites "the fundamental difference between Dicky's character and mine. I was always for pushing ahead, for expanding, for getting bigger, longer, faster, heavier - for becoming the biggest in the world. I could never just stroll along. Dicky, on the other hand, could not see the point of continually increasing our effort. 'Why not relax and stay as we are?' he would say. 'We're quite big enough already.' In this he was very like my father who hated having responsibilities and preferred everything on a small scale. I, by contrast, had much more of my mother's ambition."

Immediately after the departure of Jimmy Chipperfield, there was a reduction in size of the big top and abandonment of the hippodrome track. The Fontners and the Roman spectacle were no longer included. In their places were Chipperfield's chimpanzees, and Maximum and Minimum, equine contrasts, presented by John Chipperfield. Edward Graves (World's Fair. 3.12.1955) wrote of the last stand on Hounslow Heath, stating that, if one did not pay too much concern to the loss of the chariot racing and parade, the new set up was for several displays "considerably brighter and better." New or altered acts seen included four Digger Pugh Girls on a quadruple trapeze; Charles Illeneb (who had been mauled and seriously injured when presenting Smart's lions on 13 October) with four young tigers; a bareback riding act by Sheila Duggan, a young Fontner and three Digger Pugh girls, trained by John Chipperfield; Anne Chipperfield riding High School; Hans Brick with four chimpanzees; and Doreen Duggan showing the camels and llamas, and then with the zebras and George the giraffe at the end.

The Big Show, with its 20 pole big top and Roman chariot racing, had come to an end. Arguably, even though it had done exceptional business for its first two seasons, it was too big and too expensive to run in Britain for much longer, since its very size meant that it could not visit many of the smaller towns where Chipperfield's had done well before. But nonetheless, under Dick Chipperfield's direction, it would remain a sizeable operation, ranking alongside Bertram Mills and Billy Smart, the other members of the "Big Three," for another nine years.

Journalist Eddie Campbell sums up Chipperfield's in its heyday as "a brave, rough-and-ready show, displaying immense vitality but a whole dimension separate from the ordered magnificence of Bertram Mills." He writes, "I think there were probably five different reasons for the explosive success of the family but there is no hope of finding a universal formula because the ingredients will never be repeated. The first was the public appetite for entertainment after the six or seven years of privation during the war. *Anything* would take money. The second was the size and impact of the show, a huge thing, bursting with an almost crude vitality. The third was the huge cargo of animals. The volume on offer was enormous. Dick Chipperfield once said to me, 'If you put enough animals in one place, a crowd will gather.' He said it as though it was a family discovery which they were, much to their own surprise, in a position to implement. Fourth, there was a belief in the importance of publicity. Fifth and finally, there was a curious in-family tension which in most similar circumstances would have produced disruption and maybe collapse. The tension was between Jimmy and Dick, with Marjorie and John on the sidelines. Once, at Dundee, Jimmy and Dick and I went for a walk round the town in the forenoon. We were at some factory when two heavy doors swung open and there emerged a van which had obviously just been professionally repainted. It gleamed and looked superb. We all three stopped to let it come out and then Jimmy said, 'Dick, every wagon on our show ought to look like that.' Dick disagreed, 'The day *one* wagon on our show looks like that, we're bust.' That was an example of the tension but for some extraordinary reason with the Chipps it served rather to stimulate aspiration than to disrupt. At the time of their expansion, and until Jimmy's departure in 1955, it served somehow to fuel more and more endeavour."

Below: *the chariots in the zoo when the show played Ipswich in 1955.*

Chapter 6
1956 to 1964

Above: *Chipperfield's Circus played alongside the cattle fair in Athlone, Ireland.*

Chipperfield's Circus was again on BBC television at the start of the 1956 season, with a documentary from Down Farm. As well as the preparations for the show's departure, Jimmy Chipperfield was interviewed and talked about his new role as a farmer and his show jumping ventures with his daughter, Mary. That year's circus tour included a trip to Ireland, a major undertaking for a show of this size to cross the Irish Sea and travel in both the north and south. They originally planned to stay for eight weeks but they encountered such success that they toured for nearly five months, with lengthy stays in Belfast and Dublin. In Athlone, the circus was on the same site as the cattle fair. The scheduled return to England was delayed by being unable to get a ship because of the Suez crisis, so they wintered in Ireland and returned the following March. General Manager Bobby Thompson says that they enjoyed the visit as the Irish were so welcoming and everyone loved the circus. From an administrative point of view, he had some difficulties with getting things done on time which could be frustrating. They encountered no anti-British feelings. In 1956, Chipperfields sold three elephants - in order of size, Jimmy, Monica and Blackie (two bulls and one cow) to Fossett's Circus in Ireland, where they were presented by Teddy Fossett, or his wife Herta or her father Otto Lordini. To have three elephants was a considerable attraction for an Irish show and, when Chipperfields arrived with their 15, Fossetts reacted with a pictorial poster headed Chipperfield's Elephants but not specifying the number. The elephants stayed on Fossetts until 1958 when Herta presented them on Circus Samerei Busch in Germany, after which they were sold to Russia.

The 1956 printed programme lists these attractions: Overture, the circus orchestra under the direction of Al Podesta - the Pugh Girls, on the trapeze - Alola the jungle princess and her Bengal tigers - Britain's fastest lion group presented by Clem Merk - the Airdonis, high trapeze - spotted Hungarian stallions and spotted ponies with Henry the donkey - the Domis on the tight wire - the Peerless Poodles - the Western Spectacle with the Three Texans, Little Hubert, Douglas Kossmayer, Chief Eagle Eye and Cowboys and Indians - Fiery Jack and his useless assistant - the Three Henrys, designed for thrills - Five Valnohas, juggling on high unicycles - the Cheeky Chimps, including the stilt walking chimp - the Diaz Family, First time here, Spain's most famous clowns - the Bustons, football on bicycles - Introducing the Indian pythons - 12 Palominos and Thoroughbred Racehorses, and Sidi the wonder jumping horse, presented by John L. Chipperfield - The Only Exotic Group, introducing George the giraffe with Bactrian camels and llamas - John Chipperfield presents High School - The Elephant Spectacle, The World's Greatest, presented by Wenzel Kossmayer - Raluy and his Triple Somersaulting Car, "The World's Only" - The Queen.

The stilt-walking chimp was Charlie, a great character who was with the show until his death in 1978. He came from Paignton Zoo where he was partly trained by Alexander Zass, who had originally gone to Paignton during the war with the animals from the Chessington Zoo and Circus because of the danger from bombing. Charlie was taught to stilt-walk by Hans Brick, the trainer of great ability who was with Chipperfield's for a while in the mid-50s. The other chimps were Skipper and Bobby. Wenzel Kossmayer, who had done so much with the first elephants in the late 1940s, did not stay long this time; and the Spanish clowns did not register well with the British public and also departed. Daredevil Raluy brought a new thrill to close the show, a somersaulting car which careered down a ramp before taking off, and it was another Spaniard, his partner, not Raluy himself, who drove the car. One printing of the programme still has the address as Down Farm, Stockbridge, but the next has Oak Gardens, Wishford, near Wilton, Wiltshire, that of Mr and Mrs Chipperfield Snr.

Sally, daughter of Dick and Myrtle Chipperfield, recalls the trip to Ireland by boat, waiting at the docks and travelling in the family's big four wheeled living wagon. Her earliest memories are of going away to boarding school when she was five. Her cousin Mary had been to the same school, but had left, and she went back there to accompany Sally and her cousin Carol Stockley, who was four. Sally remembers the show with a great big tent and how there were always lots of people around. There were many Irish workers, all very wholesome and honest. There was always someone who would keep an eye on the children and everyone was very trustworthy. There was strict discipline, for very good reasons. Sally remembers running under the beast wagons where the lions, tigers and bears were, but she only did it once. It was the only time she remembers being told off by her father who was furious as she had gone against the rules and was in danger.

Below: *when the circus could not return to England from Ireland because of the Suez crisis, it played some unusual dates, such as this performance in the factory canteen of BTH in Larne.*

Left: *the dogs with Diane and,* **right**, *with Marion Larrigan, who met her husband Peter on Chipperfield's. Their daughter, Tanya, is a leading dressage rider.*

Sally recalls knowing every animal's name and she and her cousins would help in the stables at the age of seven or eight, alongside Bill Stubbs who looked after the Shires. They had to clean their ponies which they rode and led in the parade. She was encouraged to be with the animals and they had photos taken with them all the time. Bill's wife, Alice Stubbs, was nursemaid to the young Chipperfields, their caravan always being behind Marjorie Stockley's big living wagon on the family side of the ground.

For the 1956-57 Christmas season, John Chipperfield went with the horses and chimps to the Liverpool Stadium circus and, in 1957, the printed running order follows similar lines to the previous year's, with the Airellys aerial act and the Massino Troupe on the trampoline in place of the Airdonis and the Domis. Chako the almost human ape, Be Wilda the great magician and Kelly's unrideable mule were among other new features. During the 1957 season, Doreen Duggan was with Circus Scott in Sweden, presenting three Chipperfield elephants; and Franz Huby (described as Franz Hruby Triumph) showed five polar and three brown bears on the Radio Circus in France, a show which had two cage acts that year, the other being another British one provided by Sidney Howes and Robert Brothers' six lionesses and one lion. Although occasionally described as brown, as they look browny black sometimes, the bears with the polars continued to be the Canadian black ones. In the autumn, the informative book *Chipperfield's Circus* by Pamela Macgregor-Morris was published by Faber & Faber.

Chipperfield's commenced a series of Christmas shows at Bingley Hall, Birmingham, an established venue for winter circus, with the large population of the West Midlands to draw on. The 1957-58 show featured 23 items: Overture - polar and black bears shown by Captain J. Smith - Gina on the swaying anchor - tigers shown by Roger Debille - lions with Roger Debille - D. Pugh's Aerial Ballet - English Shire carthorses presented by John L. Chipperfield - The Shetland ponies, followed by Henry the donkey - the Hermanis, grace and strength combined - Marian's Pony and Dog Revue - the Astrals on the trapeze - Fiery Jack and his crazy baby Austin - three elephants presented by Dick Chipperfield - Kelly's unrideable mule - De-Vel and Pat, juggling on unicycles - Cheeky Chimpanzees presented by John Chipperfield - Les Denivers, comedy acrobatic - Western Scene with Big Chief Eagle Eye, Cowboys, Cowgirls and Davy Crockett Jnr. - The Two Grimbles, clowns - Zarak the jumping horse and his girl friends - 12 Thoroughbred Racehorses presented by John L. Chipperfield - the exotic act featuring George and Georgina the two giraffes, the Bactrian camels, the llamas and Harry the hippo - the mighty group of elephants presented by Dick Chipperfield. Like George the giraffe and the Bactrian camels, Harry the hippo came from Whipsnade Zoo. His parents, Henry and Henrietta, had been captured in Africa in the 50s and had long lives at Whipsnade, the last one dying in 1995.

Above: *Mr Pastry (left) with Tom Fossett as Grimble and Dicky Sandow as the schoolgirl.*

This season marked the return of Maude Fossett (née Chipperfield), to the show, with her husband Tom, their son Tom and daughter Shirley. Together they provided the Astrals trapeze act; Tom Jnr. was De-Vel the unicycling juggler; and Shirley was Gina in the moon. Tom Fossett Jnr. performed a comedy entrée as one of the Two Grimbles, the other being Dicky Sandow. They had put together a routine but, at the dress rehearsal, Dick Chipperfield thought that it didn't work well enough and he told them to do the old egg entrée, so they had to quickly gather together the props needed. Bill Smee, the scenic artist, also appeared as clown Pee Wee Smee, on the receiving end of many broken eggs, in the routine. In later years, as Professor Grimble, Tom was recognised as one of the finest British clowns of his generation, but his start had been the year before, when he was with the Carl Purchase Circus, operated for a short time by his uncle, Jimmy Chipperfield. With the first performance that day, Tom looked at the posters and saw "Grimble & Grimble - clowns." He asked who the clowns were and Jimmy said, "You're one of them - get made up," and a star clown was (in due course) born!

That same winter season, Doreen Duggan took the three elephants and three girls act that she'd shown in Sweden to the Bertram Mills Circus at Olympia, an important booking during which time they appeared in front of Her Majesty the Queen, Prince Philip, Prince Charles and Princess Anne. During the following summer, Doreen was with the elephants in Spain, on Circo Price, and also her brother Terry took a third giraffe, Kismet, on tour with this leading Spanish circus in a specially converted double decker bus.

The World's Fair review (4.10.1958) by Edward Graves was headed "Circus of the bright lights" and he considered Chipperfield's to be "the best lit circus to travel Britain for many a long year," also referring to the fact that a TV crew had not found it necessary to boost the lighting for a recent recording from the show. The large front included paintings by Bill Smee of the Lioness Wagon on one side and the Western scene on the other. When seen at Leeds, a fortnight stand, the programme had been augmented by the variety and TV star, Mr Pastry (Richard Hearne), whose acrobatic and knockabout comedy ability was integrated into the show. He came from circus stock, his grandfather being stud groom for Lord George Sanger who drove a team of horses in Sanger's parades. His humour was much suited to the circus.

His first appearance was to come in late through the public entrance, as if he was a member of the audience. He was accompanied by Dicky Sandow as a St Trinian's schoolgirl, constantly asking Mr Pastry to give her an ice cream. He eventually picked up a large ice cream from an attendant, asked "So you want an ice cream, do you?" and swung it at Dicky Sandow's face. Dicky ducked and the ice cream went over the attendant, who then chased them out through the curtains. Mr Pastry was in the bareback act, doing some voltige tricks, after Hubert, Anne

Chipperfield and Julie Dare had done their riding. Hubert was dressed as a miniature Davy Crockett, the Western folk hero of the day. In the Grimble and Grimble routine, it was Mr Pastry who threw up one egg only to have it crash and break on his unprotected head. He also had a go on the trampoline of the Massino troupe, and ended up proving his acrobatic ability by turning a double somersault. Mr Pastry proved to be a valuable way of enhancing attendance.

Fiery Jack, as always with a "diminutive accomplice," was presenting his comedy motor car and there was more comedy with the unrideable mule and with Chako, the "Almost Human Ape," who molested a lady, supposedly a member of the audience, removing her skirt, before ascending to the top of an inclined wire and then sliding down it, the routine known as the "Slide for Life" which he presented without the gorilla suit under the name Andorra in the menagerie on Sunday afternoons. In real life, Chako went by the name of Mr Black.

Dick Chipperfield's son, Dicky, had made his début with the lions that season, after he left Wellington School at the age of 15, working with three lionesses in a wagon cage in the style of the old wild animal presentations in the menageries. The wagon was pulled into the ring by an elephant and, once she had left the ring, the blinds on the cage were pulled up and the lionesses revealed. The trainer went in and the big cats raced round and performed jumps and pyramid groupings on slings against the bars, providing a spectacular routine, made more thrilling by the closeness of the trainer and lions. Dicky had come home from school and practised the act for two weeks before appearing before the public. He had been in the cage with wild animals before but it was the first time he'd worked an act, although it had been discussed many times previously and he'd long held an ambition to present the lions. His first shows were in Edinburgh and he was seen with the lions on television but, at the next stand, Glasgow, the local authorities felt the risk he was taking was too great at his age and so he was not allowed to appear, the authorities invoking a law designed to protect children from being exploited through "unsuitable" work. So, when Edward Graves saw the show at Leeds, his uncle, John Chipperfield, worked this act, as well as presenting the four Shire cart horses, four Shetlands and the donkey, the big liberty horse group of 12 thoroughbreds (six greys, six chestnuts) and the three chimpanzees.

Below: *the wagon cage was pulled into the ring by an elephant for "The Original Wild Animal Presentation." This photo shows the cage used for the leopards in 1961-3. At other times, a pair of oxen pulled the leopards' cage into the ring.* **Below right:** *Jack Smith, leading the elephant, and his wife, Edith Freyer, are experienced animal trainers. Their son, Emile, is a leading trainer for Sally and Jim Clubb's Clubb-Chipperfield company.*

Above: *in 1957, the pagoda balancing routine was presented in this novel way. While Tommy Fossett balanced the canopy on a cane on his forehead, eight girl riders as Indian lancers entered and handed their lances to Shirley on a rolling globe. She passed these one by one to Tom who fitted one end of them into the cups on the edge of the canopy, the other on his forehead. With all the lances in place and the pagoda canopy fully supported, Tom juggled two hoops on his arms.*

In the big cage at the start of the show, the polar and black bears were shown by Edith Freyer, dressed in a Slav-style tunic and assisted by her husband Jack Smith, and Roger Debille presented five lions in a fast moving display. Jack Smith later paraded three brown bears, and Dick Chipperfield presented the group of eight elephants being toured that year. The Tom Fossett family contributed "three specialities which fairly sparkle" - their Astrals aerial display, Shirley as Gina in the moon, and Tom and Shirley as Duballo and Jose with the juggling act and the pagoda balance.

The show also included the Digger Pugh Aerial Ballet, four girls on vertical ropes; Julie Dare showing the poodles; and the Cowboy Carousel with Jack Carson as Chief Eagle Eye and Barbara as the human target for his whip tricks, sharp shooting and knife and hatchet throwing. Last but not least, Anne Chipperfield presented the final act, the spectacular exotic group, starting with six Bactrian camels, each with a girl rider, in a liberty routine, then joined by seven llamas, Harry the hippo in a trailer pulled into the ring by the ringstaff, and George the giraffe, with a girl rider, and Georgina the female giraffe. When viewed by Edward Graves, there was also a baby camel and Mr Pastry carried in a recently-born llama. The programme includes a photo of a snake charmer, believed to be Asita, a German artiste with a snake and crocodile act, who was with the show for a short time.

Alfie Gunner, who went on to become Chipperfield's tentmaster, joined the show as a ring boy in 1958 when he was 17. Originally from Portsmouth, he was passing through Nottingham and asked the circus for a job. He was quickly promoted to being a tentman and his skills as a steel worker and welder, from two years of an apprenticeship, were put to good use. Cyril Waite, as tentmaster, and Jimmy Stockley, in charge of the transport and electrics, "ran the show," as far as moving it from A to B was concerned. Alfie remembers Jimmy Stockley: "He was a seriously hard worker; he led from the front; he never slept and he never asked you to do something he didn't do. He was an absolutely brilliant mechanic. Thanks to him, the old wagons, which weren't bad for their day, would plod on and on." Cyril Waite, married to Maureen Duggan, was "very straight - no airs and graces - and very efficient."

The king poles were erected by the advance pole crew, run then by Bob Fossett, using two sets of poles. They'd arrive at the new ground mid-week and put up a set of king poles and queen poles. Then, after the pull down of the circus at the previous ground on the Saturday night, the pole crew would arrive on the Sunday and take down that set of poles and then move on to a third ground and put up the poles for the circus to use the following week. Thus, when the circus arrived at a new town on the Sunday morning, the poles were up and the stakes were already in the ground, thus saving a lot of time building the show up.

At the time, there would be about 50 working men on the circus - seven or eight ring boys taking props in and out during the performance, 15 to 20 tentmen, a dozen grooms and two or three beast men, two electricians and mechanics and two or three on the advance pole crew. At each pull down on the Saturday night and build up on the Sunday morning in the next town, there'd also be around 20 casual workers. They needed this number of men, plus mechanical help, to lift the large canvas sections, which became even heavier when wet, retaining so much water. At the time, ring boys were paid £3 per week plus food and accommodation, and tentmen got £5. This wage was also usually reserved until the men were aged 21. There were extra payments for leading a gang of men on pull down or build up, and a £2 per week bonus for drivers. The bonus was paid at the end of the season. So, all in all, Alfie says, the pay was not too bad when you consider that tradespeople in Portsmouth Docks were on £8 per week at the time. When the show went into winter quarters, the men were on half pay of £3 per week.

During the week, the tentmen were divided into two gangs. The outside gang would work from 9 a.m. until the 4.45 p.m. matinée doing maintenance, such as welding, painting and carpentry. They'd take the big cage down after the wild animal acts at around 5 p.m. and then have a couple of hours off until the cage had to be erected around 7 p.m. for the night show at 7.30. After they'd taken the cage down again, they could get out in the evening. Each day, two or three of them were not required to put the cage up for the second show - this was their "day off." The inside gang were the gangway men. During the morning, they'd clean the seats and inside the big top and around the show, picking up any litter. Then they'd have two hours off in the afternoon before going on the doors for the two shows, taking tickets, showing people to their seats, etc., during the performances. At the winter quarters, you worked from 8 a.m. to 8 p.m. each day, including Sundays, but finished at 1 p.m. on Saturdays, when the circus arranged transport into the town for the men. Many of the men were Irish, or Polish, and Alfie Gunner remembers that he was the only Englishman at one point. A nucleus of at least a dozen of the outside gang stayed for ten or 12 years or more - among them Big John, Maxi, Major, Herman, Freddie, Meanie, Brennan (a Scot), Joe O'Neal, Danny Flynn, Vincent O'Boyle, Harry Shrimpton - and Major (John Nyhan) and Herman Purence stayed at the farm until their deaths in recent years and Vincent O'Boyle ran the gift shop in the Natal Lion Park until his retirement to County Mayo in his native Ireland in 1993.

Alfie remembers both Jimmy Stockley and Cyril Waite as trying to improve the lot of the working men: "We'd joke that the animals were treated better than the men." They made new bunk wagons and, the first year at the farm at Heythrop, in the winter of 58-59, they built bunk houses and a snooker room. That winter was a very cold one and the Heythrop farm had previously been used as a sawmill, so many of the big barns didn't have ends to them until later, giving little protection to the men working inside.

Many of the vehicles had come from the Army, including the big four wheel drive Mack and AEC tractors. Other lorries - Fodens, Thorneycrofts, Atkinsons, etc. - would be bought from the nationwide haulage company, British Road Services. "BRS scrap'em, we buy'em," the men would joke. With stands of a week or a fortnight and jumps between towns of 40 or 50 miles, sometimes less, the transport would only do 1,000 miles a year. When they went to Scotland, as they did in 1958, they'd clock up 1,500 miles but that was rare, so the transport was quite up to the job, given the attention of Jimmy Stockley and his team. As far as building and maintainence was concerned, the circus was completely self-sufficient. Almost everything, from stable tents, wallings and poles to wagons and props, was made or adapted on site. The range of specialist transport designed and manufactured included trucks to carry the seating, tractors carrying the generators or a crane, beast wagons for the wild animals, bunk wagons for the staff, horse boxes, reinforced box trailers for the elephants, the canteen bus, a wagon with a large pool for Harry the hippo, and a converted double decker bus for the giraffes.

For the winter season of 1958-59, Chipperfield's presented their second season at Bingley Hall, Birmingham, with the substantial presence of heavyweight comedy actor Fred Emney as guest ringmaster. It also marked the début of Dicky Chipperfield Jnr. as elephant presenter. The programme was: Overture - African lions with Roger Debille - The Paulos, trapeze act - Three Teddy Bears - The Silvanos, comedy acrobats - The Original Wild Animal Presentation, with John L. Chipperfield - Ron and Rita, thrills and spills on the tightrope - The Canine Revue - Thoroughbred liberty horses with John Chipperfield - Fiery Jack and Co. - The Massino Troupe, trapeze/trampoline acrobats - The Maxims, riding act - Chako, the almost human ape - The Cheeky Chimps with John L. Chipperfield - Five Biasinis, trick cyclists - Europe's Greatest Elephant Herd presented by 15 year old wonder boy Dicky Chipperfield Jnr. - Mr Fred Emney and the joey pony - The Exotic Group, camels, llamas, giraffes and Harry the hippo, presented by Miss Anne Chipperfield. The Biasini family from Italy, who contributed their cycling act and the Sylvanos knockabout table routine, was to remain with Chipperfield's for some time. The Paulos, from another famous circus dynasty, were Harry Paulo and family who also presented the Ron and Rita tightrope routine and rode in the Maxims riding troupe.

The 1959 tour commenced in Southampton, and King's Park, Bournemouth, was the stand for the Easter holiday. The programme was: Overture - Polar and black bears - Gina the girl in the moon - African lions - Three Paulos, trapeze act - Chipperfield's cart horses - Canine Review - Two Sylvanos, two men and a table - The baby teddy bears presented by Marion

Larrigan - Ron and Rita, comedy slack wire - Mixed troupe of bulls and ponies - Grimble & Grimble - Massino Troupe, trampoline/trapeze act - The Original Wild Animal Presentation, with John L. Chipperfield - The Maxims, riding troupe - The Astrals, aerial act - Troupe of thoroughbred racehorses with John L. Chipperfield - Chako the almost human ape - Duballo and Jose, juggling act - The Cheeky Chimps - Biasini Troupe, cycling act - Chipperfield's Herd of Elephants presented by the world's youngest trainer, 15 year old Dickie Chipperfield - Exotic Troupe of camels, llamas, giraffes, crocodiles and hippopotamus presented by Anne Chipperfield. The bears and lions were presented by experienced trainer Clem Merk.

Celebrity ringmaster Fred Emney was again with the show but he fell coming out of his caravan at King's Park and broke his ankle. As a result, the 20 stone star later sued the circus for loss of earnings as he alleged that it had been agreed that a pedestal would be placed outside the caravan door. As a result of his size, he had been unable to check that it was indeed there before coming out of the door. He received £850 in damages. The show visited Ireland again and the business, though satisfactory, was not as sensational as in 1956. In the 1959 programme, the permanent address was Heythrop, near Chipping Norton, the farm and winter quarters used by Chipperfield's to the present day.

Above: *a reception for the circus in Dublin in 1959. Included are John, Dicky and Dick Chipperfield (front row, right to left), Mr Black (Chako the ape), his wife and son (front row, left), Tommy, Vera, Shirley and Maude Fossett (second row, right to left), Tom Fossett Snr. and Marion Larrigan (third row, far right and third from right), as well as Freda, Anne Chipperfield, Doreen Duggan, the Biasinis, the Massinos, ringmaster Alex Clarke and family, Peter Larrigan, Clem and Violet Merk, Fiery Jack, Frank Pursell, Bill Smee and Terry Duggan.*

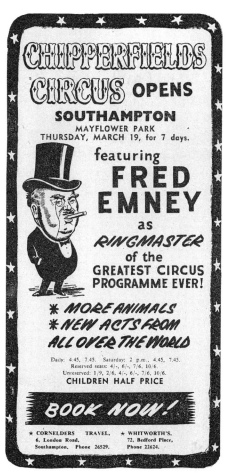

Left: *the Atora Suet wagon drawn by two oxen in the circus parade - one of several links with commercial comapnies made by Chipperfields in the late 50s and early 60s. There were also the two Henessey brandy mascots, the St Bernards, Brandy and Soda, which, like the oxen, could be seen in the menagerie and there was a tie-up with Wagon Wheels biscuits, with a covered wagon drawn by two coloured horses.* **Right:** *a press advert for ringmaster Fred Emney.*

That year also sadly saw the death at the age of 85 of Richard Chipperfield at Wishford, Wiltshire, where he and his wife had lived happily in retirement for 20 years. Eddie Campbell described him as "a very calm, reasonable and intelligent man who I found myself liking very much... I was greatly impressed by the general intelligence of the old man - nothing like the popular picture of the fairground showman."

Ringing the changes at Bingley Hall in 1959-60, Chipperfield's presented the "First World Wide Christmas Circus Festival," with new acts and animals from other sources for the third season here, as well as the first appearance of Chipperfield's crocodiles and snakes act. The programme was: Grand Parade - young Carolyn Roberts showing the "Shetland ponies presented by the Robert Brothers" - Dala and Viona, sharpshooting with bow and arrow - Miss Kitty's Dog Revue (Kitty Roberts) - juggling by Henri Vaddon, "the modern Cinquevalli" - Scott's Famous Sea Lions presented by Arthur Scott - The Toledo bulls and ponies presented by Doreen Duggan - Cele and Co., Italian clowns - Haute Ecole from Bertram Mills Circus, High School riding by John Gindl - Sydney the boxing kangaroo (from Robert Bros. Circus) - The Nile Crocodiles and Indian Snakes presented by Doreen Duggan - Interval - Les Ferri, perch act - Petersinn's Bears from Denmark - Four Kents, cycling act - Miss Ferri and her chimps - Tarzan and his mate, new aerial act - Bertram Mills' liberty horses presented by John Gindl - The Bello Troupe, Italian springboard act - Chipperfield's Elephant Ballet, from Circo Price, presented by Doreen Duggan - Finale. The clowns were listed in the programme as Jacko Fossett (from Robert Bros.), Buppo, Zeppy and Bindle. Amazingly for Chipperfield's, although there were plenty of animals, this programme did not include a cage act.

Another reason for the presence of animals from elsewhere in the Birmingham show was the staging of another major Christmas circus by Chipperfield's at Granby Halls, Leicester. The programme here listed: Overture - Polar and brown bears presented by Edith Freyer - African lions - The 3 Paulos, trapeze - The Shire Cart Horses, with Charlie, world's smallest pony - Two Sylvanos - Canine Revue, dogs and ponies, presented by Marion Larrigan - Ron and Rita - Haute Ecole with John Chipperfield - Snakes and crocodiles presentation by Zira - Pee Wee Smee directed by Bumble, making an omelette - Interval - The Original Wild Animal Presentation, presented by Terry Duggan - Fiery Jack and Co. - The Riding Maxims - Thoroughbred Racehorses presented by John L. Chipperfield - Chako, the almost human ape - Charlie the chimp - The Five Biasinis - The Chipperfield Herd of Elephants presented by Dicky Chipperfield Jnr. - The Exotic Group of camels, llamas, giraffes and Harry the hippo, presented by Anne Chipperfield - The Human Cannonball: Terry Duggan.

The 1960 touring programme included new attractions - Carmen on the solo trapeze, Iwarro Tarzan with his jungle aerial presentation, the Shipway Twins on the horizontal bars, the Rosaires on the trampoline, Sylvo (Biasini) with his comedy car, the Human Cannonball, and, for part of the season, Mr Pastry. The Original Wild Animal Presentation of two lionesses was made by Terry Duggan, and there were the Nile Crocodiles and Python - "Unbelieveable - This artist even swims with live crocodiles." At one stage of the tour, there was also Dick Francis - "the newest TV singing star." Dicky Chipperfield Jnr. presented the lions in the big cage.

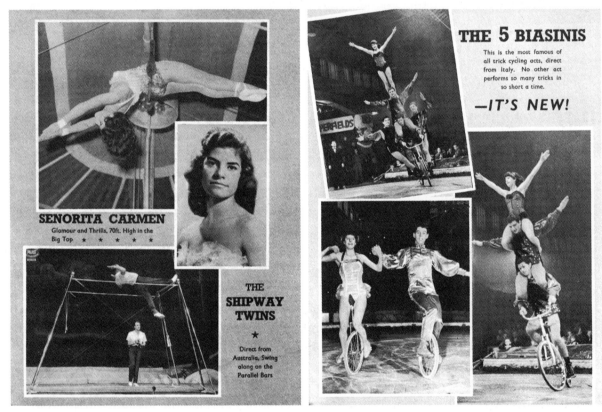

Left: *Carmen Rosaire and the Shipways in the 1960 printed programme.* **Right:** *the Biasinis.*

The circus community and the Rosaire family in particular was grief stricken when beautiful trapeze artiste Carmen Rosaire fell during a rehearsal for a TV show on Sunday 28 August 1960, watched by members of the circus and guests including Mr Pastry, who had come from hospital after being bitten on the arm by Charlie the chimp. A leather strap that was part of Carmen's rigging had broken. She died in hospital in Kingston, Surrey, the next morning. Carmen was the 18 year old daughter of Dennis and Amelia Rosaire. The Rosaires are one of Britain's most talented circus families, and Dennis and Ivor Rosaire, Chipperfield's elephant trainer in the early 50s, were brothers. Amelia was Spanish, originally a member of another famous act, the Rubio Sisters, who appeared at Bertram Mills Circus at Olympia. With his son Carlos, daughter Carmen and Alan, their midget partner, Dennis performed a comedy trampoline routine which they continued to present after Carmen's death.

Above: *the Shire cart horses made an impressive liberty act - presented by John Chipperfield. Their horses were Robin, Skipper, Duke and Captain.*

In October 1960, the first Chipperfield Corgi Toy was produced and sold in toyshops all over Britain. It was the Chipperfield's Circus Crane Truck, based on the Mack NM6 tractor, and it became the best selling Corgi Major of the year, with 58,000 copies sold. The relationship between Corgi Toys and Chipperfield's Circus began in 1959 when Mettoy's chief designer, Marcel R. Van Cleemput, visited the circus at Midsummer Meadow, Northampton, and conceived the idea of a series of circus vehicles. The Corgi Chipperfield connection, and the subsequent range of toys and models, are described in an illustrated section on page 170.

Chipperfield's fourth Bingley Hall season, in 1960-61, brought together animals from Chipperfield's and Bertram Mills' resources with human acts new to Birmingham. The programme was: Overture, orchestra under the direction of Les Dock - Bertram Mills' Bengal tigers - Gigi, monkey tricks - Dicky Chipperfield Jnr.'s African lionesses - Two Angelos, trapeze act - Military Parade, the Jack Whiteley Troupe - Equine duet from Bertram Mills - The Rosaires on the trampoline - Our playful teddy bears - Senorita Luciano and her pigeons - The precocious pups - Olympic Spectacle, Athletes in Action, also featuring the Shipway Twins from Australia - 3 Courtials, clowns from Italy - Sorelli Miletti, rolling globe act from Italy - High School presented by Nadia Houcke - Spanish Fantasy: the Toledo bulls and ponies presented by Doreen - 2 Forgione, juggling act - the Courtials - Jean Makovec, strongest man in the world - Bertram Mills' liberty horses presented by Nadia Houcke - Dicky Chipperfield Jnr. and his elephants - The Human Cannon Ball, shot from a giant cannon. The Mills tigers were presented by Bela Roucka, and the "Equine Duet" was the Big and Little horse and pony number shown by Norman Barrett. A BBC TV recording of acts from the show was made by Barrie Edgar and transmitted in February 1961, with commentary by Peter West.

In 1961, the tenting programme was broadly along similar lines as the previous year's, with Dicky Chipperfield Jnr. now in the 16 foot wagon with the two lionesses in the Original Wild Animal Presentation, and the almost human ape's name had changed from Chako to Gigi, though the man in the gorilla skin was still Mr Black. The Elleanos, a branch of the Stey family, provided two wire acts, a solo by Amando on the low wire, with a back somersault to close the routine, the other a high wire act with father in comedy role, two men, one of them Amando, and a girl. The Chipperfield animal acts of polar and black bears, lions, Shire horses, dogs, bulls and ponies, High School, crocodiles and python, liberty horses, chimps, elephants and the exotic group were blended with the human contributions of Iwarro Tarzan, the Biasini family (including the Sylvanos table acrobatics and Sylvo's comedy car), the Rosaires, the Elleanos and the Human Cannonball, to form a full and satisfying circus.

The crocodiles (in fact, alligators) and snakes were originally presented by Doreen Duggan, **left,** *and later by Freda,* **right.** *Both included swimming with one alligator in a tank on the motorised "Cleopatra's Barge." Doreen and Freda showed the act under the name Zira.*

Carlos Rosaire was presenting the bears - a new role for him - and his father Dennis was ringmaster. Dennis was no longer seen in the Rosaire trampoline routine, this being performed by Carlos with partners, the diminutive Alan and newcomer Arthur in Dennis's comedy role. It was also this Arthur, Arthur Grice, who was the human cannonball.

Right: *when Eamonn Andrews (left) related Jimmy Chipperfield's story for "This is Your Life" on BBC Television on 13 March 1961, with Matron Scott talking of his injury from Bruni the bear, Dick Chipperfield is seen with Tosca, one of his brown bears from the circus, which his son Dicky had brought to the studios. He had been helping Jack Smith train the brown bears during that season.*

Right: *Chipperfield's provided the elephants for the epic movie "Cleopatra," released in 1963 and starring Elizabeth Taylor and Richard Burton.*

John Chipperfield was an able trainer and presenter of many species of animal. He was extremely hard working, often showing four or five animal acts in each show and assisting in several others. He specialised in horses and ponies but he was also expert in working with lions, tigers, bears, dogs, giraffes and all exotic animals, elephants and chimpanzees. He also trained the young Chipperfields, including Dicky, Jimmy Stockley and his own children, in working with animals and in bareback riding.

Right: *with the pair of skewbalds in the late 40s.*
Below: *with the new Bengal tigers in the mesh cage in 1963.*

Right: *Dick Chipperfield, Charlie the chimp, Bill "Lofty: Dredge and TV personality Noele Gordon in a publicity photo for an ATV programme from Bingley Hall.*

Above: *backstage in the ring doors - as Katharyna warms up with a balance on an elephant tub, the bulls wait for their cue to enter the ring.* **Right:** *Katharyna, the ballerina on the wire.*

For the fifth Birmingham season, in 1961-62, Birmingham circus-goers saw another new programme, featuring Chipperfield's own new group of tigers, with John Chipperfield, and three leopards, Chota, Sita and Manello, presented in a new 14 foot long ornate wagon cage by Carol Cordello, who had joined the show with her husband Michael, both being keen to work with wild animals. Chota appeared in the Disney film "In Search of the Castaways" and in the Christmas TV show, hosted by Noele Gordon for ATV, this act was given a special production with Africans juggling fire torches, while Dick Chipperfield Snr. showed the tigers, with a special announcement that he was going back in the big cage for this TV show only.

With the Overture from the orchestra directed by Les Dock, the running order was: The Maxims, voltige - Fred Lony, the man with the iron jaws - Canine capers - Trio Marianys, balancing act - Carol and her leopards - The Golden Linders, gold posing act - Les French, musical clowns - Katharyna on the tight wire - High School - Chipperfield's mighty herd of elephants - Interval - Royal Bengal tigers - Les Teddys, acrobatics on the hanging perch - El Gran Tonisko, the Spanish aerial sensation - Our troupe of thoroughbred horses - The Great Lemoine, on the sloping wire - Bertram Mills' chimpanzees presented by Rudi Lenz - Two Primlettis, dive of death - The Marrakesh Troupe, Moroccan tumblers - Finale.

The 1962 tenting programme brought several changes from the previous season. The new tigers were presented by John Chipperfield, and other newcomers were Les French clowns; the Primletti family, who'd been at Bingley Hall, including Katharyna the 12 year old on the tight wire and the Primlettis diving routine; the Marianis; and the Linders. The printed programme listed: The tigers - Duo Lisboa, aerial perch - African lions with Dicky Chipperfield Jnr. - Iwarro Tarzan and his jungle trapeze - The Maxims riding troupe - The Sylvanos, comedy table acrobatics - The dog revue - Les French - The Great Katharyna - The Fantasy of the Bulls - The Marianys, roller balancing act - The Mighty Herd of Elephants presented by Dicky Chipperfield Jnr. - Interval - The Rosaires, fun on the trampoline - The Golden Linders, gold posing acrobats - Zira and her crocodiles and pythons - The Primlettis, sensational dive from 35 feet - Chipperfield group of thoroughbred racehorses - Les French and Co. - Charlie the famous chimp - The Biasinis - The Exotic Group - The Human Cannonball. In his World's Fair review (15.9.1962), Edward Graves wrote of "The charm of Chipperfield's Circus," praising "one of its very best programmes to go on the road since the post-war revival. A programme rich in individual and collective talent; well endowed with bright ideas and evocative of pleasing nostalgia, yet as modern as can be (as witness the new style of 'big cage' introduced but a few weeks back)." Constructed by Chipperfield's own staff, this was made of mesh, compared to the rigid barred sections seen before. It was hung, suspended from a metal circle with wires attached to the king poles, above the ring fence. When the lion and tiger acts were over, it was winched down into the open ring fence and covered using the hinged wooden top. This style of cage had been seen first in Britain at Bertram Mills' Circus at Olympia in the 1961-62 Christmas season. Additional acts, not listed in the printed programme, were the three leopards, now shown by Zira (alias Freda) in the wagon cage, pulled into the ring by two oxen; the two Primlettis with their motor cycle on the high wire; and Mrs Primletti with a pigeon act. The Maxims riding act comprised Anne and Dicky Chipperfield, Carlos Rosaire, Arthur Grice and comedy from Alan of the Rosaires trampoline act. Doreen Duggan presented both the bulls and ponies and the dog revue, and it was John Chipperfield who appeared with the elephant herd. Freda later took the leopards to Russia where she had the misfortune of them escaping from their cage. She was so scared of the consequences that she grabbed them with her bare hands and threw them back into the wagon.

The 1962-63 Bingley Hall programme, Chipperfield's sixth season there, contained new routines in the form of an elephant and pony revue, with the four senior elephants and four spotted ponies, presented by John Chipperfield, and a novel exotic act with Harry the hippo, ostriches and a new group of six zebras at liberty, also shown by John. The programme was: Overture, orchestra under the direction of Les Dock - Indian Fantasy, new liberty routine with the thoroughbred horses presented by J.L. Chipperfield - The Zeros, knife throwing act from Hungary - Erika and her pigeons - The Lorenti Troupe, footjugglers and balancers from Italy - Scott's Sealions presented by Arthur Scott - Luftman Family, clowns from Portugal - The Domis Domis, wire walkers from West Germany - Marion's chimps (presented by Marion and Billy Dash) - Cossack High School Presentation by Ivan Bratuchin - Elephant and Pony Revue - Interval - The Forest-Bred Lionesses with Dicky Chipperfield Jnr. - The hippo, zebras and ostriches - Frattelli Vassallo, Italian trapeze act - Franki Babusio and his model T Ford, crazy car - The Nello football dogs - Four Warachs, unsupported ladders - Gentleman Jack, pickpocket act - The Cossack Riders presented by Ivan Bratuchin - Finale.

A special Christmas Day circus was shown on the ITV network with television personality Shaw Taylor as guest ringmaster introducing Dicky with the lions; the liberty horses with Doreen Duggan; Hermane and Partner, ladder balancing; Clowns Fiery Jack with Pee Wee Smee; Robert Bros. chimpanzees with Sylvano; clowns, Les French with their boxing robot; Robert Bros. boxing kangaroo with Mr Pastry; Joe Gandey's educated pony, Tommy; the Primlettis, high wire motor cycle; Hans Peterson's Russian bears; John Chipperfield with the elephant herd; escapologist Paul Denver; the Maxims riding act and Mr Pastry's Riding Machine; and a Noah's Ark backdrop for the finale with pairs of animals including lion cubs, camels, giraffes, llamas, zebras, horses, ponies, dogs and elephants.

While Chipperfield's retained four of their senior elephants from the large herd of 12, they sold eight to the American circus giant, Ringling Brothers and Barnum & Bailey, which was embarking on a European tour in 1963, where they were presented by Hugo Schmidt, Ringling's resident trainer at the time. By a strange quirk, the elephants' former trainer, Ivor Rosaire, was also booked for the tour, with the five elephants from Sir Robert Fossett's Circus that he had presented since leaving Chipperfield's and which he had made into a very strong number indeed, appearing at Olympia with Bertram Mills Circus. Ringling's European tour was not a success and the eight elephants were presented on other continental shows, such as Circus Trolle Rhodin, and subsequently went to America with star animal trainer, Gunther Gebel-Williams, in 1969. Chipperfield elephants were appearing in his herd on Ringling Brothers' Circus in the United States for many years. When Graham Thomas Chipperfield joined Ringlings in 1993, he helped Gunther Gebel-Williams with the elephants and there were two former Chipperfield ones then - Sita, who died in 1994, and Ranée, who died in 1996. They were "great characters, as good as gold," to quote Graham, and Sita was called the Grandma elephant, who was put with younger, more boisterous ones when they needed some maternal protection and control.

Above: *two ostriches - ridden by Freda and driven in a sulky by Pam, Bingley Hall, 1962-63.*

The Chipperfield tenting show in 1963 included the début of a new group of ten baby Himalayan black bears, trained by Dicky Chipperfield Jnr. The programme listed these acts: Overture under the direction of Bernard Weller - The Maxims, voltige riding - Canine Review - Sorelle Lorenti, antipodists from Italy - Scott's Sealions - The Great Katharyna on the tight wire - Chipperfield's original leopard scena - Troupe Mariani, roller balancing - Alola and her pigeons - Les French, clown troupe - The Great Zira with her crocodiles and python - Chipperfield's elephant and pony revue - Interval - Himalayan bears - Los Duo Lisboa, aerial perch - John Chipperfield and the tigers - Lee Moyne and Partner, aerial motor cycle - Dicky Chipperfield presents the world's fastest group of African bred lionesses - El Vassallo on the high swinging trapeze - Les French - Chipperfield's ostriches and zebras - The Warach Troupe, unsupported ladder balancers - Chipperfield's thoroughbred liberty horses presented by John L. Chipperfield - The Primlettis, a breathtaking dive from 35 feet in free space - Grand Finale featuring camels, giraffe, elephants and beautiful girls. Arthur Scott was ringmaster. During the season, the Stey Troupe on the high wire were seen in place of the Katharyna/Lee Moyne/Primletti numbers. It was John Chipperfield who showed the six zebras in their liberty routine, with Harry the hippo later circling the ring in leisurely style in this display. Although listed as coming after the interval, the cage acts were invariably presented first in the show.

John's impressive liberty presentation that year included six greys, later joined in a carousel sequence by four spotted horses on pedestals, eight spotted ponies and three black Shetlands. The routine came to an end with two chestnuts at liberty and then a hind leg walk round the ring by an unharnessed grey horse. A group of new baby elephants arrived at Liverpool, and also that year, Dick Chipperfield's book, *My Friends the Animals*, was published. Around this time, the circus big top was used one evening a week for professional wrestling, which was particularly popular then, and there was a promotional tie-up with Omo washing powder where the public could see the show at a reduced price if they brought coupons on "Omo Circus Night," to boost attendances at the start of the week

For 1963-64, Chipperfields were again faithful to Birmingham audiences for their seventh annual season at Bingley Hall, with five new baby elephants, and four new polar bears joining the Himalayan black bears. The running order was: Overture, music by Bernie Weller and his circus ensemble - Mixed group of polar and black bears with Dick Chipperfield Jnr. - Illona, trapeze act - Royal Bengal tigers with John Chipperfield - Gina, the girl in the moon - David Rosaire and his perky pekes - Clown pot pourri - Alola and her pigeons - Les Rivels, clowns from Spain - Arlix, balancer from Switzerland - Tommy Turnbull on the slack wire - Chipperfield's herd of baby elephants - Interval - Devel the wonder juggler - Ferris chimpanzees - The Ferson Robles, cycling act - Les Rivels, clowns - The Lunas, low flying trapeze from Hungary - Equine Cavalcade with John Chipperfield - Trio Bedini, Italian footjuggling and acrobatic act - Chipperfield's Riding Machine - Finale.

Right: *members of the Chipperfield and Stockley families in 1964. From top to bottom: Dicky, Dick Snr., Jane, Myrtle, Anne, Sally, grandma Maude, Doris, Carol, John Snr., John Jnr., Tommy, Jimmy Jnr., Marjorie, Doris Jnr., Maryann, and Charles. This group photo was taken when Cliff Michelmore presented a feature on the circus for BBC Television.*

In 1964, the tenting show featured the Cimarros, four young men with a daring high wire act and an aerial perch duo as the Michaels. The Nicolodis acrobats from Italy were on the show, along with the Bedini Troupe, foot balancers; the Marianis, roller balancing; and Franky Babusio's comedy taxi. Clowns Tommy Turnbull, Pee Wee (Smee) and Hubert had a "cooking problem" and the Maxims provided fun and games on horseback. Animals were in a wealth of displays - including the dogs; pigeons; zebras, llamas, ponies and hippopotamus; the baby elephants; polar and black bears; the tigers; the lionesses; English thoroughbred horses; and the Bactrian camels.

Right: *George the giraffe was a feature of the show for most of the 50s and early 60s. Here he is being ridden by Freda. To get the rider onto his back, George would lower his neck. The rider would hold onto his two horns as he raised his neck and then slide down his neck into the riding position. This amazing sight, which could have been a fascinating part of the exotic act, took place backstage.*

Top: *Dicky with the new polar bears at Bingley Hall, 1963-64.*
Below left: *On tour in August 1964 at Weston Super Mare.*
Below right: *a grand mount in the track between the ring and the boxes by four adult and five new baby elephants in Swindon, August 1964.*

An announcement which caused headlines and shocked circus fans all over Britain was made when the show was in Weymouth in the summer - Chipperfield's Circus was leaving the country at the end of the season to tour in South Africa. The final pull down took place at the Oxpens, Oxford, on Saturday 26 September. A whole new adventure was about to begin.

Right: *the canvas hits the ground during the last pull down - Oxford, 26 September 1964.*

Chapter 7
On tour in South Africa

Above: *World's Fair circus editor Edward Graves (left) wishes Dick and Myrtle Chipperfield* bon voyage *on board the Windsor Castle.*

The decision to leave Britain was an interesting move. Bobby Thompson recalls that they felt they had temporarily exhausted home territory and South Africa was a 'new' country with a lot of people and not much other entertainment. There was also the rise in the power of television. Although Chipperfield's Circus, like Billy Smart's, had appeared on TV regularly and had promoted itself through both documentaries and programmes of acts from the show, the dominance of television through the two channels then, BBC and ITV, had affected many live entertainments. Britain had enjoyed three big touring circuses in post-war years and, later in 1964, Bertram Mills' Circus announced that it was terminating its tenting operation. Unlike Chipperfield's, it was closing it down completely, although Mills would continue the annual London winter seasons at Olympia for three more seasons. For 1965, only Billy Smart's of the Big Three travelling shows of Britain remained.

South Africa did not then have television, added to which its climate meant that circuses could tour all the year round, whereas in Britain the weather kept them off the road for three or four months. There were few other circuses in southern Africa, although the main one, operated by Whilma H. Wilkie, who himself had come from England in 1954, was well established, with a good reputation. Also, in comparison with the possibility of touring in some countries, English was one of the main languages in South Africa and British enterprises were generally very welcome at the time.

A partner in South Africa had been needed, to get the show into the country. When the trip was originally proposed, Stanley Boswell, who had run his own circus there for many years, was going to import the Chipperfield show. This did not work out and Mariany, a well known circus character, famous for his ability to train baboons, mentioned it to a friend who talked to Harry Shuster, a Jewish financier, who came to see Chipperfield's in England and then Dick Chipperfield flew to South Africa to finalise the deal, and Harry Shuster was connected with the circus for all the time it appeared in southern Africa.

Top: *the top deck of the Cal Agro at sea. As well as three Mack tractors, a fire tender pump trailer and a bunk wagon, one of the front door trailers can be seen top right. The derrick cranes were used to hoist some of the equipment on aboard. There were two more decks, one with loose boxes for the horses and the other for the other animals.* **Below:** *loading the Cal Agro.*

The ship chartered to transport the animals and equipment to South Africa was the Cal Agro, a big landing craft under the command of Captain Brady. Until then, it had been used to transport expensive timber from deep up the Amazon. The Chipperfields were taken aback to see an array of rifles in the captain's cabin, used, so Captain Brady said, to shoot South American Indians if they attacked the ship. It took four weeks to make the journey from England to Cape Town. John and Dicky Chipperfield Jnr. led the team on board looking after the animals. Dick Chipperfield Snr. and his wife Myrtle travelled on the Windsor Castle and the Stockley family, grandma Maud Chipperfield, Sally Chipperfield and some staff members left on 29 October on the Pendennis Castle, both faster ships which took two weeks. Other members of the company travelled on Union Castle ships. Having seen them safely on their way, Bobby Thompson flew to South Africa to be there when everyone arrived. Sally Chipperfield (now Sally Clubb) recalls taking part in the Pathé newsreel about the event, with Sally and her cousin Jane Stockley at the farm, riding camels, and helping to load the Cal Agro at Immingham Docks. Sally had left school that summer and was in charge of the dog act and she remembers promising Vincent O'Boyle, a trusted tentman and carpenter, who was travelling with the animals, ten shillings (50p) for every dog that arrived safely, and they all did. Sally did not regard leaving Britain with any trepidation. After all, her home was the circus and that was going to South Africa with them. She recalls being told it was so warm that you'll never wear a jumper again but no one mentioned some of the less appealing aspects of life there, such as tic fever or the need to buy a water purifier.

On arrival in Cape Town, the circus was based on the Foreshore, right across the road from where the ship docked. Bobby Thompson says, "The Foreshore is right at the entrance to Cape Town. You can see Table Top Mountain, with its tablecloth on top if it's misty. It was a marvellous view but we paid dearly for it later with the wind and the rain. I was always consulting the barometer in my caravan and my children's favourite phrase was 'Daddy's tapping it again'." Brian Boswell, son of Stanley Boswell, was adviser to the show right from its arrival, finding staff and helping with numerous arrangements.

The arrival of Chipperfield's Circus was an event. There was a big Christmas parade through the streets, organised by the Cape Town authorities. Chipperfield's were invited to be represented and the four big elephants were the talking-point of the parade. The show itself opened on Saturday 12 December. In the Cape Times, Ivor Jones wrote, "Acts presented in a blaze of showmanship... Last night, a large audience which included Mr Stanley Boswell, veteran South African circus personality, must surely have been of one delighted mind in voting this well-varied, fast-moving entertainment top of its class. Applause was generous and the atmosphere was charged with enthusiastic approval." The Cape Argus wrote of "animals in the pink of condition, young artistes picked from all parts of the world including some of the communist countries, and that almost legendary know-how combined to provide an evening of great enjoyment." There was a less welcome headline when the Cal Agro was impounded as the dock fees hadn't been paid, but, as Dick Chipperfield made clear in a disclaimer, this was a matter for Captain Brady and not for the circus, which had paid its agreed costs.

The printed programme lists the strong combination of animals and acts, including several which had toured with Chipperfield's Circus in previous years - The Big Parade - The mixed troupe of polar and black bears presented by Dicky Chipperfield Jnr. - El Vasallo, high swinging trapeze - John Chipperfield presents Chipperfield's Bengal tigers - The Michaels, hanging perch - Dick Chipperfield's African lionesses - The Antares, revolving aeroplane aerial act - The Maxims, bareback riding - Three Rossi, two men and a table - Canine Capers - Sorelli Lorenti, antipodists - Alola (Anne Chipperfield) and her pigeons - Carol (Stockley) and her pythons and crocodiles - John Chipperfield presents his troupe of elephants - Dilello, musical clowns - The World's Smallest Cage, Dicky Chipperfield and his lionesses - The Vasallo Troupe, unsupported ladder acrobats - John (Chipperfield) and Jane (Stockley) with their Equine Carousel - Dilello clowns - The Bactrian camels presented by Anne Chipperfield - The Cimarros on the high wire - The Biasinis, cycling act - The Human Cannon Ball, Arturo Grice - and comedy interludes by South African clown Tommy Turnbull. The orchestra was directed by Andy Janssen. The key staff listed were Richard Chipperfield, Administrative Director; John L. Chipperfield, Programme Director; Costume Supervision, Mrs M. Stockley; Personnel Director, M.E. Chipperfield; Transport Director, James Stockley; General Manager, R.R.S. Thompson; Tent Master, C. Waite; Scenic Artist and Cover Designs, W.H. Smee; Ringmaster, Ernest Maier Maine; and Publicity and Public Relations, Ken Dean.

Within days of the opening, there was yet more publicity when a gale caused massive rips in the big top which would take some time to repair. South easters like this are common in Cape Town. They call it "The Cape Doctor" as it regularly blows everything away! Circuses today, with plastic tents, have little trouble in Cape Town but Chipperfield's tent was a mature "ripe" canvas one. Undeterred, the show reorganised and continued on the Foreshore in the open air on 22 to 24 December, with the four king poles for the lights and aerial rigging, the tiered seating and the ring encircled by the canvas side wallings. The afternoon sun caused the alligators to become very lively, whereas they were usually more lethargic under the canvas. The wind returned and nearly blew the seats down and so the show pulled down and built up in Goodwood Park on Christmas Day, reopening on Boxing Day.

Above: *playing in the open air in Cape Town when winds caused massive rips in the big top.*

Sally Clubb remembers the tremendous way they were made to feel at home in South Africa, with numerous press interviews and invitations to people's homes. With the lower cost of living, the working men felt rich and a few succumbed to enjoying spirits since they could afford ten bottles of brandy a week for the first time if they felt so inclined. For one or two, this sadly led to alcohol dependence and they had to be returned home for treatment.

The first major move was the 500 miles from Cape Town to Port Elizabeth. It had been intended that the height of the transport fleet be cut down, so that the show could travel by rail, but very little had been done at that stage. In fact, only one trailer on the whole show was low enough to fit on the railway. All the rest would have to be lowered and cut down to size on site. Jimmy Stockley Jnr. recalls - "The petrol Macks could not cope with the heat and general conditions and I remember them crawling up Sir Lowry's Pass and having to walk up the

Bloukrans Pass behind our big living wagon because the road was too steep and dangerous for us to travel inside as we usually did." Alfie Gunner remembers taking five days to make the first journey in a lorry as it broke down and he and Jimmy Stockley Snr. slept in the bunk wagon which he had been towing. It was clear that many of the older vehicles could just not make the longer journeys satisfactorily, particularly if the route went through the mountains.

They continued in this way until they reached Pretoria when the show went by train to Lorenco Marques (now Maputo) and up to Beira and then into Rhodesia. The big Mack tractors were left in Pretoria and the Chipperfields bought two Bedfords and a Ford to pull their four-wheeled living trailers - those of Dick, Marjorie and John and their respective families. The Macks remained in a yard in Pretoria until just a few years ago when they were cut up. Tentmaster Cyril Waite left in Pretoria and Alfie Gunner later took on this role. On its return from Rhodesia, the show travelled by train, with the exception of the larger vehicles and some of the caravans, but the journeys often took a long time, sometimes not arriving until 3 p.m. with the train often taking a secondary route to avoid clashing with scheduled services. The vehicles would be loaded onto the train on flat trucks and the artistes travelled in compartments in carriages, but lived in their own caravans on site. Alfie Gunner used to drive the Leyland Octopus pole truck through with a dozen men so the king poles were up by the time the train arrived. When they first went by rail, the show had three train loads of equipment but this was reduced later, but transportation remained expensive and the circus had to pay cash in advance before the train would leave.

Hubert and Richard, the midget clowns, were treated like royalty wherever they went, since South Africans all knew and loved diminutive Tickey, who was a highly popular personality, with his own circus at one time.

On tour, the men who'd come with the show from England lived in bunk wagons and they were augmented by black Africans recruited in Cape Town. At one time, Alfie Gunner remembers that there were 200 staff but this number was not needed and they soon selected a crew of 40 who could move the show twice as fast as the 200! There were 25 ex-military bell tents for them to live in but this number soon dwindled as they were left behind or caught fire. Alfie Gunner experienced severe culture shock when first working alongside the black Africans. He went to wake one of the men in the morning and realised he was shaking a dead body, the man having been knifed in the night. Another man was burnt to death after a row with his girl friend. She returned to the circus at night and poured petrol over his tent and set fire to it. The circus ended up with a very good team of workers but there were some shocks and surprises along the way.

The show continued to attract enthusiastic reviews. In Johannesburg in April 1965, the Sunday Times reviewer wrote, "There has not been such a massive collection of animals under one roof since the floating of the Ark Transportation Company." He was enthusiastic about the lions - "most excellently presented, and were more lithe and alive than the usual somnolent carnivores we are accustomed to" and he considered the "equestrian finale was really something, with the huge ring of circling horses round the central tableau, and on the ring itself, the trotting Shetlands and midget ponies, and the air full of thudding hooves and a thick cloud of sawdust." In Rhodesia (now Zimbabwe), a critic hailed it the "Best circus ever... From start to finish this circus grips the attention of every single member of the audience. It has often been said of circuses that if you've seen one you've seen them all. But this cannot be said of Chipperfield's. Their entire approach to every act is different to any of those we have seen before," and the writer thought "Dick Chipperfield's two lion acts are definitely the fastest, most dangerous and most magnificent lion acts we will ever see in Rhodesia." He continued, "The clowns brought shrieks of laughter from the crowds but unfortunately we didn't have nearly enough of them. There could have been more clown acts as these clowns looked as though they could carry on all night. Dilello, the continental clowns, brought a standard of music I haven't heard before in any circus."

Left: *Carol Stockley + python.* **Right:** *John's baby elephants, Jimmy Stockley on the right.*

There was a tragic accident on 19 July 1965 in Salisbury, Rhodesia, when Arthur Grice the human cannonball was killed. Instead of being propelled across the ring to the safety net, he dropped out of the cannon when the explosion was heard. A verdict of accidental death was recorded. His widow Fatima and the entire company were devastated. His body was flown to England and the funeral took place on 31 July at the North London Cemetery.

On its return from Rhodesia, the circus played in the Ice Dome in Durban for six weeks while a new big top was received. This was a 140 feet round four poler, compared to the 180 feet big top with four king poles and eight queen poles. The tiered seating had to be cut down and other adjustments made to the poles and rigging. There were new lattice steel king poles, made in Mozambique, which were lighter to lift than the old tubular metal ones. The new big top was easier to handle but, as Dicky Chipperfield put it, "we all thought it looked so small."

The human acts in the 1966 programme in South Africa were almost all new, as the show had to be changed substantially since the circus visited many of the places it had gone to during the previous year. With Brian Boswell as ringmaster, the printed programme lists: Overture (Andy Janssen again directing the orchestra) - Polar and black bears presented by Dicky Chipperfield - Miss Theres on the trapeze - John Chipperfield with the Bengal tigers - Logano, contortionist on the trapeze - Dicky Chipperfield's African lionesses - The Maxims, riding act - Sally Chipperfield and her canine acrobats - The Sforzi Troupe, juggling on the slack wire - Anne Chipperfield and her pigeons - Dilello clowns - Charlie the chimpanzee presented by Dicky Chipperfield - John Chipperfield and the liberty horses - Chipperfield's wild west horse spectacle presented by Jane Stockley - Intermission - Gentleman Jack, the world famous pickpocket - Chipperfield's troupe of elephants, Doreen Duggan and the elephant girls - Trio Dinos, strength and balance in gold - Dilello, musical clowns - The troupe of Bactrian camels presented by Miss Anne Chipperfield - The Marilees, high flying trapeze from the USA - Finale. The show was again presented by National Entertainment Productions (Pty.) Ltd. Family films show Brian Boswell presenting the bears and John or Dicky with the tigers.

The pickpocket Gentleman Jack was a Dane with a routine involving members of the audience whose pockets he picked with remarkable skill and in a most entertaining way, taking wallets, watches and glasses as well as removing ties and pairs of braces. He was retained for the 1967 programme which also featured the solo British musical clown, Don Saunders, whose efforts to play the piano and as a kilted bagpiper had made him a great reputation at the Great Yarmouth Hippodrome Circus and with Bertram Mills' Circus in the 1960s.

Above: *Brian Boswell with Chipperfield's tigers.*

The 1967 printed programme lists: Overture - The new mixed group of black panthers and leopards presented by Dick Chipperfield Jnr. - Dick Chipperfield's African lions - Introducing Don Saunders - The Spanish Fantasia, beautiful girls and thoroughbred horses in an equestrian display - Miss Louise, limbo dancer - Fiery Dick (Dicky Chipperfield) and Co., comedy motor car - Gentleman Jack, pickpocket - Sarina (Sally Chipperfield) and her canine friends - Professor Grimble, the "fabulous" magician - The Chipperfield liberty horses presented by Miss Jane - Interval - The Lunas, low flying trapeze act from Hungary - Messrs. Speedy and Hubert - Charlie the Chimp - Lew Pawloks, French trapeze act - The Two Karans (Carol Stockley and Anne Chipperfield), balancing with the pagoda and sword and dagger - Don Saunders, musical clown - Hubert - The Chipperfield elephant and pony ballet presented by John Chipperfield - The Riding Machine, "Here we see the experts and the not quite so expert." The ringmaster was R.V. Moore and tentmaster was A. Gunner, with advance administration and publicity by Miss A. Baillie and J. Florees.

The new act of black panthers and leopards had been developed the previous year by Dicky Chipperfield, with a total of 15 animals at one stage. These included spotted leopards from Africa and black panthers from Java. In a big cage set up in the zoo, Dicky spent hours with the small cats and trained them in eight months to an astonishingly high standard. The routine included a lot of close work with the animals and of particular interest were various tricks which had rarely if ever been seen before - the lie down, initially with five leopards and black panthers on top of the trainer; the stepping-stone jump by a black panther from one pedestal onto the trainer's back and then to another pedestal; and a long jump by black panther Mowgli straight at the trainer, to land in his arms with his head on Dicky's shoulder.

There was some diversification with other linked businesses. Coventry Zoo was planned and built in 1965-66 on land leased from Coventry Council, with Dick and John Chipperfield and Stewart and Jill Banks as partners. The Banks later took it over completely. The Chipperfields provided the animals, including lions, tigers, bears and camels, some of them, including Harry the hippo, returning to England from South Africa. Harry spent the rest of his days in Coventry. The zoo offered visitors in the large Midlands city a good range of large mammals, notably those most popular with the public. The enclosures for the lions and tigers were partly made from sections of circus big cage. These tall sections, with a cross at the bottom, came from Bertram Mills' Circus and had been acquired by Mills when they bought a group of lions from top French trainer Alfred Court in the 1930s. The lions were shown for Mills by Pat Bourne at Olympia and by Cilla Kayes on tour.

Above: *Jane Stockley with the horses.*

Around the same time as Jimmy Chipperfield's success with the Lions of Longleat at Lord Bath's Wiltshire estate at Easter 1966, Chipperfield's Circuswas involved in two lion parks in South Africa. The first park was built near Johannesburg with the landowner as partner and the family subsequently sold out to that partner. It continues to do well today. The Chipperfields also invested in a substantial game reserve in Natal which opened as the Natal Lion Park. Here, just off the Umlaas Road, families from Durban and other towns and villages could go on safari, driving their own cars through the park and seeing lions, giraffe, zebra, eland and other game. The park was managed by Jimmy and Marjorie Stockley.

During 1967, the decision was taken to return to Britain with the circus. The best of the South African business had been enjoyed in the first two years and it had not proved possible to use the tours there as a springboard to further international visits, as Dick Chipperfield had once proposed. In some respects, Chipperfield's Circus had been too big for South Africa, which really had only four sizeable centres of population, Johannesburg, Pretoria, Durban and Cape Town. Dicky Chipperfield today reflects on what would have happened, had they stayed, since, he says, "the other shows were definitely suffering as Chipperfield's Circus was so much better." Travelling there was vastly different to Britain, necessitating moving much of the show by train. The average UK journey had been 40 or 50 miles, with 100 mile jumps a rarity, whereas in South Africa trips of 400 or 500 miles were the norm. The sudden dangers from weather, such as gales, tornadoes and twisters which would sometimes occur with little warning, caused headaches too. They found that the big top needed to be replaced every year, as the sun bleached the canvas and rotted the stitching so quickly. Nowadays, with big tops made of plastic, this would not be such a problem. In addition, enjoyable though life in South Africa undoubtedly was, they were a long way from the circuses in Britain, in Europe and America, so providing animal acts to them from their large collection was more difficult, and they missed the interaction with other circuses and circus people which was an essential part of their business. The decision to return was a difficult one, as many of the animals could not leave the country, due to travelling restrictions caused by laws relating to African Horse Sickness. Thus, the magnificent collection of horses and ponies, and the exotic group of camels, had to remain in South Africa.

Left: *Anne Chipperfield with the pigeons.* **Right:** *Maryann Stockley practising the trapeze.*

The circus had a growing number of wild animals, new tigers as well as the established lions, bears, leopards and tiger groups. Dicky Chipperfield Jnr. departed with his leopards and panthers to England in September 1967, while on Chipperfield's Circus Brian Boswell showed the bears, the lions and the original group of tigers. Brian had quickly become a key man in the running of the show and he later married Jane Stockley, who had taken over the showing of the liberty horses. For the family, the events of 1967 were in some ways similar to those of 1956. Dick, Marjorie and John had a total of a dozen children. While some were still very young, the elder ones were wanting to participate in the running of the show. Some conflict and some change were inevitable.

Right: *the final build-up in South Africa, at Kingsmead in Durban, the test cricket ground car park. Charlie the chimp lends the tentmen a hand, as tentmaster Alfie Gunner looks on.*

Chapter 8

Back to Britain and into the 1970s

Dicky Chipperfield Jnr. was featured with Billy Smart's Circus during its long autumn stand on Clapham Common, London, in 1967. His group of leopards and black panthers attracted a lot of attention and was hailed as a "superb cage act" by World's Fair correspondent Don Stacey, who had taken over from Edward Graves after his death in 1965. At that time, Smart's visited Clapham Common annually and always changed the programme substantially, to provide Londoners with a new show to see. The old rivalry between the Smarts and the Chipperfields was perceived by some when Dicky was billed solely as "Richard" in the printed programme, the name Chipperfield not appearing, and, in the reprint, Don Stacey "knighted" him as "Sir Richard and his Jungle Furies." As Richard, he appeared on the Christmas Day Billy Smart's Circus BBC TV programme, recorded at Clapham, and the act was favourably talked about as being different as well as showing an impressive rapport between trainer and wild animals.

For the Christmas season, Dicky and the panthers were at the King's Hall, Belle Vue, Manchester, in a strong programme. He hit the front page of the Daily Mirror under the headline "Just playing!" with a photo session with 18 year old model, Drusilla Robinson. Black panther Mowgli leapt at Drusilla, hurling her to the ground, but she was freed within 30 seconds. She suffered cuts on her neck and face and Dicky commented, "Mowgli was only playing, and things got a little out of hand. He did not attack her. Her injuries would have been ten times more serious if he had." It had been intended that the act would travel in 1968 with one of Europe's leading shows, Circus Williams in Germany. But Dicky had lost some animals on the ship due to illness, so he wanted to check that the management would pay the agreed salary if there were fewer leopards in the group. He flew to Cologne but was unable to speak to the circus owner, Carola Williams, and the manager said that they'd have to let him know about the salary when he arrived. In view of this uncertainty, the act did not make the trip to Germany and Dicky joined other members of the family in arranging the return of the circus lions, tigers, bears, elephants, dogs, alligators and Charlie the chimp to the farm at Heythrop, near Chipping Norton, and the establishment of a Lion Park at Lord Gretton's estate at Stapelford Park, near Melton Mowbray, Leicestershire, which opened at Easter 1968.

Big cats such as tigers and leopards were sold to Robert Brothers' and Sir Robert Fossett's circuses and a new group of six tigers was bought by Billy Smart's where experienced trainer Charles Illeneb presented them. The tigers had been bred on Chipperfield's Circus in South Africa and trained by John Chipperfield. However, perhaps because of professional pride, Charles Illeneb altered the routine before it was included in Smart's shows from 1968 through to their final tour in 1971. He was assisted by Peter Hodge, who became better known as trainer Marcel Peters.

During the summer of 1968 Doreen Duggan took the four senior elephants to the Great Yarmouth Hippodrome Circus where they were partnered in the original Elephantasia routine by four girls, one of whom was Sally Chipperfield whose dog act had originally been programmed too. Bob Fossett was running a summer circus on the stage at the Pavilion Theatre in Rhyl and Dicky presented the leopards and black panthers there as well as Charlie the chimp and the alligators. Bob Fossett had previously worked for Chipperfield's in the 1950s, in charge of the advance pole crew. Dicky's panthers were featured in the Cirque Royal building in Brussels for the 1968-69 winter, working for the management of Sabine Rancy and her husband Dany Renz, both experienced equestrians from old established French circus families.

In March 1969, it was reported that Coventry Zoo, founded by Dick and John Chipperfield in partnership with Stewart and Jill Banks, had been purchased for £100,000 by the Chipperfield brothers of Weymouth, and Terry Duggan, Billy Chipperfield's brother-in-law, had been appointed its manager.

Left: *Dicky with the leopards at Rhyl in 1968.* **Right:** *Tommy Fossett as Grimble with Menyus Lunas (right) and Peter Sandow (left) in the omelette entrée in 1969.*

Chipperfield's Circus was back on the roads of Britain at Easter 1969 in Leicester. "Returned from their African tour" proclaimed the posters and, having left the previous big top and seating behind, a new outfit had been purchased from the Circus Moreno in Denmark. This was a six pole green big top with tiered seating, which had been used for some years by Moreno before its demise. Although smaller than when last seen in Britain, the show offered a full and entertaining programme, with the return of many artistes who'd worked for Chipperfield's Circus before. There were no liberty horses, since John Chipperfield was training a new act, but the excellent educated horse routine of Joan Rosaire and Goldy was featured. With Les Dock on saxophone and directing the three piece band, the acts were: three polar bears and four Himalayan black bears with Doreen Duggan - Miss Peggi (Lorenz), solo trapeze - Dicky Chipperfield with his five black panthers and three spotted leopards - Dicky Chipperfield and five lionesses - clowns Peter Sandow, Roger and John - The Two Lunas, aerial act from a swinging moon - Trio Lorenti, juggling, footjuggling and unicycling from Italy - Sally Chipperfield and her Poodles - Grimble & Co., Tommy Fossett as Grimble in the egg smashing routine, with Peter Sandow and Menyus Lunas - Joan Rosaire and Goldy the wonder horse - Interval - Doreen Duggan with the Nile crocodiles - Charlie the chimp with John Chipperfield - Gentleman Jack, pickpocket - Omar Rabati, young Moroccan contortionist - Doreen Duggan with three Chipperfield elephants and girl riders - Tommy De Vel and Vera (Tommy Fossett and his wife, Vera), juggling and unicycling - Franky Babusio and his comedy taxi. Clown John swapped roles by becoming ringmaster John Moore early in the season.

In late September, the equine content received a further boost when the Mohawks bareback riding act joined the show at the end of their summer contract at the Hippodrome Circus, Great Yarmouth. The Mohawks comprised Ken MacManus, his wife Clara (née Paulo), their daughter Evelyn and son-in-law John Darnell, and their immaculate and colourful riding routine was a stirring addition to Chipperfield's programme for several years.

Early in 1970, Dicky Chipperfield gathered together a score of lions for a new lion park being opened by their relations in Portrush, Northern Ireland. This included six male lions from the circus group previously shown by Amédéo Gérardi who had died following injuries received during an attack by them on Cirque Sabine Rancy in France.

Left: *the Alcaraz Troupe on the trampoline in 1970, with Pepe on the left.* **Right:** *Tommy Chipperfield started showing the horses in 1970.*

Chipperfield's Circus opened its 1970 season at Runnymede, near Staines, on 26 March, in time for Easter. The same big top was used but there was a new front, with paintings by Bill Smee of the leopards and panthers on one side and the elephants on the other. The programme was: the polar and black bears - Shirley on the aerial ladder - the leopards and panthers - clowns Peter Sandow, Roger and Terry Hanleo - the lionesses - Two Waldos, aerial perch and voltige - Sally Chipperfield's poodles - The Zaracal, three handed balancing and acrobatic act - Phil Enos and his comedy car - Tommy De Vel and Vera, juggling and unicycling - Interval - John Chipperfield and his new group of four spotted liberty horses - Hanleo the fire eater and Margaret Marshall with a snake and three alligators - Grimble's comedy entrée with Tommy Fossett as Grimble, with Peter Sandow and John Chipperfield Jnr. - John Chipperfield with the three elephants, ridden by Sally, Shirley and Maggie - The Five Alcaraz, Spanish troupe with a combined springboard and trampoline act - Charlie the chimp, with John Chipperfield - The Four Mohawks, bareback riding - The Riding Machine, with volunteer riders.

Dicky Chipperfield Jnr. presented all three wild animal acts at the start of the show, having increased the lionesses to eight. John Moore was ringmaster, Ken MacManus the house manager, and Les Dock led the band. Terry Hanleo, who had replaced the programmed fire eater Tagora injured in a car accident, left early on and the crocodiles were presented by Margaret Marshall and later by Roger, swopping his clown outfit for a space-age costume.

During the 1970 tour, Tommy, second son of John Chipperfield, had made an impressive debut when he often presented the spotted liberty horses, trained by his father. A new baby elephant arrived, the first of a new herd. The family called her Kamala, the same name as the first elephant bought by Dick Snr. in 1947. Peter Sandow met his wife, Pepe, who was a member of the Alcaraz family, and Peter joined the troupe before they went on to establish their own comedy acts as well as having two talented daughters, Sandra and Sophie. During the season, Werner Steibner joined the wild animal department, taking over the presentation of the bears. He was keen to show wild animals and had worked as a groom and assistant for top trainers Henri Dantes and Gerd Siemoneit in his native Germany and had come to London when Gerd appeared at Bertram Mills' Circus at Olympia in 1965-66 where he met his English wife, Clare. An important newcomer was Janet Thomas who came to work on the aerial ladders, ride the elephants and help present the crocodile act and who later became a member of the family when she married Dicky Chipperfield.

Top: *in 1970 with the ex-Moreno big top.* **Below:** *in 1971 with the new four poler in Bristol.*

In 1970, Chipperfield's Circus provided animals for the zoo in the Dreamland, Margate, that year, with Doreen Duggan managing this enterprise.

For the 1971 season, Dicky Chipperfield had been persuaded by president and producer Irvin Feld to join the three ring Ringling Brothers and Barnum & Bailey Circus in America, presenting his lions and also the leopards and panthers. This was a marvellous booking which acknowledged the importance and entertainment value of these two contrasting wild animal displays as well as Dicky's own ability as a trainer and presenter. The animals were shipped early in the year and, after rehearsals, Dicky opened with them on 22 February. The group of lionesses was increased to ten animals and the press comments included "Intrepid Englishman Stars... Circus Premières Panthers" and "Chipperfield's poise and unruffled cool in the cage will remind you of greats like Buck or Beatty" (referring to big game hunter Frank Buck, who, although he was featured with Ringlings, didn't actually show big cats, and to Clyde Beatty, who for several decades was a household name lion and tiger tamer with a wild-style act). During the year, Werner Steibner began to present the leopards and panthers regularly. He had first done this back in the autumn of 1970 in Romford when he worked them as a result of a £1 bet with Dicky. Having looked after them for some months, he knew them and all went well in the routine until the final trick. Black panther Mowgli jumped into his arms but his weight took Werner by surprise and knocked him down. In a flash, Dicky was in the cage but Mowgli did not attack his new presenter... and Werner won his £1 bet. The wedding of Dicky and Janet was celebrated in Las Vegas, in the same place where Elvis Presley was married.

The 1971 tour opened in Bristol and the good business experienced for much of the previous two years was indicated by the presence of a brand new four pole white big top, made by Stromeyer in Germany, and Bill Smee had painted tigers on the front in place of the leopards. The new tent was larger than the Moreno one but it was full to bursting on several occasions over the Easter weekend at Durdham Downs. There were again three cage acts to open the show, with a new group of six tigers (four old ones and two newcomers) shown by Dutch trainer Jean Michon, and with 16 year old Tommy Chipperfield showing a new group of six young lions and lionesses. Anne Chipperfield, as Charmian, introduced her display with free-flying macaws and cockatoo. This featured a balance of a pole on her forehead, with Kiki the cockatoo on top of the pole, while she ascended and descended a fixed ladder. Doreen Duggan was with the show at the start of the season, showing the bears and the elephants, but soon left to manage the animal side of the Stapelford Lion Reserve.

The programme was: Overture by the Les Dock Trio - two polar and four black bears with Doreen Duggan and Karl Brenner - 2 Papado Sisters on the aerial ropes and Jane Brenner, aerial anchor - Six Bengal tigers with Jean Michon - Di Lello clowns - Tommy Chipperfield with the lions - Two Waldos, aerial voltige - Sally's poodles and pony - Phil Enos's comedy car - Charmian's exotic birds - Two Josés, juggling and plate spinning - John or Tommy Chipperfield with six horses - Interval - Belios Brothers (three men, one girl), fixed bar act - Di Lellos, musical clowns - five crocodiles and one python presented by Eve Lynn (Evelyn Darnell of the Mohawks) - Charlie the chimp with John or Dick Chipperfield Snr. - El Vaquero, solo low wire act - Chipperfield's three elephants - Four Dakotas, red Indian display by the Di Lellos, with twin vertical rope climbing, lasso work and hoops - The Mohawks, bareback riding - The Riding Machine. The ringmasters were John Chipperfield Jnr. and Jimmy Stockley Jnr., joining the show from South Africa, with run-in clowning by Little Arthur.

Top left: *Dicky with high wire walker Werner Guerro by the Liberty Bell parade wagon on Ringlings.* **Below right:** *the Riding Machine on the tenting show, with John Chipperfield on the horse, Marius Biddall (left) and Jim Clubb and Karl Brenner on the rope.* **Below left:** *the summer of 71, left to right, Mike Tunnicliffe, Carol Stockley, Jim Clubb, Sally Chipperfield, veterinary student Wyn Buick, Tini Michon, Jimmy Stockley, Anne Chipperfield and, kneeling, David Jamieson.*

A regular visitor was Mike Tunnicliffe and it was not long before Mike became engaged to Anne Chipperfield. Before the show went to South Africa, Mike had worked with Dicky, helping to train the baby bears, and he was now a garden designer. Anne and Mike were married on 27 November in Southampton. On holiday with the circus during the summer of 71, as well as myself, were Wyn Buick, in his final year of his vet's course at Cambridge, and Jim Clubb, in his last year at King's School, Rochester, and with a burning - and realistic - ambition to become an animal trainer. One night in Christchurch, there was a storm and somehow the alligators managed to escape into the nearby River Stour. Four were found quite quickly, much to the relief of the local fishermen, but one called Charlie lived unseen in the river for a couple of weeks. He was spotted by an angler and wrapped up in netting until a rescue team from the circus could arrive from the next town, Southampton, after which he rode on their laps on the back seat of a car as they returned him to the show. November 1971 marked the last stand of the final tenting tour of the mighty Billy Smart's Circus, and several after-show parties took place between the two companies, friends from Smart's, such as Patricia Antares, travelling from Clapham Common to Chipperfield's at Leyton and Enfield.

In December, at the end of the Ringling season, Dicky and Janet flew back to England, with the lions following by ship. While Dicky could have opted for the personal financial security that Ringlings offered, he wanted to return to play his part in the family business. Werner Steibner and the panthers were flown by Jumbo jet to Paris to appear in the prestigious Gala de la Piste, a performance which gathered top acts from all over the world at the oldest surviving circus building, the Cirque d'Hiver, which was opened in 1852. Now operated by the Bouglione family, as famous in France as the Chipperfields are in Britain, this historic setting, not far from the Place de la République, was a fine venue for the act's memorable return to Europe. They only just made it in time, however, as the props for the act were not available and Werner had to appropriate other pedestals from Bouglione's own acts. The show went well and, after the Christmas season in Paris, the panthers subsequently appeared in Circus Krone's building in Munich and on tour in Spain in 1972.

The Rainbow in London was well known at the time as a venue for rock concerts and it was on the stage of this theatre that Chipperfield's Circus presented its 1971-72 winter show. The family was constantly on the lookout for good venues to stage the show and the deal struck with the Rainbow management was that they would provide the theatre and the publicity and Chipperfields would put in the programme and the lighting. As it turned out, this was not such a good deal for the circus as this meant that the theatre would gets its percentage of whatever was taken at the box office, less publicity costs, whereas as Chipperfields had to pay all its salaries and other expenses before making a profit. The Rainbow had formerly been the Finsbury Park Astoria, one of the largest music hall theatres in London, and the circus fitted in well amongst the ornate statues and paintings of Eastern scenes. Unfortunately, the business was not as good as hoped, possibly because of late publicity, perhaps due to the reputation the Rainbow had as a rock venue, not for family entertainment. The show was a full one, using the height of the proscenium arch to good effect and with the number of animal acts only slightly reduced because of appearing on a stage. Indeed, the ring was 31 feet in diameter, compared to the 42 foot standard size, and the stage had to be strengthened to take the weight of the elephants. After the Les Dock band's overture, ringmaster Rex Gray and six circusettes introduced the show with a dance number, for which they had their own pianist, bass player and drummer. Rex Gray was well known for providing floor shows and cabarets and, became a great circus enthusiast, providing dancers and production numbers for circuses, such as those run by Peter Jay in the 1980s at the Great Yarmouth Hippodrome and Blackpool Tower. The acts were: the six tigers with Jean Michon - The three Santus, French jugglers at the front of the stage - Tommy Chipperfield with five lions - The Two Ritzas, aerial act by Ronnie Paulo and his wife - The Internationals, comedy trampoline by Marius and Violet Biddall and Violet's sister Clara Cook (née Sandow) - Sally's poodles and pony, with Jimmy the monkey -

Charmian, parrots, cockatoos and macaws - four spotted horses with John Chipperfield - interval - the Circusettes - comedy wire walker Brian Andro - Six Santus, cycling act - Two Barcias, balancing and adagio couple - Pythons and four alligators, mixed with magic with doves, by Anne Chipperfield, Tini Michon and Jim Clubb - Les French clowns with their boxing robot - Charlie the chimp with John Chipperfield - The Three Gambys, French high perch act - John Chipperfield and the three elephants, ridden by Sally, Janet and Tini - The Riding Machine - Finale with Rex Gray and the Circusettes.

Opening at Hay Mills, Birmingham, the 1972 tenting tour featured the regular animal displays with the two Collins from France on the high wire; Brenda Larenty on the low wire, Phil Enos and his comedy car, the Three Anastasinis diabolo jugglers, and comedy interludes with an escaped gorilla and equally human camel; two spots by the large Micheletty family from France, with their nine handed trick cycling routine, and juggling as the Seven Ricos; and the Mohawks riders. Run in clowning was by Colin Enos, son of Phil, and Frank Bailey, and John Chipperfield Jnr. was ringmaster. Jim Clubb, who had joined the show as an apprentice wild animal trainer, was presenting the alligators and python, in which he was assisted by Sally Chipperfield who in turn had Jim's help with her poodles, pony and monkey. He also showed the bears for the first few weeks until John Chipperfield Jnr. took over.

Left: *Sally Chipperfield and her poodles.* **Right:** *Carol Stockley with Oryx in 1974.*

Brenda Larenty's wire act had made its début at the Fairfield Halls, Croydon, Circus during the previous Christmas season. It was of a high standard, as befitted the daughter of such professional artistes, her Hungarian father, Alexander having had his own springboard act, and her Russian mother having been with the Naitto Troupe. She made her entrance from a large shell which gradually opened to reveal the ballerina within - a charming contrast to the more robust items on the programme.

During the season, Carl Fischer Jnr. joined to show the bears and the elephants, while Doris, daughter of John and Doris Chipperfield, took over the birds as Anne was expecting a baby. John Moore had re-joined as ringmaster; and, once the lions had done their six months quarantine from their American trip, Dicky mixed these nine with the six to make a total of 15 lively lions and lionesses which provided an exciting display, the subject of special posters at the time. Joe Cates and an American Twentieth Century Fox TV unit had been in Europe during the summer, with Bert Parks introducing a host of shows. These included Chipperfield's in Britain, with the family animal acts and also young Sally Ann Duggan seen practising with four small lions and a tiger, a scene which caught the imagination of audiences and became quite widely requested for re-runs in the States. Recordings were also made at the Hippodrome, Great Yarmouth, and Dicky Chipperfield presented the bears, tigers and lions in the big cage in these shows.

In 1972, the Jimmy Chipperfield family had promoted a large show under the title Circo Enis Togni, the big top and seating having been bought from this major Italian outfit. Jimmy's daughter Mary was the featured star, with a whole range of animals and good quality human acts. Business had not been satisfactory, notably because the Togni name was not known at all to the British public so, when the show played Clapham Common at the end of the season, the title Mary Chipperfield's Circus was used for public performances and for two recordings for Thames Television which were for Christmas 1972 and Easter 1973 transmission. The original Chipperfield's Circus felt that having another big circus bearing the name Chipperfield would create problems for it and so legal advice was taken and an injunction taken out. The case seemed to be made stronger when even the World's Fair newspaper had a front page headline on 3 February 1973 stating "Chipperfield's will not tour this season," referring to the fact that Jimmy and Mary Chipperfield were not running their circus that year but the headline was taken at least by some as implying that it was the original Chipperfield show that was not touring.

For the 1972-73 winter, Chipperfield's returned to the scene of earlier successful seasons, Bingley Hall in the heart of Birmingham, and enjoyed excellent business, with plenty of packed houses and large parties. Tommy or John Chipperfield Jnr. was presenting the polar and black bears with Dicky following with the six tigers and then a further enlarged group of lions, 18 in all, with another three males which had come from America. John Chipperfield's horse routine had been enhanced by the solo chestnut Arab, Oryx, resplendent in white plumes and harness, in the jumping and hind leg pirouetting routine with four girls holding the gates. Oryx appeared before the six spotted stallions at liberty. As well as the usual animal routines, the programme included the Mazans, Hungarian revolving acrobatic carousel, and an aerial rope act by Miss Mazan; Miss Linda (Burger), from Switzerland, with a polished solo trapeze act and upside down walk in loops suspended from the roof; the Biasinis, back with three numbers, their well known cycling act, Marina Biasini on the low wire, and the three Porto Ricos, knockabout acrobatics with a table by Giovanni and Serge Biasini, with Serge's wife, who was also Doris Chipperfield's sister. The comedy numbers were the Internationals on the trampoline, with the traditional clowning by kilted Marius Biddall going very well, Phil Enos with his car, his son Colin as run in clown, and the Riding Machine.

The 1973 season brought a big Bulgarian troupe to Chipperfield's - the Kehaiovis, a ten strong springboard routine of quality, who also presented a perch act as the Sofias. For the main act, they wore shirts and shorts and were promptly christened the "football team." Their presence was short-lived as there was a dispute about accommodation and they departed. The comedy was well catered for by Tommy Fossett as Professor Grimble, with his wife Vera and Carl Orry, Phil Enos's comedy car, and the Brizios clowns from Italy and Germany, who provided a slosh act with plenty of energy. Vivianna, baby daughter of Mr and Mrs Peter Althoff of the Brizios, was christened in October in the big top. The programme featured Brenda Larenty on the wire, and on the aerial ladder, and Tommy De Vel and Vera's juggling act and the Chipperfield animals.

As well as the large group of lions, the tiger act was now 11 strong, and there were new baby Indian elephants, making a herd of 11, the three senior elephants plus eight younger ones in training. A second Chipperfield lion act, comprising five lionesses, was presented by Gordon Howes on a summer tenting circus put on by Gordon and Mike Austin in partnership with Mike Denning and Billy Wild, under the title Denning & Wild Circus Supershow in conjunction with Circus Olympic, using the old Chipperfield-Moreno six pole big top. The engagement of Sally Chipperfield to James Clubb was announced when the show was at Dartford, Jim's home town, in August.

Above: *Jimmy and Marjorie Stockley on the steps of their living wagon around 1956 or 1957.*

When Chipperfield's Circus returned to England, Jimmy Stockley Snr. had remained in South Africa, running the Natal Lion Park and Game Reserve, with his wife Marjorie. Their daughter Carol and son Jimmy worked in Britain with the circus as well as spending time in South Africa. On 31 May 1973, Jimmy Snr. died at the age of 57, following an incident with a black wildebeeste (bearded gnu), part of a group from the Orange Free State that were being inoculated against tic fever pending release. He received a blow to his chest. At the time, it did not seem serious but internal bleeding developed and he died four days later - a sad end for a great family man who loved Africa and wild life as much as he did. His son remembers being with Chipperfield's Circus on Southsea Common at the time. He had just come out of the ring from working the three big elephants in the evening show when he heard the news.

After the winter in Portugal and the Canary Islands, Werner Steibner and the panther act enjoyed a considerable success on the Swiss National Circus Knie during 1973. Knie is generally acknowledged as the finest one ring circus in the world, with a total change of programme every year as it visits the same cities and towns. The booking of Dicky Chipperfield's panthers was a tribute to the excellence of the act in itself. More was to come when the celebrated Swiss zoologist, Dr Heini Hediger, devoted a substantial part of an illustrated scientific paper to the interaction between man and panther in the display.

Below: *Mowgli the black panther makes a long leap into Steibner's arms on Circus Knie.*

Dr Hediger, former director of Zurich Zoological Gardens, wrote in Image Roche (No. 62 published in 1974) of the "extreme tameness and, in the animal-psychological sense, literally boundless reciprocal trust" and, in considering the jump by black panther Mowgli into Stiebner's arms - "Only complete familiarity and trust make possible such a leap... The panther must feel sure he will make a comfortable and safe landing, while the trainer must have the assurance that the panther will not use his claws. In the panther's circus environment, the trainer thus represents neither prey nor treetrunk, but a *partner* to be taken care of."

Thames Television recorded two shows from the original Chipperfield's Circus at Clapham Common in November, both hosted by BBC Radio One disc jockey Ed Stewart as ringmaster and with a TV band directed by Alan Braben, and, with the legal wrangle between the families settled and forgotten, Mary Chipperfield was in each programme. The one for Christmas included Mary with nine Chipperfield tigers (the first time she had shown an all-tiger act), Dicky with 15 lions, Tommy with the six spotted stallions, the Brizios slosh number, John Chipperfield with four new baby elephants, Dicky with Charlie the chimp, Tommy De Vel and Vera's juggling and unicycling, and the Flying Tonitos. The programme for Easter 1974 had John Chipperfield Jnr. with the polar and black bears, Dicky with the group of five lionesses, El Tonito on the tight wire, Sally's poodles and monkey, James Clubb and the alligators and pythons, Tommy with the three large elephants and girl partners, Mary's own Big & Little routine with a Shire horse and Shetland pony, Tommy Fossett's comedy as Grimble, and Shirley Fossett in a revolving aerial hoop.

For the Christmas 1973 season, Manchester's Belle Vue Circus featured the horses, presented by Tommy, and a herd of seven elephants presented by his father, John Chipperfield. The routine involved four baby elephants later joined by the three older ones with girl riders. For Chipperfield's own season at Bingley Hall, Birmingham circus goers could see: Gordon Howes with five lionesses and one lion, Pharoah - clowns Colin Enos and Sonny Fossett - Dicky with ten tigers - Miss Bonita (Orry) on the trapeze - Jimmy Fossett Company, whip cracking, fire eating, drumming and knife throwing in red Indian costumes - Sally's dogs and monkey - Anne's parrots and macaws - Dahli Dahli and Co., clowns from the Mariani family with a slosh act involving a portrait painter - Sammy the sealion with Clare Steibner - Three Oscais, Hungarian trampoline act - Joan Rosaire and Tracy, double High School, followed by Joan with her palomino, Silver, the wonder horse - Mary Chipperfield's llamas, zebra and camel, presented by James Clubb - Interval - Four Amaros, from the Bradfort family, acrobatics from the Russian swing - Mary Chipperfield's Big & Little, presented by Joan Rosaire - The alligators, snakes and magic presentation by Jim Clubb and Sally Chipperfield - Four Bradforts, perch act - Four baby elephants presented by Dicky Chipperfield - The Riding Machine. Gordon Howes was ringmaster and musical accompaniment was by Les Dock, on organ, and his son Billy on drums. Later George and Alison Jones provided the music.

The 1974 tour commenced with an amazingly muddy start on a new ground in Basingstoke and also included a long summer stay in the centre of Brighton, on land owned by the railway. At both venues and elsewhere, excellent business was enjoyed. The programme included the Valla Bertinis, Czech cycling troupe, with their second number as Duo Malaris, jugglers, and the Flying Icarus, four handed flying trapeze act from South Africa, who also contributed an aerial perch routine and an illusion display, including the transformation of a girl into a tiger. David Konyot was the new ringmaster. Although from two famous circus families, David had carved a promising career for himself as a stand-up comedian, including starring in the West End in "Pyjama Tops." He joined Chipperfield's as a result of a light-hearted wrangle at the Circus Reunion when it was suggested that he wouldn't last a tenting season. He proved them wrong and later went on to develop an award-winning clown troupe. The Mohawks riding act returned as did Phil Enos with his comic car. The band was George Jones, organ, his daughter Alison on drums and Pete Burrell on sax. Dicky and Janet's son Richard was christened in Swansea in June.

From the Thames Television shows. **Top left:** *the Mohawks.* **Top right:** *the Ballans.* **Centre left:** *Jacko Fossett and Little Billy with the Rex Grey Girls.* **Centre right:** *guest ringmaster Roy Hudd and Charlie Cairoli.* **Below:** *Emilien Bouglione's horses and ponies.*

Werner Steibner presented the panthers with Circus Busch-Roland in Germany and Gordon Howes took the five lionesses to Ireland where they toured with Duffy's Circus.

Thames TV recorded two further programmes, this time in a new six pole green big top at Croydon. The Christmas show featured Dicky with 11 tigers, the Mohawks, Yuri and Tonia Gridneff's ladder balancing, Leigh Marsh's poodles, the Robertos trampoline act, the herd of 11 elephants with Jimmy Stockley Jnr., paint and paper entrée by clowns Jacko Fossett and Little Billy, and the Palacios with a superb double lane flying trapeze act. For the Easter programme, there was Dicky with his new group of five leopards, Emilien Bouglione with two liberty groups, one of four grey horses and another a Maxi-Mini combination with six matched horses and ponies, the Flying Alizés, the Bratuchin Cossack riders, Tommy Chipperfield with five baby elephants, footjuggler Jean Claude and Yvette, and clowns Jacko Fossett and Little Billy. Both shows were hosted by Ed 'Stewpot' Stewart. The new big top looked splendid but a torrential downpour revealed serious flaws in the waterproofing, so much so that the band almost went on strike, until large pieces of plastic sheeting were found to protect them.

Sally Chipperfield and Jim Clubb were married on 1 December at St Margaret's Church, Darenth, near Dartford, after which they honeymooned in South Africa, visiting the family's Lion Park in Natal and a whole host of zoos, parks and circuses. There was no Chipperfield winter circus that year but Gordon Howes did take the group of tigers to Circus Hoffman which appeared on Shepherd's Bush Green. Hoffman's own group of male lions was also featured and trainer Colin Timmis encountered difficulties with them, on two occasions being rescued by the intervention of Gordon Howes and fellow trainer Dave Freeman when the lions attacked him. Two Chipperfield animal acts went to the Austrian National Circus Jacobi-Althoff in 1975, these being Gordon with the tigers and Doreen Duggan with the five young elephants, while Werner Steibner continued with Busch-Roland in Germany with the panthers, and Clare Steibner and Dave Thomas (Janet Chipperfield's brother) went to the Far East with a crocodile act and Sammy the sealion, returning in the summer.

New acts with Chipperfield's for 1975 were the Aeronas, Hungarian aerial duo who also worked as the Two Mischkas in a balancing number, and two acts from France - the Ballans, with their turn of the century eccentric cycling, and the Pauwels musical clowns, Pepet and his sons Charlot and Marquis, who also appeared as knockabout sailors as Trio Johnson. Tini Michon, daughter of Jean Michon, and Silvana Ballan performed on aerial ropes. Tex Whiteford was musical director. A new four pole blue big top was purchased and used from early in the tour. There were various developments in the wild animal acts, with more leopards and tigers in training, a new group of five male lions on the show, and more polar bears about to join the bear group. All this activity indicates the industry that Dicky Chipperfield and his team were applying to providing animal groups for Europe's circuses. For a few autumn dates, an added attraction was the "Planet of the Apes," a group of actors on horseback with scenes from the popular movie. Business at Blackheath was exceptionally good, but it usually was for the circus, with or without the extra talking point, so the "Apes" were not retained.

The Thames TV shows were recorded at Epsom in November and comedy star Roy Hudd was the guest ringmaster. For Christmas 1975, the show featured Dicky with 13 lions, Roy Hudd with a comedy camel, the Ballans cycling act, the Laners cowboy routine, the two Hermans perch act, Mary Chipperfield with six liberty horses from Circus Knie, Gene Mendez on the high wire, star clown Charlie Cairoli and Company with their slapstick act, and Mary Chipperfield with her five African elephants. In the 1976 Easter show were Mary Chipperfield's five tigers, leopard and two lionesses, John Chipperfield Jnr. with six polar and three black bears, John Snr. with a new routine by three big elephants and three liberty horses, strength juggler Markus and Rosita, Charlie Cairoli and Co. slapstick clowns, Mary with her zebras and ponies, the Laners spaghetti comedy, and the Flying Saltas on the flying trapeze.

Mary Chipperfield's four appearances demonstrated her versatility with a range of animals but they were even more remarkable because she worked with a broken arm. During some filming, the horse she'd been riding fell and crushed her arm, resulting in a nasty break. Undaunted, she presented the animals with her arm in plaster, the only concession being that she didn't ride High School, substituting her zebras and ponies liberty act. For these appearances, Mary was literally sewn into her costume by her aunt Marjorie Stockley (née Chipperfield) who was visiting from South Africa. As she returned home on 11 December, she collapsed and died, a sudden and untimely end for a fine lady who had played a full part in the family's success.

Right: *Marjorie sews Mary into her costume for the TV shows in November 1975.* **Below right:** *the Pauwels knockabout routine as the Trio Johnson, left to right, Marquis, Charlot and Pepet.*

Chipperfield's tigers and elephants were in the Bouglione's winter circuses in Paris. Werner Steibner took over the tigers from Gordon Howes, and Doreen Duggan showed the five young elephants, firstly at the gala shows organised as Christmas treats for children and families of factory workers at the Porte de Versailles exhibition halls and then in the historic Cirque d'Hiver building. In the meantime, the original leopards and panthers were in quarantine at the farm, since they had been booked by producer Dickie Hurran for Blackpool Tower in 1976.

Chipperfield's Christmas Circus was presented under the big top at Shepherd's Bush Green, London. With the four piece band led by John Benham on drums, the show comprised: five polar and two black bears with John Chipperfield Jnr. - Dicky's new group of six spotted leopards and one black panther - Dicky with ten lions - Silvana Ballan, aerial rope - Sally and Jimmy's poodles and monkeys - Duo Mariany, head to head balancing - Peter Sandow's comedy taxi - John or Tommy Chipperfield with the horses - Interval - Flying Saltas - Miss Ayleen, contortionist - the Ballans cycling act - James Clubb and company with the alligators and pythons - Mariany clowns - Tommy with six elephants or John with the elephants and horses - The Riding Machine. Dicky took the lions to Belle Vue, Manchester, for a few days for an American TV recording, during which time Jim Clubb presented the leopard act.

On 20 February 1976, Silvana, daughter of Mr and Mrs René Taggiasco-Ballan, was married to Jimmy Stockley at St Mary's Church, Chipping Norton, followed by a reception at the Quiet Woman Hotel. Many of Silvana's family were present from France and Jim's sister, Maryann, was at the wedding but sisters Jane and Carol were in South Africa, though they were reunited with the newlyweds courtesy of an international phone call.

The 1976 touring show brought back the Ballans and the Pauwels acts and newcomers were Aimée Santus, solo trapeze and footjuggling, the Lunas in the aerial moon, and the Hungarian Biros family, with a four person handvoltige number and seven in the combined Risley-springboard act. Dave Benson and Laila were the Konchaks, presenting the alligators and pythons, and Jim and Sally Clubb presented their two new brown bears in a full routine. As well as the bears, leopards, lions, dogs and monkeys, horse and elephants on Chipperfield's Circus, the company also provided animal acts elsewhere - Gordon Howes had five lionesses and a lion and a group of five new tigers on Courtney's Circus in Ireland, his sister Barbara presented the three baby elephants in Portugal, Doreen Duggan had the five young elephants on Cirque Amar in France and the six spotted horses had been sold to the show, and Werner Steibner showed the eight leopards and black panthers at Blackpool Tower. In April, two of the cage acts went to Paris for an engagement with a big circus put on by Jean Richard and the Bouglione family. These were the 11 tigers, presented by Wolfgang Heppner, and the polar and black bears, shown by Tini Michon, but the programme was over-booked, there were contractual difficulties and the acts returned to quarantine at the farm.

The tenting show did good business, with exceptional attendances again at Bristol. Jim and Sally Clubb's son, James, always known as Jamie, weighed in on 4 July at nine and a half pounds. The five elephants had returned from Cirque Amar since, by some quirk, the show had two elephant acts, the other being Mary Chipperfield's African elephants shown by William Voss who also presented her big mixed group of wild animals. Tommy took over the five elephants on the Chipperfield show. In August, Dicky Chipperfield had an operation on his knees which kept him out of the ring for some weeks and Jim Clubb presented the leopards and a group of six lions. Jim was already involved in the poodles and monkey revue, and in showing his brown bears, as well as helping with the elephants and the Riding Machine. Jim got used to hearing people in the audience say, "Oh no, it's him again," when he made yet another of his six appearances! For one week, he even had to show the alligators and pythons again as Dave Benson was away, but he managed to persuade Charlot Pauwel, the white face clown, to take over for a few days. The Pauwels also introduced the Six Peppets, an old-time acrobatic number involving the three men and their wives in human pyramids.

Below left: *Jim Clubb with the leopard group.* **Right:** *Gordon Howes presenting the tigers.*

In quarantine at the farm, there was the bear group, plus three new young polar bears which had come from Moscow Zoo, and the big tiger group with several cubs. At the time, Chipperfield's Circus owned a total of 31 tigers, most of them born and bred by them. Dick Chipperfield Snr. was training four young tigers in a small cage built up in the zoo, assisted by John Benham, who'd qualified as a solicitor but who nursed a keen ambition to train wild animals. John Chipperfield Snr. was training a new liberty horse group, with Oryx and three other chestnut Arabs accompanied by a delightful cream Shetland pony.

On 28 October, the show opened on Shepherd's Bush Green, London, and the group of leopards and black panthers that Werner Steibner had shown at Blackpool Tower were back on the circus and Dicky Chipperfield took them over again. All went well at the first performance until the lay down with four lying on Dicky on the ground. First one then another black panther attacked him and seriously mauled him as he called for help. John Chipperfield Snr., his father Dick Chipperfield, Jim Clubb and others went to his rescue and drove the panthers off and Dicky was taken from the cage and to hospital for his wounds to be treated. He was soon back on the show but the attack was undoubtedly the worst mauling of his life, made all the more unsettling in view of the superb relationship that Dicky, and subsequently Werner Steibner, had enjoyed with the leopards before. Dicky felt that they lost that closeness with them when they did six months quarantine in the winter of 1975-76, prior to the Blackpool season, and Dicky had taken them over again after Werner had shown the act exclusively for five years, so the change must have been unsettling enough to provoke the attack. The show did well for the rest of the stand and audiences cheered Jim Clubb when he presented the other leopard act, unaware that it was a completely different group of animals..

Amazingly, within a couple of weeks, Dicky was presenting a revised act, with the seven from his new group joined by four from the old one, including black panther Mowgli, for the Christmas TV recording for Thames Television at Croydon on 19 November. This included the 11 leopards with Dicky, Mary Chipperfield with her own group of five tigers, the Six Herculeans old time acrobats, Sally and Jimmy with their poodles and monkeys, Los Alamos Western act, Mary with four African elephants, the Bruksons on the low wire, the Bubi Ernestos clowns, and the Flying Leotaris. The Easter show, recorded on 21 November, included Dicky with a combined group of 15 lions, the Bubi Ernestos clowns, the Flying Tonitos, the Charly Ross Trio novelty diabolo act, the Lunasz aerial moon act, the Brumbachs sword and dagger balancers, and Tommy Chipperfield with eight elephants. The green oval six pole big top was used, as this was larger for the TV crew than the usual blue four poler. Christopher Palmer was again producer and director and the special TV orchestra was directed by Alan Braben. Disc jockey and TV personality David Hamilton was the guest ringmaster. British wild animal trainer Marcel Peters had visited the show at the time, to arrange for the purchase of six young tigers for a new act he developed for the Dutch Circus Toni Boltini, for whom he also trained a big lion group.

I remember particularly a journey in a snowstorm to Chipperfield's on New Year's Day 1977 under the big top in Coventry. Tommy Chipperfield was showing a group of eight lions that day as he was taking them to Blackpool Tower for the summer, and he also presented the new liberty act. Sally's dogs were shown by Violet Biddal and Maryann Stockley because Sally and Jim were at Austen Brothers' Circus for the winter season at Granby Halls, Leicester, where they showed the two brown bears, Lester's jockey monkeys with two monkeys and two ponies, and the pythons and alligators act.

For the 1977 summer tour, there were new specialities in the persons of the Marquez Family, three men and a girl on the springboard, who also provided Dino Raffles on the rola rola, as well as the return of Peter Sandow, with his comedy taxi. With Jimmy Stockley or John Chipperfield Jnr. as ringmaster, the programme was: Overture by the four piece band, sax, trumpet, organ and drums - seven polar bears and one black bear presented by James Clubb - Dicky with ten tigers - Dicky with five lions and lionesses - Silvana Stockley on the aerial rope

- Sally and Jimmy with their poodles, monkeys and ponies - Dino Raffles, rola rola - Two Lunas, aerial moon - Four Arab horses and cream pony, with Doreen Duggan - Interval - Alligators and pythons presented by the Konchaks, Dave Benson and his wife who also included knife and hatchet throwing in the routine - Jim Clubb's brown bears - The Marquez Family, springboard acrobats - Eight elephants presented by Doreen Duggan - Peter Sandow's comedy taxi - The Riding Machine. As well as the polar bears in the act, the new youngsters were being trained by Dicky and Jim Clubb. Doreen Duggan had taken over the horse and elephant acts as Tommy Chipperfield was away at Blackpool Tower with the lions. Gordon Howes returned to Courtneys in Ireland, with the lion group enlarged to nine animals, and a group of six tigers. Werner Steibner returned during the summer but his attempt to take over the original leopards went badly wrong when black panther Ingua attacked him and he had 45 stitches in his face. John Chipperfield Snr. had become ill during the summer and leukaemia was diagnosed. As a result, John and his wife Doris no longer travelled with the circus, spending time at their house at the farm and undergoing treatment in hospital.

During the back end dates, three new acts were introduced - Maryann Stockley on the low wire, a group of four Arabian camels shown by Dick Chipperfield Snr., and John Chipperfield Jnr. with his old English sheepdog, Blue, which he showed as a roadsweeper, the dog enjoying this romping comedy routine which John Snr. had trained.

Tommy Chipperfield was seen with the group of nine lions at Billy Smart's Circus in October, for the BBC TV recording of the show to be broadcast at Easter 1978. Because of Chipperfield's own rival shows for ITV, Tommy was given his uncle Dick's showname Ricardo in the BBC programme. In November, Thames TV recorded their usual two shows, this time from Ewell, Surrey, again with David Hamilton as guest ringmaster. The Christmas one included Dicky with ten tigers, the Cata Polen springboard troupe from Poland, illusionist Lee Pee Ville and company, glamorous sword and dagger balancer Rogana, James Clubb's three Russian bears, clowns Bocky and Randell, and Tommy with the herd of 11 elephants. The Easter show included Cata Polen's adagio act, Dicky with the polar bears and Yogi the black bear, clowns Bocky and Randel, contortionist Miss Matilda, Gerard Edon on the trapeze Washington, Bobby Roberts Jnr. with Robert Brothers' six elephants, and the Two Munoz, excellent high and low wire act with both forward and backward somersaults on the wire. This was to be the final Thames Chipperfield TV circus. In 1978, Thames started televising shows from Billy Smart's big top, while the BBC made programmes with Robert Brothers' Circus.

Chipperfield's provided the main animal acts for the Belle Vue Circus in Manchester in 1977-78, with Doreen Duggan and eight elephants, Tommy and the horses and Dicky with the featured attraction, 14 lions and lionesses.

Jim and Sally Clubb realised their ambitions to run their own show, firstly for a winter season under the title "Chipperfields presents the King's Hall Circus" in Derby, which did very well in the hall which was a swimming baths during the rest of the year (the pool having been boarded over for the circus). As well as their own bears, dogs, monkeys and ponies, they bought the group of five lionesses which Gordon Howes had presented in Ireland. Their touring circus opened in Banbury on 27 March 1978 under the title of Sally Chipperfield's Circus, in a two pole blue big top. Although modest in size compared to the original Chipperfield show, it gave good entertainment in a more intimate setting with a company which included Tommy Chipperfield for the first few weeks before he joined Robert Brothers' Circus to train a group of tigers for them. Just a few days before the opening, Chipperfield's favourite chimp, Charlie, died on 22 March at the farm, a remarkable character who lived to well over 30 years of age.

Gordon Howes took a different group of five lions, from Dicky's big group, to Courtneys in Ireland in 1978 and he also took the three baby elephants. Tragedy struck on 1 April when he was practising the lions. He backed into one inadvertently. It felt threatened and attacked Gordon, his injuries proving fatal. Aged 38, Gordon was an all-round circus man. His father was Captain Sidney Howes, whose lion act was a feature of Robert Bros. Circus for many years and then with Gerry Cottle. Gordon was experienced with elephants, chimps, and bears as well as with lions and tigers and he had been a ringmaster, clown, and acrobat. His death devastated his family, his wife Barbara, their children Barbara, Paula and Michael, his sister Barbara, and his parents, Syd and Jessie, and shocked circus folk and fans around the world.

The 1978 Chipperfield Circus, when seen in Reading in September, included the Bruksons wire act, with their second number with a springboard as the Darix, Manuel Gonzales on the rola rola, and British aerialist Sebastian on the trapeze Washington and, as Gerone, performing sword and dagger balancing. Dicky Chipperfield showed the bears, tigers and lions, with Alex Storey, who was his assistant for the bear act, presenting the group of five Arabian camels. Dick Chipperfield Snr. presented the liberty horses, and one of them was ridden by a girl for High School. Anne Chipperfield's pagoda balance and exotic birds were in the programme as were John Chipperfield's comedy dog, Blue, Peter Sandow's taxi and Jimmy Stockley with ten elephants. Senior elephant Mary had died earlier in the year. The bear act numbered nine - eight polars and one black Himalayan, Yogi. Silvana Stockley was ringmistress for the first half and Anne's husband, Mike Tunnicliffe, was ringmaster for part two.

John Chipperfield Snr. died on 13 November 1978, after a long struggle with leukaemia, and he was buried alongside other members of the family at Wishford on 17 November. The announcement of his death on the front page of the World's Fair referred to his training of a large number of species of animals, adding "but pre-eminently he was the horseman of the Chipperfield family and one of the best British circus horse trainers... His loss to the Chipperfield's Circus, and to the circus in general, is a great one."

Sally Chipperfield's Circus had done well on its initial tour but it encountered disappointing business on its return to King's Hall, Derby, for the 1978-79 winter. The same could be said for the original Chipperfield show which was at Liverpool Stadium, the first winter circus there since the 1950s. The programme included the animal acts alongside the return of Brenda Larenty on the low wire and also as Solitaire on the aerial ladder, and the Danish family Haddie, with three acts, Miss Agnette, contortioniste, Miss Isabelle, solo trapeze, and a four handed cycling number with the girls and two men. Clowning was by Brum (Tommy Cook) and son Shaun and wife Mary, and by the Swiss clown Alfredo, formerly with the famous Chickys troupe. Working with the local radio station, Radio City, Chipperfield's staged a special performance for 1600 children, including 100 blind boys and girls. Radio City provided headphones to each blind child, with Billy Butler and Norman Thomas describing the acts.

In 1979, Dicky Chipperfield devoted himself to creating a new lion group and to various TV commercial and film jobs. Around this time, these included an advertisement for diamonds with black panther Mowgli, who was also in the Kenny Everett show with Cliff Richard, and with a polar bear for a Paul McCartney video. The breeding and training of big cats also resulted in providing tigers for Circus Corty Althoff in Germany, where Werner Steibner presented them, and lions for a group on Cirque Pinder-Jean Richard, trained by veteran Victor Saulevitch and presented by Yann Gruss. The three baby elephants were sold to Ashton's Circus in Australia but they never reached their destination. The ship taking them was routed via the Cape of Good Hope, with a stop in Cape Town. Even though the elephants were off-loaded to another vessel in the harbour, they were technically deemed to have been on South African territory. Australian government regulations prohibited the import of animals from Africa because of the perceived danger of bringing diseases from there. A legal wrangle ensued but there was no way round the problem that was acceptable to the Australian government, so the three elephants were taken to the family's park in Natal.

The circus went out late, in June 1979, having been waiting for the new red and blue four pole plastic big top made by Italian manufacturers Canobbio. Dicky and his lions were featured in a big summer circus at the National Exhibition Centre, Birmingham, while the lions and tigers acts on the touring show were shown by Dave Freeman, son of George Freeman Biddall,

Left: *John Chipperfield and Blue.* **Right:** *Anne Chipperfield with her macaws.*

latterly elephant presenter on Sir Robert Fossett's Circus. As well as the animal acts, the show included the Mariannis equilibrists, Los Carmellitas on the aerial cradle, and Peter Sandow's comedy taxi. In the summer, vandals set fire to the stable tent in Weymouth and the elephants and horses were burnt, some badly. It took them many weeks to recover and, in the autumn, Sally, the elephant that Dick Chipperfield had bought as a baby in 1947 died, leaving only Lelia of the senior elephants, plus five medium-sized ones. Continuing with the same programme, augmented by Mataus as Spiderman on the cloudswing, the show played a very successful winter season under canvas at Enfield in Christmas 1979 into January 1980.

In 1979, Jimmy Chipperfield's Circus World had been launched, providing a third touring circus with the Chipperfield name in Britain. This featured Mary Chipperfield's animals, presented by her sister Margaret and by Carl Fischer Jnr., and they had a successful three month season at the Great Yarmouth Hippodrome Circus building, in conjunction with its new owners Jack and Peter Jay. At the same time, Mary herself, with a further collection of animal acts, was co-starring with musical clown Charlie Cairoli at the Blackpool Tower Circus for the third year, before returning to Jimmy Chipperfield's Circus World for a London season on Clapham Common which included a Royal Gala in front of Princess Anne.

By the end of the 1970s, there were fewer members of the Chipperfield family involved in the original circus. Dick Chipperfield Snr. continued to direct the show, along with his wife Myrtle, and their son Dicky. Dick and Myrtle's elder daughter Anne and her husband Mike Tunniclife remained in key positions, but their younger daughter Sally and her husband Jim Clubb had started Sally Chipperfield's Circus. John Chipperfield Snr. had sadly died and his son Tommy was training animals elsewhere, including a fine tiger act for Robert Brothers. John Chipperfield Jnr. was on the circus. Marjorie and Jimmy Stockley Snr. had died and by 1979 their children were pursuing careers away from the original show. It was agreed that Dick Chipperfield's share in the Natal park be exchanged for the Stockley share of the circus. Brian and Jane Boswell tour Brian's Circus in South Africa while Jimmy Stockley Jnr. has established a successful film and TV animal business.

The British circus scene too had changed. Although the Billy Smart family had stopped touring its gigantic circus in 1971, there was a good market for live circus which others, with medium sized operations growing considerably in the early 70s, were able to satisfy. As well as Chipperfield's, these included new shows like Gerry Cottle, Austen Brothers, and Circus Hoffman, operated by the Mack family, and established outfits such as Robert Brothers and Sir Robert Fossett. But the 1980s were to see further changes for traditional circuses and initiatives by some, most notably Chipperfields, to take their shows to other parts of the world.

Chapter 9

Hong Kong to New Zealand - World Tours in the 1980s

The 1980 Chipperfield Circus opened to excellent business in Banbury, with the Biasini family returning with their cycling act, their knockabout routine on a table as the Trio Puerto Rico and with young blonde Gabriella, one of the new generation of this Italian family, on the aerial rope. American clown Phil Enos, who had been running his own show as Eno's Circus, was also back, with his comedy car, and his daughter Pam presented her footballing boxer dogs. Eliane Baranton, wife of Giovanni Biasini, contributed her stylish footjuggling, and the Philadephia Flyers on the flying trapeze joined the programme mid-season.

Right: *Phil Enos was back in 1980 with his comedy car.*

The stone-age epic movie "Quest for Fire" was filmed partly in Scotland in October and November. A total of 14 elephants were recruited, from Chipperfield's Circus, from Mary Chipperfield's resources and from Sir Robert Fossett's Circus, and they appeared as mammoths, complete with hairy skins and fibre-glass tusks. Two of Dicky's lions were also engaged, to appear as sabre-tooth tigers, complete with extra fangs which fitted onto their canine teeth. Needless to say, they were very tame and amenable to permit this.

Below: *part of the sit-up by all 17 lions and lionesses in Dicky Chipperfield's group.*

Dicky Chipperfield's lion group numbered 17 and was exceptional for the range of tricks, including close solo work such as the head in the mouth or sitting astride one and dramatic group routines. Among these were various jumping sequences and also the fan, where 14 lions and lionesses walked round the ring in line, and a sit-up on the floor with all 17. Dave Freeman worked with Dicky and usually presented the lions, and it was intended that he take them to the United States in 1981 for a contract with the Hamid-Morton Circus, a three ring show playing large buildings and sports halls. Dicky himself showed the act at the Monte Carlo Circus Festival in December 1980, winning the Prix des Amis du Cirque de Monaco, the Circus Friends of Monaco, while his cousin Mary Chipperfield was named La Dame du Cirque for her acts with her liberty and High School horses, ponies, zebras and elephants. Dave and the lions went on to Eindhoven, Holland, for a Christmas date but there were difficulties handling such a large group in the wings of the theatre there so they reluctantly withdrew from the booking.

For the 1980-81 winter season, good business was again enjoyed at Enfield. The programme was even more biased than usual towards animals, with young German trainer Thorsten Kohrmann presenting Mary Chipperfield's novel farmyard act with pigs, goats, dog and donkeys, and her pygmy hippopotamus, Jorrice, as well an exotic group of camels, Highland bull, Ankoli cow, zebroid (a cross between a zebra and a pony), and jockey monkey, added to Chipperfield's own bears, tigers, lions, macaws, horses, and elephants. Charles, youngest son of John Chipperfield Snr., presented his comedy car, aided by his brother John. There was Chipperfield's own illusion act, ending with the substitution of a leopard for a girl, and Graham Thomas Chipperfield, eldest son of Dicky and Janet, made his debut at the age of 11 with a rola-rola act. The main acrobatic act was the foot juggling and ladder balancing of the Italian Perris family, brother and two sisters, who had also been among the prizewinners at Monte Carlo. Unfortunately, bad luck again hit the elephant herd, with two of the younger ones becoming ill and dying after they ate part of the new plastic tent.

During 1980, Sally Chipperfield's Circus had continued to do well in its third season, with a programme of improved quality, and for the winter it was seen at Bingley Hall, Birmingham. Tommy and Charles Chipperfield had taken Chipperfield Brothers' Circus out for a few weeks during the summer but they encountered difficulties and, later in the year, Tommy went to Australia as wild animal trainer for Ashton's Circus. Jimmy Chipperfield's Circus World went out for a second touring season, this time with Mary Chipperfield as the star with her animals, but it did not continue travelling after a second stay at the Great Yarmouth Hippodrome. In 1981-82, the Austen Brothers Circus used the Jimmy Chipperfield's Circus World title, while Mary concentrated on training and presenting her own wide array of animal acts.

Dicky Chipperfield's big lion act was shown in America by British trainer Marcel Peters in the USA - first at the Hamid Morton Circus and then as a special attraction at Sea World in San Diego. The 1981 Chipperfield tour was notable for having no lion act, but there were nevertheless two cage acts, the polar and black bears, presented by Alex Storey, and the tigers presented by John Chipperfield. Dicky added a third cage act later, with a new group of leopards and jaguars, including the black panther Mowgli from his original group, with the lie down on top of Dicky and jump into his arms. Newcomers to the show were the Oporto family from Portugal with musical clowning and a Risley act as the Diaz Brothers, the Biros on the flying trapeze and with their Risley-springboard act, clowns Chipper and Beano, and John Chipperfield's comedy car. Louise Gerard presented the liberty horses and rode High School.

John Chipperfield showed the three Indian elephants, and in August, he took elephant Meena to the Alps as part of a historic scientific study under the patronage of Chris Bonington and Professor Sir John Butterfield of Cambridge University. They re-enacted the crossing the Carthaginian general, Hannibal Barca, made in 218 B.C. when he attempted to destroy the power of Rome by marching his army and 37 African elephants from Spain across the Alps into Italy. The scientific expedition went at the same time of year and by what is believed to be the original route. The aims were to help towards a radio telemetry system for monitoring endangered species, including elephants, in the wild, in conjunction with the Universities of Oxford, Melbourne and Birmingham, and to find tangible evidence of Hannibal's march by archaeological investigation during future trips.

Chipperfield's Circus returned to Enfield in November, rather than at Christmas, as it had the two previous winters, since Dicky and leading circus proprietor Gerry Cottle had created a joint venture for a bold initiative in presenting a combined international Cottle-Chipperfield Circus in Ocean Park, Aberdeen, Hong Kong. It was a case of acting swiftly to conclude a lucrative deal. They had heard that a British circus was being sought to go to the colony and so faxed Ocean Park to find out more. Dicky, Gerry and shipping expert John Smith then flew over to discuss it further and, when they returned to England, there was a fax from Ocean Park confirming the deal. They opened on 19 January 1982, initially for eight weeks but this was extended to a total of 15 weeks, after which they went on to the Portuguese colony, Macau, on the Chinese mainland, for a further four weeks. Gerry and Dicky wrote after the opening, "Business is fantastic. The reception we have had is unbelieveable." The show was presented in a huge blue four pole big top, formerly owned by David Smart. It featured Dicky Chipperfield with his tigers and his group of 16 lions; John Chipperfield with the elephants; 8 Beskidy Polish springboard act, also appearing with acrobatics on the Russian pole; The Swinging Cottrellis, handbalancing by Willy Cottrell assisted by his wife Joanna; clowns Sonny Fossett, Wee Bean and Colin Enos; strongman Ivan Karl; The Flying Carrols, flying trapeze act with three girl flyers from Las Vegas, their second act, the Michelle Duo on the aerial perch; Gene and Eleanor Mendez on the high wire; Gerry Cottle's Superkids on the trampoline; Barry Frost's Circus Band; and Maxello's London Showgirls, Maxello being Max Butler who produced the show.

The first season in Hong Kong. **Left:** *Gerry Cottle (left) and Dicky Chipperfield.* **Right:** *the people of Hong Kong flocked to the show.*

Above: *the entire company from the first Cottle-Chipperfield season in Hong Kong in 1982.*

When it opened, the clamour for seats was amazing. During the Chinese New Year (25 January to 7 February), four shows daily were given, at 11 a.m., 2 p.m., 5 p.m. and 8 p.m., and, with extra chairs, 3,899 people were seated. There were still many who were desperate to get into the show and on one day an estimated 10,000 people were turned away. Seat prices were 75 dollars (£7.50) for box seats and £5 for all other seats. A special free bus service operated from the centre of Hong Kong to the circus site. In the first two months alone, the box office takings were over £1 million.

The show was promoted as "Gerry Cottle's Circus starring Richard Chipperfield Jnr." and it was presented by Circus Americano Ltd., a company jointly owned by Dicky and Gerry, and promoted by Ocean Park Ltd. The park is on the south side of Hong Kong and includes a magnificent aquarium and dolphinarium. It was many years since a Western circus had played in the colony and the credit for pushing the idea forward must go to Peter Hulme, then in his first year as Commercial Director of the park. The organisers had many obstacles to overcome, including strict requirements on operating licences, work permits and import licences for the animals. The costs of transporting an entire circus were high as they included the big top, seating, equipment and caravans in containers, and the tigers and elephants, by ship from Britain, and the lions by air, coming from America.

They returned for a second season in November 1982, presenting a completely new show, from 16 December to 10 April 1983. In a survey among Hong Kong circus goers, polar bears had scored highly and so Chipperfield's polar and black bears, presented by Marcel Peters, and leopards, jaguars and black panther Mowgli with Dicky Chipperfield, were featured strongly, along with more aerial thrill acts. Ringmaster Ian Dey returned, introducing the acts in both Chinese and English, and Max Butler staged the show again, with a new musical director, Pete Burrell, in charge of the five piece band. The programme included the French Santus family, with juggling, comedy vaulting and trick cycling; British aerialist Sebastian on the trapeze and with his Supa Nova Space Rocket; the Cherifian Troupe of Moroccan tumblers; Clowns Sonny Fossett, Willie Cottrelli and Wee Bean, paper hanging entrée with plenty of paste and water; Sonya Burger, trapeze and upside-down walk across the top of big top; The Great Marco, from

Above: *the company for the second Hong Kong season in 1982-83.*

Holland, Marco Peters on the space wheel; Kubler's seven chimpanzees; The four London Showgirls on aerial ropes; and comedy interludes by Sonny Fossett and Company, including Colin Enos and Paul Cook. Marco Peters and his brother introduced a big illusion act, in place of the Cherifian Troupe, which was with the show when it moved on to Kallang Park, Singapore, from 28 April to 26 June. After Hong Kong, Dicky Chipperfield returned to England and Ron Marshall took over his group of leopards and jaguars.

On 12 May, Aga, a five year old lioness, escaped during a performance of the small circus owned by Charles Weight, then showing in Didcot, near Oxford. She was free for more than six hours, ending up in a garage. As Aga was originally from Chipperfield's and because they were based nearby, Dicky was called in and a cage was set up around the garage. Dicky crawled into the darkened garage as police marksmen watched in disbelief, and then led her back to her cage at 1.30 in the morning. He commented, "I had never done this before and it was quite an experience. It was very dark in there and she was snarling at me. But really she was just frightened and saying she wanted to be helped... I got very close to her to make the right noises. Quite quickly she stopped making a fuss and became calm."

Chipperfield's Circus in 1983 saw the return of the Belgian clowns, Les French, with two clown routines, an egg and plate smashing entrée and their classic boxing robot, with a musical finale. Leader Rene Chabre's wife, Christiane Gruss, contributed a stylish aerial rope act, and the Biros were back with their flying trapeze and Risley-springboard acrobatics, and there was a four handed Arab tumbling act. Charles Chipperfield showed the three elephants while his brother, John, worked the seven tigers and Dicky the 15 lions. Sally Ann, daughter of Doreen Duggan, presented the four chestnut horses and cream pony. Mike Tunnicliffe was ringmaster. There were four young circusettes, recruited from Oxfordshire Job Centres, resulting in lots of publicity, and they contributed a dance routine and rode the elephants.

During the winter, Chipperfield's big cats were seen in the two Christmas circuses presented by Roberts Brothers' Super Circus, operated by Bobby and Tommy Roberts Jnr. At Belle Vue, Manchester, Dicky presented his 15 lions in the Exhibition Hall, while at Kelvin Hall, Glasgow, Ron Marshall showed the tigers. The polar and black bears were in Paris. Sally Chipperfield's Circus had another successful season at Bingley Hall, with a complete change of programme, but after the circus had left the hall was gutted by fire on 15 January, thus ending a long history of winter circus presentations in the heart of Birmingham. This also marked Jim and Sally Clubb's final Sally Chipperfield's Circus, as their Clubb-Chipperfield company devoted itself to training animals for films and television, and Jim Clubb developed a remarkable number of cage acts which have been featured with the world's top circuses, notably Knie in Switzerland, Roncalli, Busch-Roland and Krone in Germany, Louis Knie in Austria, Arlette Gruss in France, Ringling in the USA, and Kinoshita in Japan.

Chipperfield's enjoyed a very successful tour of Ireland in 1984, encountering many people who remembered the show from its last visit in 1959. During a three week stand in Dublin, a new big top was introduced. Made by Italian manufacturers Canobbio, this was 138 feet (42 metres) in diameter, larger than the previous big top. It was easier to erect, with electric-powered winches for raising the king poles and lifting the cupola. By the Dublin stand, 13 cubs had been born, nine lions and four tigers. The programme again included Les French and the Biros, with the addition of the Michaela Kaiser Cossack Riders, Michaela also appearing on the aerial rope. Sally Ann Duggan continued to show the horses and, with her brother Alex, the elephants, while the cage acts were John with the six polar bears and Himalayan black bear Yogi, Dicky with 13 tigers and then 14 lions. Les French provided another routine, a poetic one in contrast with the usual robust Chipperfield fare, with Tony and Christiane Gruss as Harlequin and Columbine, blowing giant bubbles. In the autumn, the Biros departed and were replaced by the Flying Rochelles from South Africa and Franco di Angelo on the cloudswing. There was an attempted robbery on the box office trailer in Londonderry but the gang could not have reckoned with the fact that Dicky Chipperfield was sitting out of sight within. Taking them by surprise, he knocked the gun from one robber's hand and they fled.

Financed by the success of the Irish visit, Dicky was keen to return to the Far East, and began to make arrangements for a two year tour, taking in the capitals and major cities of countries where a Western style circus would be a great novelty. The four pole big top was extended to a six poler, 56 x 46 metres, with built-up seating for 4,000 people, and new lighting and effects purchased. Dicky formed a joint venture with Malaysian entrepreneur Paul Lee and they opened in Jakarta, Indonesia, at the end of June 1985 to fantastic business. Max Butler produced the show, with his Maxello Showgirls, and the acts were the polar and black bears, tigers, lions and elephants, Flying Carrols, Gene and Eleanor Mendez on the high wire, the Bauer family on high swaypoles and motorbike on the high wire, the Perris footjuggling and ladder balancing, the Di Lellos musical clowns and Football Boys jugglers. The Chipperfield horses and pony were not taken on the tour, largely since they did not have particular appeal to Far East audiences, and so they were sold to Tommy Roberts Snr. of Robert Brothers' Famous Circus where they were shown for many years and indeed two were featured there over ten years later.

Writing in King Pole magazine, Hugh Leech reported that the show was extended beyond the 28 August scheduled close. He commented, "The reader who is used to our English climate can have no conception of the sort of conditions under which Richard (Dicky) Chipperfield and his entourage are operating. Not only is the temperature in the mid-nineties, but far more relevant is the very high humidity (over 90%) which has a very debilitating effect on everyone. As Richard said, 'It's no use trying to get the locals to work at our pace, we have to slow down to theirs.' The more credit to them for their result."

Tentmaster Mathias Kluger (formerly of the Cimarros high wire act) told Hugh that the big top was filled to capacity on most nights and particularly at weekends, with four performances on each Sunday alone. The only drama suffered on the trip out was wrestling with a force nine gale in the Arabian Sea, causing the loss of a trailer which was not lashed down securely enough on deck. Hugh wrote, "Charles Chipperfield, the transport and maintenance manager, and Casey Owen, the wild beast superintendent, will have their hands full in moving the show around the Far East. But judging by the smart appearance of the wagons and the excellent state of health of the animals, they are more than up to their task."

The show moved to Surabaya in Indonesia before going to the Philippines, firstly in the Araneta Coliseum, seating 20,000, and then in the big top. In Singapore, the circus was sponsored by McDonalds restaurant chain and opened on 31 January 1986, closing at the end of March. A schedule of 14 shows a week (four on Sundays) was extended to 20 during holiday periods.

While there was again no original Chipperfield Circus in England in 1986, Chipperfield Brothers' Circus took to the roads that year, directed by Tommy and Charles Chipperfield working with the Biasini family.

Moving to Bangkok, Thailand, Chipperfield's Circus opened on 15 April at the Hua Mark Stadium, with the big top further extended to an eight poler to seat 4,000 people more comfortably. Originally planned as a four week stay, the Bangkok date was extended until the end of June. Alfie Gunner rejoined Chipperfields when they provided a big top for the four week season of Holiday on Ice in Singapore. A tent was bought from Circo Moira Orfei and extended to an eight poler, 83 x 75 metres, seating 7,500. The weather presented difficulties for the circus in Bangkok, this time with rain causing severe flooding, before it departed for its next dates in Taiwan.

Above: *putting up the eight pole big top for the first time in Bangkok.*

The Chinese promoter in Taiwan was responsible from arranging all the import papers while Dicky Chipperfield was back in England, booking acts for future shows, and he arrived in Taiwan to find that the elephants did not have the correct papers to be landed. The shipping company was threatening to destroy them and the only compromise Dicky could negotiate was to transfer them to a large barge in the harbour while the documentation was sorted out. They visited the elephants and their groom every day on the barge to ensure that they were all right. The Taiwanese authorities steadfastly refused to let them land, so a return to Bangkok was considered, but they would not grant export papers as they hadn't come into Taiwan. The officers concerned would not grant export licences until they were satisfied with the import licences. A Catch-22 situation. Eventually, the only way out was that the British authorities agreed to accept them back in Britain and, once a ship had been found, the elephants returned home. In the meantime, Chipperfield's Circus was to go to Ocean Park, Hong Kong, from December 1986. After two weeks at the Chipperfield farm, the elephants were inspected by a fully qualified vet and then went back on board ship to Hong Kong, where they subsequently appeared with the show. In November, a British newspaper headlined a story claiming that the elephants had been "imprisoned" in their travelling quarters for three months and a 25,000 mile voyage, a misleading suggestion which ignored the fact that they had been fed, watered and looked after by experienced staff and were in fine shape. Dick Chipperfield Snr. was quoted as saying, "Quite clearly the reporter who produced such an emotive attack on us has not even seen the elephants!"

The elephants appeared alongside daredevil star Elvin Bale from the USA; the Flying Cavallinis, double lane flying trapeze act, with one of the girls working a Roman rings aerial act; the Cretzu, 12 strong springboard and perch act; the Brizios clowns; Maxello's Showgirls; Dave Freeman and the lions; and Sally Chipperfield's pigs, presented by Alex Larenty, son of Doreen Duggan, who also showed his dustbin dog. The orange and blue big top was a 45m x 70m oval tent, capable of seating 4,500. The business was not as good as during those early visits with Gerry Cottle and there were other difficulties. Elvin Bale had been a featured artiste with Ringlings in the States for many years, At Ocean Park, he presented three routines including a thrilling solo trapeze act and a motorbike on the high wire with his sister, Gloria. When performing his human cannonball number on 8 January, Elvin hit the ground, not the giant inflated airbag, resulting in injuries which paralysed him from the knees down. Trapeze star Mark Lotz took over on 23 January but he fell from his trapeze on 3 February, having been performing his own act and the human cannonball. Gloria Bale remained, performing the motorbike on the high wire routine with one of the Cretzu. A report in the South China Morning Post said that Chipperfield's Circus was putting "some of the right sort of magic back into the circus yesterday with a fung shui ceremony to get rid of a spell of misfortune... Richard Chipperfield, under instructions from a Taoist priest, led his entire staff around the circus ring burning incense. The circus staff were then led outside the big top to make offerings at an altar laden with fruits and three roasted pigs. Mr Lee Wah, the priest who officiated at yesterday's ceremony, said he had taken special care to place the altar pointing in the right direction so as to bring the circus performers the best of luck."

Simultaneously, Chipperfield's London Circus was appearing in Korakuen Stadium, Tokyo, Japan, from 24 December to 15 February. The show was held in a large tent which covered a quarter of the Baseball Stadium, using the arena's seating which faced the raised ring and stage. The strong programme starred Mary Chipperfield, with her Dutch Friesian horses, and an exotic group of African elephants, buffalo, zebras, pygmy hippo and Nicholas the giraffe, and included Dicky Chipperfield's 11 tigers, presented by Horst Merkl; Streicher's seven chimps; Supanova rocket aerial act; Gartner's three elephants; the Stroici springboard troupe and aerial ballet; Sally Chipperfield's black bears presented by Jennifer Solomon; juggler Victor Ponche and Sylvia; and the Flying Ramos, with the triple somersault by Bruno Ramos being specially applauded by the Japanese. Rex Grey provided his Showgirls and choreographed the circus which was accompanied by Nick Capocci and his Anglo-Japanese band and ringmastered by David Hibling. Interestingly, at the request of the promoters, there were no clowns, in spite of the Japanese enjoyment of slapstick and broad comedy.

Right: *the poster for the Japan season.*

On 3 March 1988, Dick Chipperfield Snr. died at the age of 84. He had been actively involved with the circus and with animals right up to the end, training tigers and breeding mules. In King Pole, his son-in-law James Clubb wrote, "It is an interesting indication of his position in the world at large that there were major obituaries for him in all the quality daily newspapers: Daily Telegraph; The Times; The Guardian; and The Independent. He was always an animal man and a circus man. Whereas other circus owners (e.g. Smarts, Mills) have come into the business and subsequently gone out of it, Dick Chipperfield would always have remained in it, changing and adjusting the style and size of his shows - and taking it to new countries - but staying faithful to traditional circus and never, ever contemplating removing animals - or indeed a business or family life without animals."

Right: *Dick Chipperfield Snr. with George the giraffe in the early 1960s. Giraffes were one of his favourite animals.*

After the close of the Tokyo and Hong Kong seasons, Chipperfield's Circus then moved to South Korea, opening in Seoul in March, until June and then back to Manilla in the Philippines. The Korean programme included 14 tigers with Horst Merkl; 14 lions with Dave Freeman; the three elephants; the Brizios clowns; Alex Larenty with Sally Chipperfield's black bears, and his dustbin dog; Ivanov's space wheel; the Urbans flying trapeze act, springboard and aerial perch acts; Los Guerros on the high wire; juggler Sorin Monteanu; and Pete Burrell's Band. One of Chipperfield's big tops, with seating for 4,100 people, was used in Malaysia from December 1987 for a tour of the People's Republic of China Circus, performing in the cities of Penang and Johore Bahru for an 11 week run. The circus itself opened in New Zealand on 28 December for a seven week tour taking in both North and South Islands, closing on 7 February. The programme in Auckland included: Gwyn Davies directing the band; John Chipperfield with the tigers; Miss Gitty, aerial rope; Dave Freeman, as Dave Corillo, with the lions; The Great Savan (Navas backwards), juggler; James Clubb's Canadian black bears presented by the Romanoffs; The New Dollys, cycling act; The Wheel of Death by the Duo Ivanoff; Flying Navas, featuring the triple somersault; The Brizios, decorating entrée; The Great Khavak and his crocodiles; The Nicol Brothers, footjuggling; four elephants from Bullens in Australia; and the crossbow act of Guy Tell.

Dicky Chipperfield returned to Indonesia in 1988, presenting the show under the Royal London Circus title. This was the programme in Jakarta in August: Supanova aerial rocket by Gerry and Joan Russell, and Gerry's sword and dagger balancing; the Spanish Tonito family with flying trapeze, trampoline, Risley and aerial rope acts; Jackie Althoff's bears; a troupe of football dogs from Holland; Duo Christal, aerial cradle act from Spain; Duo Ivanoff, space wheel act from Bulgaria; the Cardinalis clowns; John Chipperfield with the tigers and the lions; and Graham Thomas Chipperfield with his juggling act and showing the three elephants. The show moved to Taipei for 20 weeks from 12 October.

In early 1989, Dicky announced that he had sold his circus, including the lions and tigers, to his former partner Paul Lee who was continuing to run it as the Royal London Circus in Taiwan. Dicky sums up running a circus in the Far East as follows, "If you had a sponsor or promoter who knew how to advertise, you were sold out. But the danger is that you need a powerful promoter to get you in and out efficiently. If business is not as good as the promoter wanted, he has the power to close the show and not worry about the legal implications, so it could be like living on a knife edge. Our record showing for one day was 60,000 people in Manilla in the Philippines but the best business overall was in Indonesia which was unbelievable. South Korea probably provided the poorest business of the tours."

In 1989, Dicky was busy training new tiger and lion groups with his son, Richard, while his polar bears were with Courtney's Circus in Ireland for a short while and then sold to Jim Clubb of Clubb-Chipperfield to incorporate into his new mixed group of bears. Graham was showing the three elephants on Charles Chipperfield's Chipperfield Brothers' Circus. Dicky helped his cousin Mary with the opening of her new circus at Pleasureland, Southport, and presented his new lions there for a few weeks, and then in September a brand new production of the original Chipperfield's Circus was announced as opening in December - "The First Great Britain and Ireland Tour for Five Years." In the planning stages, Dicky worked with Peter Featherstone, former managing director of Austen Brothers Circus, and the letterheads and publicity material, including the Irish posters, have a strong Austen Brothers feel to them.

Using a new red and blue Canobbio big top (38 x 40 metres), Chipperfield's Circus returned to Ireland, opening in Cork on Boxing Day for the Christmas and New Year holiday until 7 January, followed by Limerick and Athlone, reaching Northern Ireland on 8-11 February with a stand in Newry, followed by Londonderry, Limavady, Ballymena, Newtownards, Lisburn, Downpatrick, Drogheda, Navan, Longford, Portlaoise, ending in Carlow on 1-6 May.

The strong programme contained: Overture by a six piece Polish band - Dicky's new tigers - Israeli clown Shiganio - Dicky or John Chipperfield with eight lionesses - Miss Annabella (Anne-Claire Schofield) on the solo trapeze - Mary Chipperfield's six spotted ponies presented by Peter Althoff - Shiganio's musical entrée - Four Kolosz, old time acrobats from Poland - the three elephants presented by Graham Thomas Chipperfield - Interval - Flying Souza from Brazil - Shiganio - Mary Chipperfield's exotic group of camels, llamas, zebra and Sonny the giraffe presented by Peter Althoff - Graham Thomas Chipperfield's juggling act - The Brizios, painting and decoarting entrée - The Irades Troupe from Poland, nine-person springboard act - Finale. After the first few towns, the Polish band departed and the Casablanca Troupe of seven Moroccan tumblers was added at Lisburn.

Graham Thomas Chipperfield had been showing the elephants in the Far East but in Cork he unveiled the springboard tricks which he had been practising for some time. Norwegian circus fan Tor Olaisen, writing in the Irish magazine Circus, said, "The act included one elephant propelling Graham from a springboard, Graham making a back somersault and landing on a second elephant. This was one of the best elephant acts that I have seen for quite some time."

Jimmy Chipperfield died after a long illness caused by cancer on 20 April 1990 at the age of 78. As well as his circus career, he will be remembered as the man whose knowledge of animals, of Africa and of what the public wanted, led to the revolutionary introduction of safari parks, where people drove amongst wild animals in their cars, commencing at Longleat in 1966. He was the twentieth century equivalent of Carl Hagenbeck, the German animal dealer and zoo director, who took the keeping and presentation of exotic animals a quantum leap forward last century by acclimatising them in open-air, 'natural' enclosures, bounded by moats, rather than in heated inside cages. Significantly, Hagenbeck too had been an animal trainer, with animal acts and a major travelling circus among his interests. In the 20 years prior to his death, Jimmy's circus involvement had been largely through his daughters Mary and Margaret and their animals and, in 1986, he and Rosie had moved from their house in Hethersett, near Southampton, to Mary's headquarters, Croft Farm at Over Wallop.

Terry Duggan, from the large family of sisters and brothers that joined Chipperfield's in the late 1940s, died on 4 May. His passing was a shock as he was only 54 but cancer had claimed another victim. After showing the lions and working with the giraffes and as a human cannonball on Chipperfield's, Terry went to Sir Robert Fossett's as a wild animal trainer in the 1960s, later managing Coventry Zoo and then developing a gripping aerial routine with his wife Tamara (née Tovarich). They and their children performed their aerial and acrobatic acts on circuses in Italy, France and Malaysia until early 1990 when Terry's cancer was diagnosed.

The inclusion of animals in circuses and zoos has been the subject of some controversy in Britain. Lobbying from organisations such as the Royal Society for the Prevention of Cruelty to Animals has persuaded many councils to ban circuses with animals from their traditional sites, leading circuses to use privately owned grounds. The RSPCA funded an independent scientific study by the animal behaviour expert, Dr Marthe Kiley-Worthington, who spent 18 months visiting circuses large and small, including Chipperfield's. Her book, *Animals in Circuses and Zoos - Chiron's World?* (Little Eco Farms Publishing, 1990), makes clear that she believes animals in circuses should not be banned and that she saw no cruelty in the training, performance and transportation of circus animals but that she considered that there should be more training, to provide stimulation, and that routines should be more imaginative. She also stated that there must be exercise areas for animals such as big cats and elephants, recommendations which reputable circuses, keen to show clearly their love of animals and interest in their welfare, in Britain and elsewhere, have followed. But the debate continues, fuelled by organisations intent on a virtual ban on all 'wild' animals being kept in zoos or circuses, no matter how well they are looked after and how interesting their captive environment, and countered by others who believe that captive-bred animals can be kept correctly away from the wild, where animals are often subject to the increasing demands of the human population for land and the horrendous attention of hunters seeking elephants' ivory, rhino horns and parts of tigers for oriental 'medicine'.

Above: *Chipperfield's tigers, with Gary Ambrose, in their exercise cage on the touring circus.*

Although business in Cork had been good, the Chipperfield Circus Irish tour closed early as the bad winter weather caused major difficulties, as well as keeping many of the public away. On returning to England, Graham and the elephants and his juggling act, plus the tigers, presented by David Sherwood, went with Charles Chipperfield's Chipperfield Brothers' Circus again for the rest of the 1990 season, although he was incapacitated for some weeks when he broke his leg, when a springboard trick went badly wrong. Charles's elder brother Tommy and his wife Marilyn had joined Tom Duffy and Son's Circus in January 1990 with their tigers and other animals. This has proved a long and successful association with this leading Irish circus as they have trained and presented numerous acts, including lions, tigers, bears, ponies, goats and other farmyard animals, dogs and reptiles.

For the 1990-91 winter, Gerry Cottle and Peter Featherstone agreed with Dicky to promote a circus under the Chipperfield name at Crystal Palace, London. This starred Graham with the elephants and presenting the lions for the first time, with a full traditional British programme, including that Chipperfield favourite, the human cannonball, in the person of Hungarian Oochie Tabak. In King Pole, I wrote of Graham's elephant act: "His style is effective and different and, to quote one observer, 'He's a real showman.' Wearing a bright red-stoned tailcoat and white gloves, he first appears to be more like a conjuror than a circus artiste but he is soon directing the elephants, using his voice and no whip or stick, as he rides standing on their backs, or, for sit-ups, on their heads. After the standard routine, two elephants take part in the springboard display. This is notable for the free run-up that Meena takes before pounding down on the springboard to catapult Graham in the air. The elephant is quite clearly responding to his vocal directions - and rewards when the feats are accomplished. The second elephant, Kamala, on whom Graham lands after his back somersault, is also staying in position on voice direction. The two people standing near her are there to catch Graham should he fall, not to direct the elephant."

The excellent business indicated that the Chipperfield name and style of circus was still more than capable of drawing the crowds. Equally significantly, it heralded a new era of Chipperfield's Circus, with Dicky hiring the valuable brand name and co-presenting the shows with other proprietors. This proved to be a good arrangement, giving Dicky time to develop further wild animal groups and to foster the careers of his sons, Graham and Richard, as well as operating a tent hire business, providing big tops for concerts, parties and other functions.

Below: *Graham Thomas Chipperfield's elephant act at Crystal Palace.*

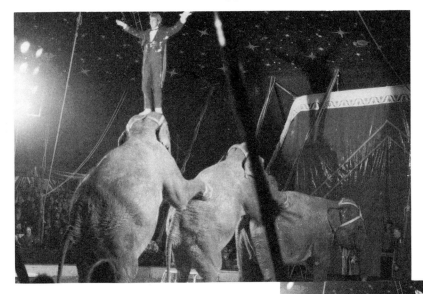

Chapter 10
In the 1990s

From 1991 to 1996, Chipperfield's Circus in Britain was presented by Tony Hopkins. Tony was a schoolboy circus fan who went to teacher training college before making the transition from circus as a hobby to circus as a successful career. He worked with the advance publicity department at Robert Brothers' Circus and did promotion and administrative work with Sally Chipperfield's, where he developed his interest in wild animals by being one of Jim Clubb's assistants when he was training young leopards and black panthers. After several years learning about the business, working for these leading names, in 1983 he began Circus Fiesta, an attractive, medium-sized show, with a good programme of British and continental artistes and animals. By 1990, he was keen to expand further and put on a stronger show but he considered that he had probably reached the business limitations of the relatively unknown Fiesta name. He therefore responded positively to the suggestion made by Brian Austen that he talk to Dicky Chipperfield about presenting his show as Chipperfield's Circus. Brian was formerly owner of Austen Brothers' Circus and now runs a highly successful tent hire and seating manufacturing company and is a director of the company touring the Moscow State Circus in Great Britain.

The 1991 Hopkins-Chipperfield joint venture proved to be a successful one, with takings over £1 million, the first year being described as a "Record Breaking Tour of Scotland and Northern England." Visiting Scotland was rewarded with good business partly since Chipperfield's had not visited Scotland for some time. Tony's input resulted in a different style of Chipperfield's Circus. The shows were more balanced, with more emphasis on comedy and some production and, while the animal numbers remained among the highlights, there weren't as many animal groups as before. The 1991 programme was headlined by the Hungarian Richter family, with a five-handed jockey riding act, "elephant barber" with an elephant shaving a volunteer from the audience with hilarious results, and acrobatics with three Indian elephants; the Ayalas, from Columbia, on the high wire; Chipperfield's six tigers with Gary Ambrose; Mona Lisa Gerbola, solo trapeze; Rebecca Austen's footjuggling; Clubb-Chipperfield's baboons with Jennifer Solomon; Duo Europa, handbalancing; Mark Austen with exotic animals; and the Europas band. The Konyots musical clowns were included at the start but departed in Scotland, and Peter Sandow and family with their comedy acts were brought in.

The following year, the Richters, Ayalas, Sandows and Rebeccca Austen acts were joined by young Russian clown Dimitri Kuklachev with his domestic cats (Dimitri being the son of star clown Yuri who'd trained the new cats for his Blackpool Superdome season the previous year) and by 18 year old Richard Chipperfield, son of Dicky and Janet, making his début with a new group of five lionesses and one lion. Sandra Sandow appeared as Sandrina on the aerial hoop and her sister Sophie presented the exotic animals. With interest in the Kevin Costner Robin Hood movie still high, there was the "Legend of Sherwood Forest" production, with the company, the Richters riding act and the Romberos knife throwing act, with Craig Bowden as Robin Hood. There was new lighting in evidence and a new big top, like Tony's previous one, from Cirkus Merano in Norway. The show, which brought a modern touch to its traditional, gutsy circus fare, was produced by David Hibling. By the autumn, the Romberos had departed and Frank Endrix, Belgian juggler and unicyclist, and the Black Scorpions, tumbling, limbo dancing and hoop diving, were included.

For a couple of towns only, Enfield and Salisbury, a second Chipperfield's Circus was presented by Tony Hopkins that year in April-May, using the old big top in a show ringmastered and produced by David Hibling and featuring Mary Chipperfield with her animals. On 23 April, Prince Michael and Princess Michael of Kent took their daughter Gabriella to the circus at Enfield as a birthday treat for her. Gary Ambrose and Chipperfield's tigers were with Chipperfield Brothers' Circus that year incidentally.

Right: *Prince and Princess Michael of Kent with ringmaster David Hibling and, left to right, Roger Cawley, Janet, Mary and Dicky Chipperfield. The Royal party greatly enjoyed the show after which they met all the artistes and toured the stables.*

Dublin's prestigious Point Theatre was the large venue for a Chipperfield Circus from 2 to 16 January 1993, with Richard Jnr. with his lions and the three elephants, the tigers with Gary Ambrose, the Eagles riding troupe from the Witney family, Gandey's horses and camels presented by Carol MacManus, the Michels Spanish musical clowns, the Zemganos, revolving aerial rocket, the Black Scorpions, Duo Diamond, rola rola, and ringmaster David Hibling.

For the 1993 touring season, Tony Hopkins retained the Richters with their riding and elephant acts, the Black Scorpions and the Peter Sandow family. Comedy was well catered for, with Peter and Pepe's two main routines, the taxi and the ghost entrée, and many appearances by the young French clown, Mathieu, who'd trained at Annie Fratellini's school in Paris before two years on Cirque Arlette Gruss, the leading French circus. Tony's own group of six chestnut Arab stallions had been trained the previous year by Margaret Chipperfield, who showed them that season, and Gary Ambrose was back with Chipperfield's six tigers. The second half was given an African theme, entitled Spirit of Africa, and included glamorous Jana with Clubb-Chipperfield's alligators and pythons. The show was accompanied by a four piece band and introduced by ringmaster Derek Masters.

The show was successful in the sixth annual Circus Awards, organised by the Circus Friends Association of Great Britain, whose members see thousands of circus performances each year. They are invited to vote for the Best Circus and the best acts in five categories, aerial acts, comedy, equestrian, etc. In October 1993, it was announced that Chipperfield's Circus had been voted Best Circus, with 35% of the vote, and the Black Scorpions were voted the Best Ground Act, with their lively acrobatics presented in such an invigorating way, and Chipperfield's tigers with Gary Ambrose the Best Animal Act. Chipperfield's became the third show to win the Best Circus award, the previous winners being Gandey's (1988, 1989, 1990) and Peter Jay's Superdome Circus in Blackpool (1991 and 1992).

It was back to Ireland for the winter, including King's Hall, Belfast, from 26 to 31 December, and then The Point Theatre, Dublin, again, from 2 to 16 January 1994. Ringmaster David Hibling introduced the award-winning tiger act with Gary Ambrose, Tony Hopkins's own horses now presented by Sally Ann Roncescu (née Duggan), Hans Pedersen's sealions, Russian clown Oleg Markhov, Peter Hoffman's African elephants presented by Philip Hansen, Sandrina on the aerial hoop and Robert Foxall on Roman rings, Peter Sandow and Company's ghost entrée, the Nikol Family from Spain with their juggling and Icarian acts, French clown Mathieu, and the Navas from Ecuador, a five handed flying trapeze act with a strong routine including the triple somersault, two double passages and an attempt at a triple with twist.

For its 1994 tour, the circus by now had a complete set of impressive tiered seating, with individual moulded plastic chairs, designed by Brian Austen's company to fit the 36 metre big top, as well as a large foyer tent for the refreshment kiosks. To help the artistes, the stables and prop tent were joined to the back of the big top, and trainers of the four animal groups - the tigers with John Chipperfield, the horses with Sally Ann Roncescu, Folco's three African elephants with Alex Larenty, and the sealions with Hans and Vicki Pedersen - were always on hand to talk to the audience after the show, an important and valuable way of keeping the public informed about how circus animals are cared for and trained. Again the comedy side of the show was well catered for, with Bulgarian musical clowns Denny, Harry and Company seen alongside the regular acts of Peter Sandow's family. The Bulgarians were replaced by the Michel clowns during the season, this family also providing the entertaining Risley act of the Rampin Brothers. Five young men from the Hungarian State Circus presented two acts, as the Kigassi on the springboard and as the Hunors with an aerial casting act. Zana and Mina Hassani performed a lively illusion act under the name Novikova, and Paul Hill was ringmaster. For the second year, Chipperfield's won the Best Circus award.

On 29 May 1994, Maude Fossett (née Chipperfield) died on 29 May at the age of 86. She was the last of her generation of the Chipperfields, her brothers, Dick, Jimmy and John, and sister Marjorie, all pre-deceasing her. Her husband Tom Fossett had died some years earlier, on 15 September 1989, aged 76. Maude had lived with daughter Shirley (Gina the girl in the moon) in St Anne's, Lancashire, and she was buried near the Fossett family base in Henley in Arden, Warwickshire.

Business was not so good during the Christmas season at Stockon-on-Tees. This was seen in an innovative documentary for The Open University on BBC Television, about the financial and management issues of running a touring circus. During the 1995 tenting tour, Saturday audiences seemed to be affected by the new National Lottery which took sufficient disposable income to deter at least some families from coming to the circus. The acts from the Kigassi/Hunors, the Peter Sandow family, Michels/Rampin Brothers, and Hans and Vicki Pedersen's sealions were again featured, with Sally Ann Roncescu presenting the horses and Mary Chipperfield's group of two African elephants with two zebras, and a cage act, either Richard Chipperfield Jnr. with his new tigers or Gary Ambrose and the older group of six, or Suzanne, daughter of Mary Chipperfield, with her lions and tigers. Igor provided several run-ins to aid the smooth running of the show which won the Best Circus award for the third time, and the liberty group was voted Best Equestrian Act, a tribute to the investment by owner Tony Hopkins and trainer and presenter Sally Ann Roncescu. On the day of the reception when they awards were presented, Peter and Pepe Sandow celebrated their 25th wedding anniversary and also at Lincoln the children of circus manager Craig Harris were christened under the big top.

Below: *Sandy Davidson (right) presented two of the 1995 Circus Awards at Lincoln - that for Best Circus to Tony Hopkins and that for Best Equestrian Act to Sally Ann Roncescu.*

Above: *Peter Sandow's comedy taxi - a regular feature of the show from the 70s to the 90s.*

Myrtle Chipperfield, widow of Dick Snr. and mother of Anne, Dicky and Sally, passed away on 17 September 1995 at the age of 74. She had played a leading role in the running of Chipperfield's Circus for five decades, looking after the booking office and dealing with financial and management issues which were more wide ranging than her programme credit of "M.E. Chipperfield - Personnel Director" would suggest. The funeral took place at Wishford.

Tommy Fossett, son of Tom and Maude Fossett (née Chipperfield), died at the tragically early age of 58 on 23 January 1996, following several months of ill health through a brain tumour. The family aerial act, the Dernos, and his solo juggling and unicycling, with his first wife Vera, and comedy as Professor Grimble, had been frequently featured with Chipperfield's Circus in the 50s, 60s and 70s, and he was with Sally Chipperfield's in the early 80s. He married his second wife Elaine in 1984 and they developed a successful schools programme. In recognition of Tommy's lifetime achievement, Sandy Davidson, President of the Circus Friends Association, presented his President's Award posthumously to Tommy. His widow Elaine accepted it at the Circus Reunion in Blackpool on 23 February 1997.

Chipperfield's Circus in 1996 was produced by French clown Mathieu Dallant and there were several new features - the Hungarian foursome, the O.G. Boys, with a comic skipping act dressed as sailors, their trick cycling as Knights of the BMX; the classic revolving aeroplane aerial act by the French trio, the Antares, who'd been with Chipperfield's in South Africa in 1965; Anita Souza on the aerial rope; and Novikova, illusion act presented by Mina Hassani - alongside the comedy contributions of the Peter Sandow family and clown Igor, the horses with Sally Ann, Pedersen's sealions and Richard Chipperfield Jnr. with his group of 12 young tigers. Although there were no elephants for the first time, the show won no less than three CFA awards that year - for Best Circus, for the fourth year running, for Best Equestrian Act, for the second year, and with the tigers winning the Best Animal Act award.

Tony Hopkins was involved in another joint venture during the autumn of 1996, when he presented a short season of Billy Smart's Big Top with Gary Smart and his parents, Ronnie and Kay Smart, in Bristol and Blackheath, London. Using the magnificent Smart big top and equipment, the programme of quality acts was well received. There were no animals in the show, as with the Chinese State Circus and Moscow State Circus presentations in Britain that year, but circus traditionalists were distressed by comments reported in the press from Billy Smart's that the public did not want to see animals in circuses any more, particularly as at Blackheath, they were just a few miles away from Chipperfield's Circus on Wanstead Flats, which was doing good business with its traditional emphasis on animals! In 1997, Tony presented his show under the Gerry Cottle's Circus title, by arrangement with Gerry, whose current projects include the Circus of Horrors, the hit of the Edinburgh Festival in 1996 and run by his three daughters, Sarah, April and Polly, and presenting the third annual tour of the successful all-human version of the Moscow State Circus in the United Kingdom, with his partners Brian Austen and Peter Featherstone in the European Entertainment Corporation.

Chapter 11

The Rising Young Stars...
of Ringlings in America and Europe's finest circuses

While the original Chipperfield's Circus in the 1990s has continued to attract audiences in Britain to its unique traditional show presented in a modern way, members of the latest generation of the illustrious family are also making an impact in circuses around the world.

Following the 1990-91 winter season in Crystal Palace, Graham Thomas Chipperfield took the lions and elephants to Cirque Christiane Gruss in France for two years. This is a medium sized show run by Rene Chabré, leader of Les French clown act, and his wife Christiane, a member of the famous Gruss circus family. During his stay there, Graham was able to develop his presentation style with both the lions and elephants, as well as presenting an exotic act comprising a camel, llama and Ankoli cow. Graham was invited to perform at the Cirque de Demain festival in January 1992. This event is an opportunity for the acts of the "Circus of Tomorrow" to be seen by a wide audience of circus enthusiasts, directors and agents. The human acts performed in the historic Cirque d'Hiver building in the heart of Paris and the animal routines were shown in the big top of Cirque Arlette Gruss (Arlette being Christiane's elder sister) in Massy, on the outskirts of the capital. Graham's personality came over well and he was awarded the bronze medal for the lions and the silver for the elephants. During the 1992 tour, arrangements were finalised with Kenneth Feld, President and Producer of the Ringling Brothers and Barnum & Bailey Circus, for Graham to join the show in December, initially with the group of lions, to be enlarged to ten animals.

Graham opened with the Red Unit of the gigantic American show at the Expo Hall of the Florida State Fairgrounds in Tampa on 1-3 January 1993. Ringlings have two circus units - the Red and the Blue, each with a different programme - touring halls in the United States on a two year cycle. Thus each city or town receives a visit from a different Ringling show each year, as each Unit's production is changed every two years. Graham joined the Red Unit which had starred the great animal trainer Gunther Gebel-Williams for 22 seasons until his retirement from the ring at the end of the 1990. Gunther is nonetheless very active on the Red Unit, holding an executive position, and working with his son, Mark Oliver Gebel, who was presenting the elephants, zebras and horses. Graham became firm friends with Gunther and Mark, helping them with their animals and practising together, and they supported Graham in his first season in the States. In particular, working with a big herd of elephants, 15 to 20 of varying ages, was a good introduction for Graham to managing a large group of these intelligent animals.

During a practice session on 24 February in the American town of Norfolk, Graham was attacked and badly mauled when he was mixing some new lions into his existing group. A fight broke out between two lionesses and, as he attempted to break this up, male lion Sheeba attacked him from behind and inflicted considerable wounds to his back. Graham's assistant, Tony Hughes, got the other lions out of the cage and went to his rescue - prompt action which Graham is quoted as saying "quite possibly saved my life." He was also wearing a leather jacket which prevented even more serious damage. Tony Hughes came from Liverpool and he had worked with lions for several years in England and Ireland before joining Chipperfield's. Dicky, Janet and Richard Jnr. flew to the States immediately, and they were all eternally grateful to Sigrid Gebel, wife of Gunther Gebel-Williams, who stayed with Graham in hospital until they arrived, sitting on a wooden chair through the night. When Sigrid, a former top model in her native Germany, said with quiet authority, "I will speak with the doctor," who was also German, she ensured that Graham got the best attention. Graham was in intensive care for some time and Richard Jnr. presented a smaller group of lions until his brother was fit enough to return to the big cage, when he showed a total of eight, rather than the planned ten.

Above: *eight days after Graham's accident with the lions in 1993, left to right, Richard David Chipperfield, Graham Thomas Chipperfield and Mark Oliver Gebel.*

For the big opening in Madison Square Garden, New York, on 25 March, there was a massive street parade in celebration of 200 years of circus in America. At the first performance, one of the lionesses bounded across the cage towards Graham in mock attack as cued by him. She hit Graham's stick which was pushed into his face, knocking his two front teeth out. In spite of these initial difficulties, Graham enjoyed working in America and Ringling audiences took to his fast moving and exciting presentation of the lions in traditional Chipperfield style.

Graham moved as planned to Ringling's Blue Unit for its new show in 1994. Five more lions arrived from England and in six weeks Graham mixed some of them with his group, forming a team of ten working well together. He was reunited with the three Chipperfield elephants, Meena, Lechmee and Kamala, and his solo act with them, including the springboard tricks, was featured in the show, a separate number from the big Ringling elephant herd's act.

The Ringling circuses travel by train and the artistes and staff have their own living compartments. At the start of the season, the accommodation for Graham, who was new to the Blue Unit, was still being completed, as were the rooms in the other half of his carriage for elephant trainers Ted Svertesky and Patricia Zerbini and their two children. This meant they had to stay in hotels, which was less convenient, and, since they had children, the accommodation for Ted and Patricia was finished first. When the show moved from St Petersburg and Orlando on 13 January 1994, a catastrophe happened when the train crashed and 19 of the 53 carriages were derailed. Sadly, two artistes, Ted Svertesky and clown Ceslee Conkling, were killed, and 15 injured, although luckily the carriages carrying the animals were all undamaged. A helicopter carrying a TV crew, filming the accident, crashed, seriously injuring the pilot. With amazing good fortune, Graham and Dicky, who was visiting him, were not on the train, as they were driving overland when the crash happened - Graham's carriage, half of which contained his compartment and half that of Ted and Patricia, had been totally destroyed.

Graham was back in New York in March (having changed Units from the Red to the Blue) and his acts were enthusiastically reviewed by circus expert Herb Clement: "Things happen when this young circus star is in the ring... Chipperfield is 'miked' so that audiences can actually hear him talking to his charges. This enhances his routines enormously." Elephants featured heavily in the show that year, with Romeo and Juliette, two babies born and bred by Ringling on its Florida elephant farm, creating a lot of interest when they appeared in a birthday production number. Elephant boss Bill Buckles Woodcock, one of the most experienced American elephant trainers, left in March 1995 and Graham was asked to take over the management and presentation of the complete Ringling elephant herd on the Blue Unit. He was the youngest elephant department head since Smokey Jones some 40 years before. At first there were 21 elephants, including the babies and their mothers, but, with some animals returning to the breeding farm, a group of 15 was retained. Graham found the first eight months very hard, with the added responsibility, but he put together a new crew of trainers and grooms and soon everything was running well.

Above: *a superb action photo of Graham with his lions on Ringling Brothers' Circus.*

Co-presenting the herd in 1996 with Graham were Californian David Polke, who first worked with elephants with Gunther Gebel-Williams, and Argentinian Danielle Raffo, the fifth generation of his family in circus and the same age (27) as Graham.

In 1996, with a new production of the Blue Unit, which starred Airiana the Human Arrow, Graham was more heavily featured with his various appearances. He perfected a double back somersault from the springboard, or teeterboard, to the back of an elephant. To do this, he needed more power than Meena could produce when she ran up and put her foot down onto the end of the board for the single somersault, so he trained a Ringling elephant to stand up on a tub and then come down with both front feet onto the teeterboard.

When they started to train this trick, Graham and Buckles Woodcock worked together to get the elephant to jump off the prop onto the teeterboard. Graham said, "It took a long time to get it right... we kept snapping teeterboards, or I'd be sent way up too high in the air!" He has also introduced Rambo the tiger to American audiences. He originally came to the States from England when he was three months old, having been bred by Chipperfield's. Rambo had been looked after by the girl friend of his brother, Richard, so he was very tame and gentle. In their efforts to keep him that way, Rambo moved in with Graham and his girl friend Rebecca, who works in the press and public relations department of Ringlings. They were staying in hotels at the time as the train accommodation was not ready and had quite a few adventures every night, getting Rambo in past the front desk. The hotel managements didn't really mind, even when he got bigger, and he'd enjoy sleeping on the bed and having a shower or a bath. Graham wanted Rambo to ride on one of the elephants in the show and he carefully introduced the young tiger cub to his four best ones. Two didn't like the look of the striped cat and his own elephant Kamala wasn't much keener, but Ringling elephant Susan didn't mind him. So every day, Graham would hold Rambo in his arms and go for a ride on Susan. The tiger literally grew up riding an elephant, so it was second nature to him. Susan had been with Ringlings for ten years, having come from another circus, and she was the elephant that Graham rode during the parades in the show.

Above: *Graham presented the Ringling elephants at the Capitol Building in Washington.*

Graham delights in working with and talking about the elephants - "gentle, lovable creatures... You can connect with them emotionally... they're so intelligent and I've never had one try to injure me, whereas lions are predatory animals to start with and the accidents I've had have given me an understanding of just how dangerous they can be, though it's not the animal's fault - that's the way lions are" He grew up with the three Chipperfield elephants and now knows every one of the large herd on Ringlings well. He reflects that every one of the 15 is older than him. "The happier and healthier they are, the better it is for me. I would do anything that I can for my animals. We have 20 people working for me, looking after them. The animals come before everything else. Whatever I need, I get. Ringling employs two veterinary surgeons - Dr Houck, the leading vet in the world for elephants, and Dr West, who's training with Dr Houck. There are 35 Indian elephants at the Ringling breeding centre, and seven babies have been born. Every elephant is different in character, and on tour we make things as relaxed and comfortable for them as we can, with exercise areas (using electric fencing) during the daytime." They exercise them in three groups, otherwise there can be disagreements between them sometimes. In late 1996, Graham started training miniature horses to work with four of the elephants, two Chipperfield ones and two from Ringling's herd, for the new show in 1998. The horses are named after rock stars, such as Buddy and Elvis.

Left: *Graham, Jay Leno and Gunther Gebel-Williams.* **Right:** *Janet, Rambo and Dicky.*

Graham has a contract with Ringling until the year 2000 and, with the new production in 1998-1999, he will be joined by his brother Richard with his group of 12 tigers. These were all born at Chipperfield's, and the company continues to breed many lion and tiger cubs each year. One tiger cub was a special guest at the Royal Review of the Princess of Wales's Royal Regiment, the Queen's and Royal Hampshires, on 9 June 1993, and a photo of Princess Diana, the regiment's Colonel-in-Chief, with the cub was chosen for the regiment's Christmas card.

The Ringling schedule is a challenging one, with only ten days holiday in December during the two years of the production run, but less than this when there is a new production to be rehearsed. Graham has always wanted to be a performer and enjoys working with such a big and dynamic show. "Ringling has changed a lot in three years. It's very modern in its lighting and music, more of a show, more theatrical," he says. "The 1996 production was a big jump forward. There are 6,000 individual lights, 15 spotlights, laser lights and a dome in the ring doors which is full of lights. The sound system is amazing with speakers all over the arena, so the sound is the same at the top of the seats as down in front of ring two. The build-up for the Human Arrow is breathtaking, with fireworks on steel cables and medieval-style costumes for all the company. The costume worn by the giant - a man on stilts underneath the outfit - cost $40,000. There's a huge dragon, made of very light polystyrene, on one elephant, and me with Rambo the tiger on another. Then the big crossbow on wheels is brought in and the Human Arrow, Airiana, all in white, is shot 75 feet across the arena - reliving man's dream of flight!"

Graham is also an experienced media representative of the circus, appearing on local and national TV and radio on countless occasions. He has been on the Tonight show three times, with Jay Leno, and Good Morning America, as well as CNN News and in newspapers and magazines such as USA Today. One of the most popular events was the Salute to Congress with 13 elephants performing a long mount in front of the Capitol Building in Washington. This was part of a mini performance in the grounds on 5 April 1995 to commemorate the 125th anniversary of the opening of the Barnum show. Politicians Robert Dole and Newt Gingrich were honorary ringmasters. Right from the start in the States, Graham's friendly approach and talkative manner made him a natural favourite in the media, but he's also had training from Ringling's PR team, including hours and hours of closed-circuit TV practice. "It's very important to be able to talk about the circus, to put it across properly and to be able to deal with every question. We must portray what really goes on. With my involvement with animals, it's important that the public is educated about how I work with them. Ringling pays a lot of attention to education, inviting the press to training sessions. We have visits from colleges, universities and vet schools, to watch training and ask questions, with positive reactions."

On the other side of the Atlantic, David and Suzanne, the children of Mary Chipperfield and her husband Roger Cawley, are well established in the family business. David took over his mother's group of tigers after her tour in 1993 with Circus Knie and he has successfully presented them in France, Holland and Switzerland. Prior to that, he showed lions in Spain and presented African elephants, and lions and tigers, in England, as well as showing his equal interest in things mechanical by acting as transport manager for a major circus. In 1997, he realised an ambition by starting his own touring circus, Cirque David Chipperfield, in France, which commenced in St Malo at the end of January, before moving to Belgium. This featured eight tigers, African elephants, horses, ponies and a group of exotic animals including a giraffe.

Suzanne Chipperfield has inherited her mother's love of horses and appeared in a BBC TV children's circus riding High School in 1984. She trained as a hair stylist with Vidal Sassoon before returning to the circus, with horses on Cirque Arlette Gruss in France and in the Fridrichstadtpalast in Berlin and with her lions and tigers at Peter Jay's circuses in Great Yarmouth and Blackpool, Cirque Alexis Gruss in France and Circus Krone in Munich. She showed her versatility in the 1996 Blackpool Superdome circus for Peter Jay when she appeared in five displays, with horses, ponies, elephants, zebras, Nicholas the giraffe and a farmyard act with pigs, goats, sheep, cow and hens.

Left: *David Chipperfield with African elephants Rosa and Opal.* **Right:** *Suzanne Chipperfield with Nicholas the giraffe at Peter Jay's Superdome Circus in Blackpool.*

Dicky and Janet's son, Richard, made his début in 1992 with a group of lions at the age of 18 on Chipperfield's Circus and he presented them and the elephants on Fossett's Circus in Ireland the following year. He worked with his father on an ambitious routine with a large group of tigers which was first seen on Chipperfield's Circus in England in 1995 and Richard's 12 striped cats won the Best Animal Act award in 1996, before departing for France and Cirque Arlette Gruss in November where they were a great success during the show's Paris season and on tour in 1997. Cirque Arlette Gruss has become established as one of Europe's leading circuses, with new and imaginative productions each year by Gilbert Gruss. It has the knack of presenting each act to its best advantage, with superb lighting and evocative music, played by its Polish band. Small wonder that the excellent routine by Richard's tigers was greeted with standing ovations and critical approval in a country where circus is appreciated as an art form and where the public is well informed about circus and not afraid to show its feelings! Richard and the tigers were specially released by Mme. Arlette Gruss to appear at Prince Rainier's Monte Carlo Circus Festival from 28 January to 4 February 1997, where they won the Prix Circus Royale, presented by its proprietor Frank Gasser from Australia. In 1998-99, Richard will join Graham with Ringling's Blue Unit in the USA, with the young Chipperfield brothers a special feature with their tigers and elephants.

With these members of the current generation doing so well, the future of this famous family in circuses with animals seems to be well assured.

Below: *right to left, Madame Arlette Gruss, Richard with his prize from the Monte Carlo festival, and Arlette's husband, Georgika Kobann.*

Appendix 1
Chipperfield Collectables

There are many Chipperfield items which have become highly prized by collectors. The selection on the opposite page comprises, from top to bottom -
- several Corgi Classic Chipperfield vehicles, produced in 1994-95
- posters for the circus in 1970 (left) and 1995 (right)
- Chipperfield's Circus News, the free promotional newspaper, this issue from 1957
- A4 landscape programme cover used for 1994-95 winter, 1995 and 1996 (left)
- programme cover used from 1959 to the start of 1963 (centre)
- the Chipperfield calendar issued by Corgi for 1995
- a greetings card from the Royal West of England Academy, using the painting by Louis Ward of the Biasini cycling act on Chipperfield's tenting show in 1959 to 1962
- four of the vintage cameo vehicles issued by Corgi in 1996 (bottom left)
- the crane truck and animal cage, the first Chipperfield Corgi toys, issued in 1960 and 1961
- poster cards, these two published by Aardvark in 1990
- the Corgi advance booking office, the third Chipperfield toy, issued in 1962
- a Chipperfield's Circus badge, issued for the Japan season in 1986
- two Chipperfield's horse brasses (right) - an elephant and the tiger riding the elephant. There are two versions of the elephant brass, one showing one tusk, the other with two tusks.

There are also Chipperfield phone cards and a Royal Doulton plate. Now that circus memorabilia is more highly prized, specialist dealers in entertainment and the performing arts often have circus sections and London auction houses, such as Sothebys, have sales including circus material. Because so much good material was produced relatively recently, in the 1940s-1960s, it is still possible to find items in second-hand shops, car boot sales and by advertising in magazines such as Exchange and Mart, even though so much circus advertising matter is by its nature highly ephemeral and relatively few items survive. The Merchandising Department of the Circus Friends Association (see page 190) sells circus memorabilia old and new.

Books, Programmes, Videos, Posters

Books. *High Endeavour* by artist Edward Seago (Collins, 1944) tells of Jimmy Chipperfield's struggle to join the RAF during World War Two and contains some of Seago's illustrations, including fine portraits of Jimmy and Dick, although their surname is not included. The children's novel *Wagons and Horses* (Collins, 1955) by Olivia Fitzroy is based on Chipperfield's Circus just after the war. *Chipperfields' Circus* (Faber & Faber, 1957) by the equestrian writer Pamela Macgregor-Morris tells the story up to the mid 1950s. Dick Chipperfield's *My Friends the Animals* (Souvenir Press, 1963), concentrates on the animals he trained and worked with as well as the family's history. A spate of books followed Jimmy Chipperfield's development of the safari park from 1966, including *The Lions of Longleat* (Cassell, 1969) by the Marquess of Bath and Jimmy Chipperfield, *David in the Lion's Den* (Cassell, 1969), a book of photos of Roger and Mary Cawley's young son, David, Mary Chipperfield's *Lions on the Lawn* (Hodder, 1971) and *Lion Country* (Hodder, 1972), plus Jimmy Chipperfield's excellent autobiography, *My Wild Life* (Macmillan, 1975). The last three went into paperback editions. There are two editions of my *Mary Chipperfield's Circus Book* (Jarrold, 1979 and 1989), both full of colour and black and white photographs.

Programmes. Chipperfield programmes before the war seem very few and far between. Many of the smaller circuses did not have printed programmes in the 1930s and before. Even some of the larger ones only had a folded sheet, giving the running order. Likewise, only one catalogue of a Chipperfield menagerie has been seen.

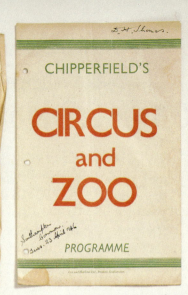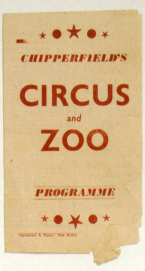
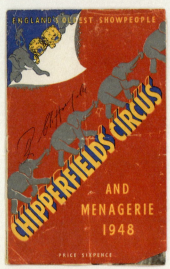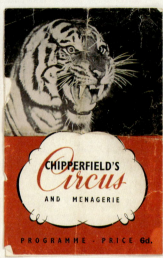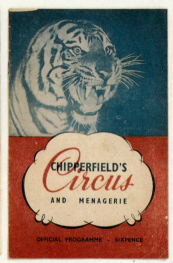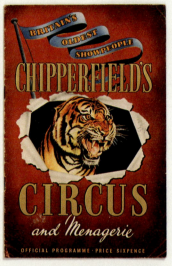
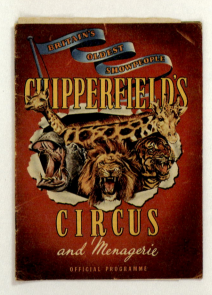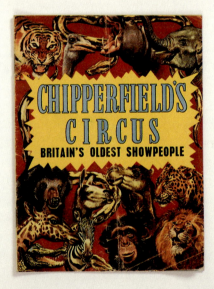

Opposite page - programme covers. Top row: *Catalogue of Chipperfield's French Menagerie, circa 1903, 8 pages (pp), text only • 1938 or 1939, folded sheet • 1946, folded sheet • 1947, folded sheet.* **2nd row:** *1948, 8pp • 1949, 8pp • 1950, 16pp • cover used for 1952 to 1958, usually 24pp, after 1956 with dated running order sheet tipped in.* **3rd row:** *cover used from 1959 to the start of 1963, 24pp, usually with dated running order sheet tipped in • cover from 1963 to 1966, 24pp, with running order printed on the centrespread • cover used for Bingley Hall, Birmingham, Christmas seasons, including 5th, 6th and 7th seasons, 16pp.* **4th row:** *covers for Bingley Hall, Birmingham, Christmas seasons • 1960-61 • 1959-60 • and Granby Halls, Leicester, 1959-60, 16pp.*

From 1949, the circus used a cover design with a tiger's head. Initially a black and white photograph, this became a piece of colour artwork for the full colour covers used from 1952 to 1958, with a variety of shades of red as the background. There are differences in each year's programmes, which are undated, and sometimes there is more than one version each year. This cover was the work of resident artist Bill Smee who also created that for the wider programmes used from 1959, with two giraffes, a lion, tiger and Harry the hippo bursting through a red background. Not many of these programmes are dated, although the tip-in printed running order usually did have the year. There were new programmes, or running order sheets, for each of the winter building seasons. Another Bill Smee painting, with numerous animals' heads, was introduced in 1963. In South Africa, there is a different programme for each of the three years - 1965, 1966 and 1967 - with two formats (one larger than usual) for the final year, although the content is very similar.

Another Bill Smee cover was used on the return to Britain, in 1969 and 1970, and the next programmes had colour photographs on the inside pages. From 1973, there were two main programmes used, one from 1973 to 1975 and the other from 1976 right through to a poster version in 1984. These concentrated on photographs and information on the animals, with the booked-in acts shown in tip-in running orders which were regularly updated. Each of the Cottle Chipperfield seasons in Hong Kong in 1982-83 had a full colour programme but there were few for the Chipperfield Far East dates, Singapore and Japan in 1986 being exceptions. When presented by Tony Hopkins from 1991 to 1996, there were several full colour programmes. For the Thames Television recordings from 1973 to 1977, folded-card tickets gave details of each programme to be seen.

Newspapers. Chipperfield's Circus News, the four page free promotional newspaper, began in 1953 and continued until 1962. It was edited by the show's publicity manager, Bill 'Lofty' Dredge. There were printings for most major towns on the tour, with several thousand produced of each issue, but how many survive today? For example, the Circus Friends Association Archives contains issues for Gillingham (1953), Liverpool and Birmingham (1954), Cheltenham (1956), Leeds (1958) with Mr Pastry, Norwich (1961) with Zira's crocodile swim, and Southsea (1962) with the Great Katharyna on the wire.

Route Cards. Printed post cards, giving the show's route for four or five towns ahead, with the dates, phone number and number of miles between grounds, were produced during the 1952, 1953 and 1954 seasons.

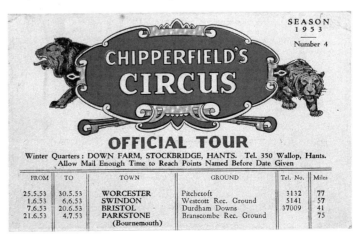

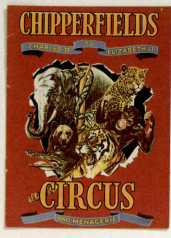
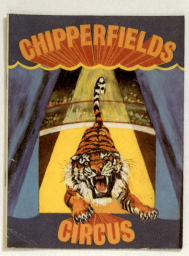
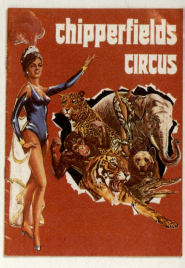

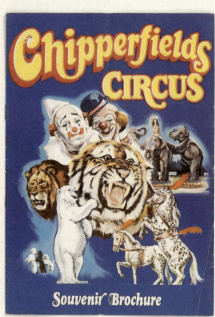

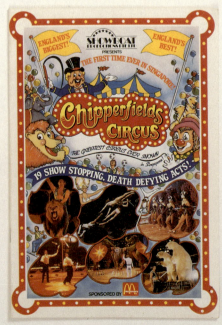
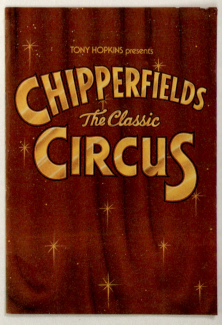

Opposite page - programme covers. Top row: *1967 (South Africa), 16 pages (pp) • cover for 1969 and 1970, 16pp • 1971, 16pp, the first programme with colour photographs • cover for 1971 and 1972, 16pp.* **2nd row:** *cover for 1973 to 1975, 16pp, with running order sheet tipped in • cover for 1976, 1980, 16pp or 12pp, with running order sheet tipped in, and 1984 folder poster version • Cottle-Chipperfield, Hong Kong, 1982, 20pp.* **3rd row:** *Cottle-Chipperfield, Hong Kong, 1982-83, 36pp • Singapore, 1986, 24pp • Chipperfield's Circus presented by Tony Hopkins, 1993 and 1994, 16pp.*

Videos. Two videos, one of the 1950s and the other of the 1960s in South Africa, using movie film from the Stockley family collection, and other Chipperfield items, are available from Alf Gunner, P O Box 8, Southsea, Hants PO5 2AY, in UK/European and American VHS.

Above: *youngsters and the Shetlands before the parade in 1956 or 57, left to right, Jane, Jimmy and Carol Stockley, Sally and John Chipperfield. Note the big format posters on the lorry behind.*

Posters and Handouts. Chipperfield's Circus has used a great range of colour posters. Few exist now from before World War Two. Those that can be seen on contemporary photos are either textual or, if pictorial, they are often stockbills showing a circus theme, so the circus in question would have its own name over-printed. During the war, Chipperfield's animals appeared in various shows and can be spotted on posters for the Sandow family's Poole's Caucasian Circus and several stage circuses in theatres.

From 1946, as Chipperfield's Circus grew larger, the quality and range of posters developed. Several designs listing 'all the acts' were used, often with small variations and some with photographs of the acts.

Most posters were the standard double-crown (30 x 20 inches) size, with occasional smaller sizes.

Chipperfield's, like other circuses, especially in the 50s and 60s, used large versions of their posters on hoardings and walls and also on their own vehicles. Sadly, few if any of these giant posters survive today.

The specialist poster printers, W.E. Berry of Bradford, worked with many of the touring circuses, including Chipperfield, Mills and Smart, to create new designs. Berry's service includes the over-printing of the town and date information in black on the batch of posters for each stand. Chipperfield's Circus had many features which were excellent subjects for pictorial posters. There were many different handouts, some in full colour, others in one or two colours.

A selection of posters appears on pages 156 to 169. • Page 156: a rare poster of Flying Officer Jimmy Chipperfield and his tigers - 1946. • Page 157: all the acts poster - 1949. • Page 158: the four pole tent - 1952. • Page 159: a revised version with the eight pole tent - 1954. • Page 160: Ranée the tiger on the elephant - 1952. • Page 161: Raluy's double human cannonball - 1952 to 1954. • Page 162: Roman chariot racing - 1953. • Page 163: Raluy's car - 1956 to 1957 • Page 164: the exotic group - first version with zebras and kangaroos - early 1950s. • Page 165: the exotic group - second version with two giraffes and Harry the hippo - late 1950s/early 1960s. • Page 166: all the acts - 1954; Zira and the crocodiles - 1962; Fantasy of the Bulls - 1962; pictorial all the acts - 1964. • Page 167: the lioness wagon - 1959. • Page 168: Dicky Chipperfield's leopards and black panthers - 1969. • Page 169: Far East dates - Singapore - 1986; Hong Kong - 1986-87; Bangkok, Thailand; and New Zealand - 1987-88.

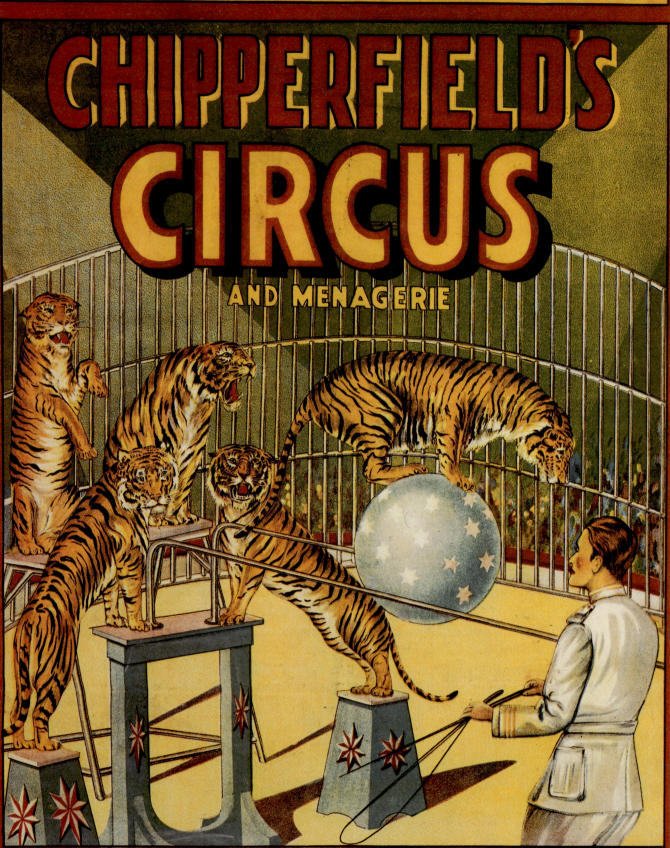

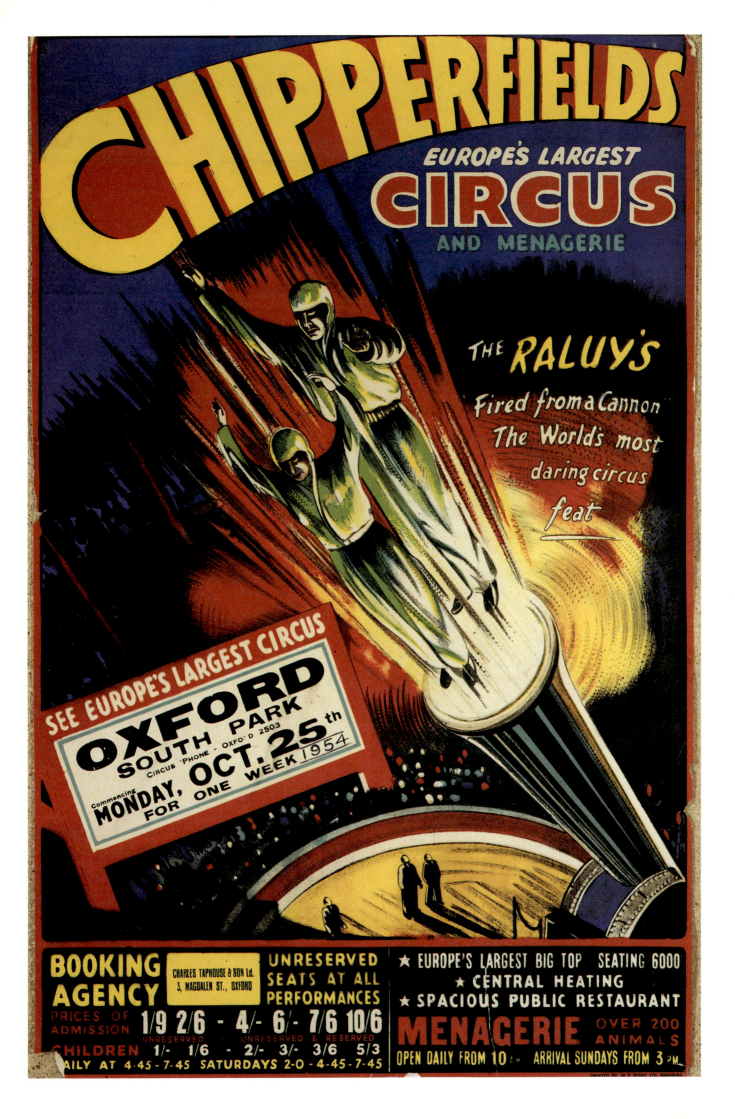

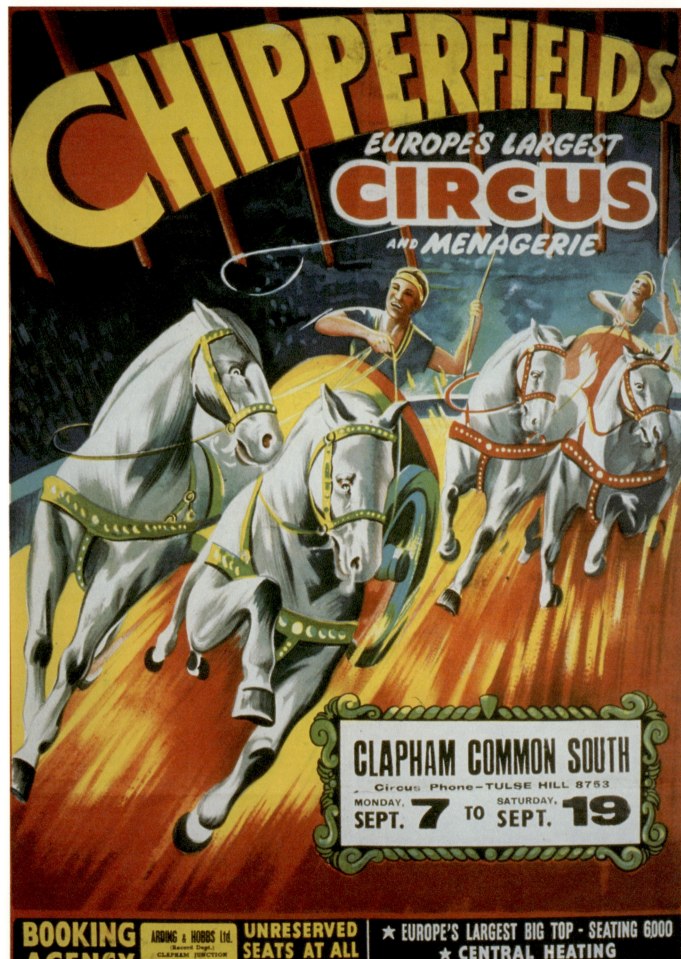

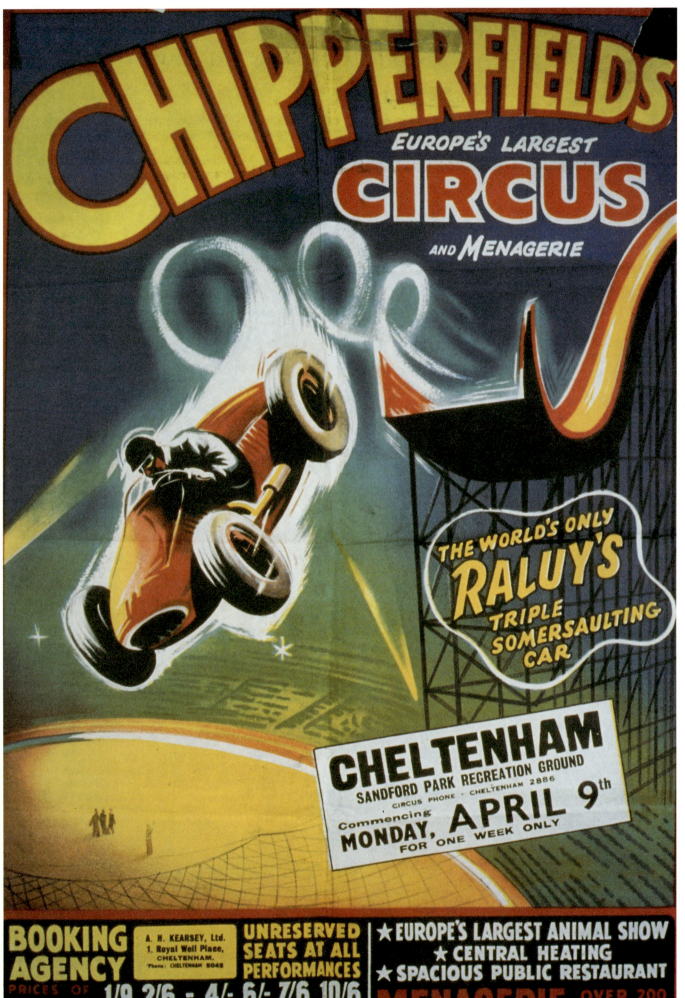

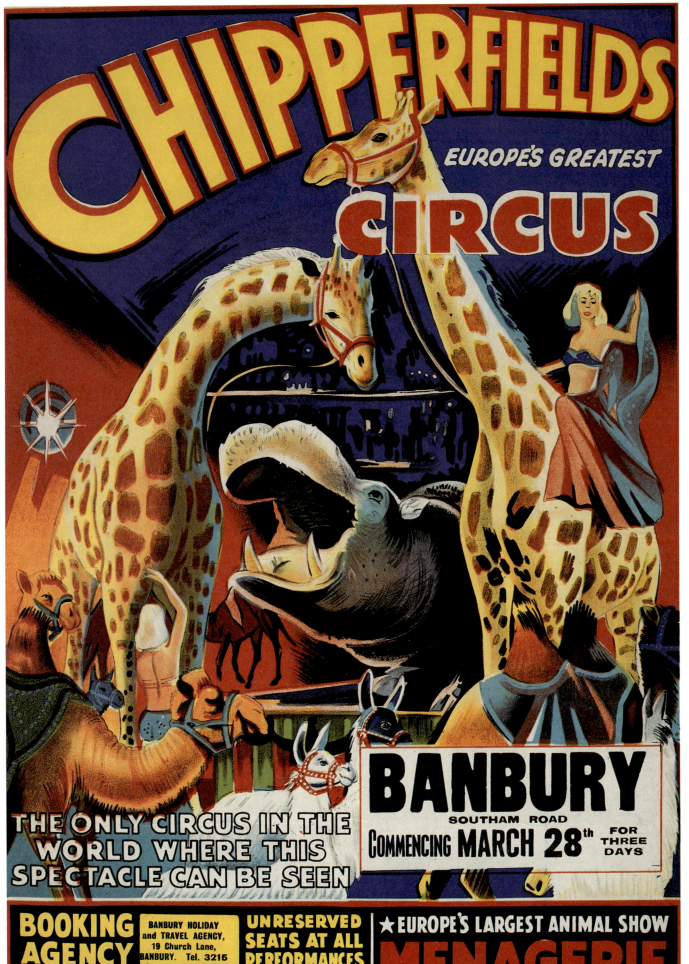

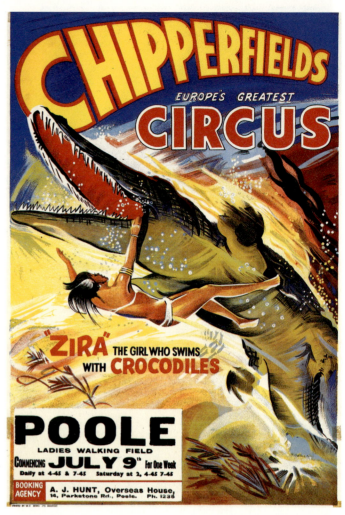

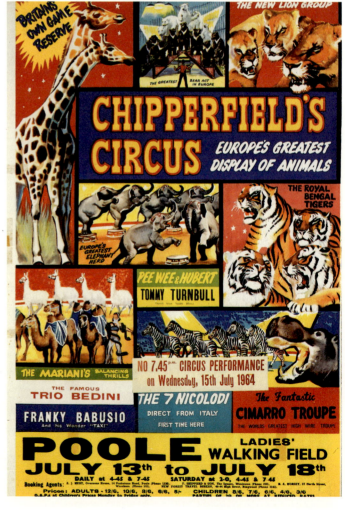

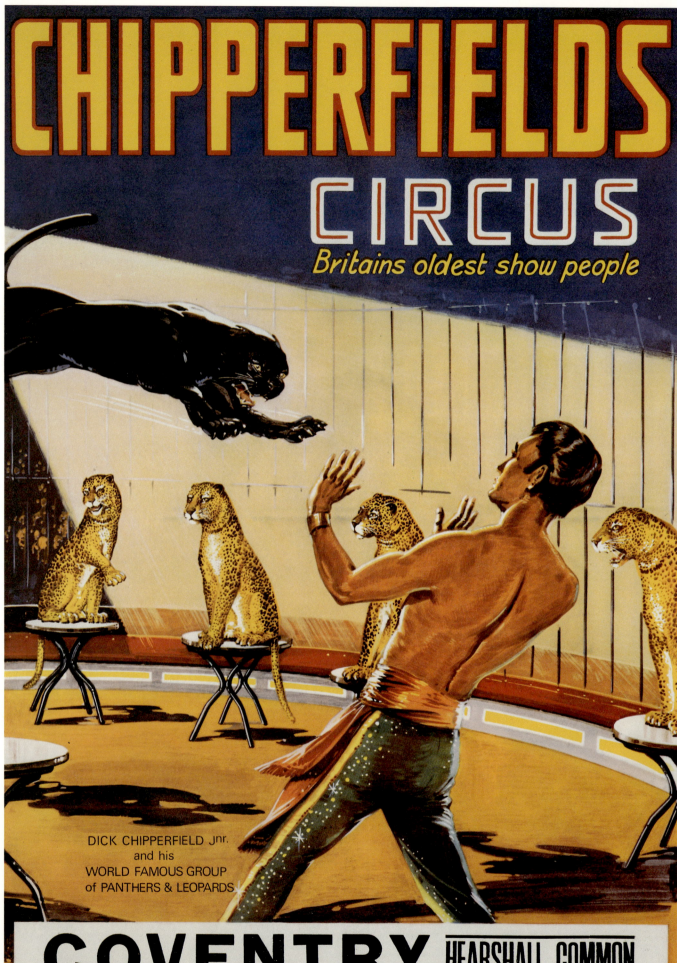

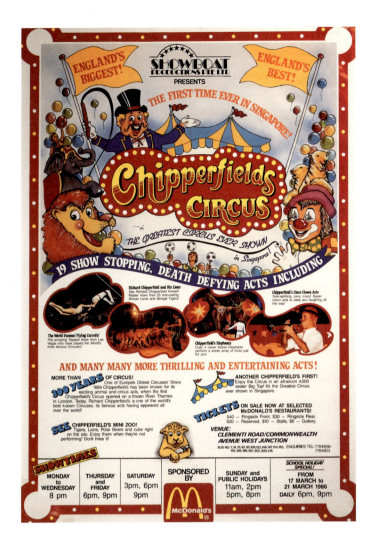

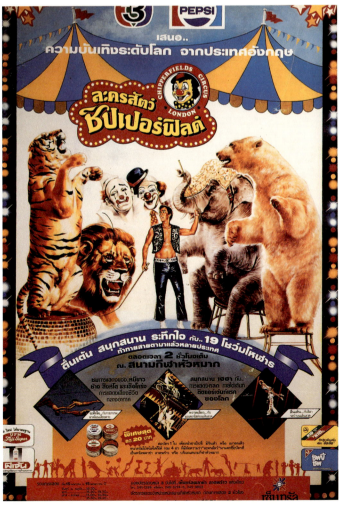
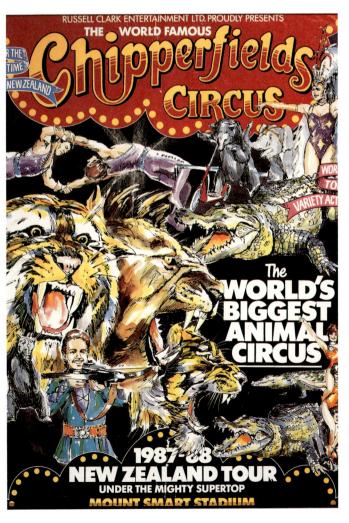

Chipperfield Corgi Models

Above: *the crane truck and animal cage were the first two Corgi vehicles to be released.*

The Original Range

The name of Chipperfield is known the world over for its circus, and equally well known in just as many places is the Corgi Toy. It was fitting therefore that these two household names came together to form one of the most well known and now much sought after collections of diecast toys, renowned for their fine attention to detail, and technical innovation. The Corgi Toy was developed in the years 1954-56 by the Mettoy Company, which had premises at Northampton and Swansea. The name Corgi was chosen for several reasons. It was a sturdy little Welsh dog, and the Corgi range would be produced in Swansea, Wales. Secondly, the name of the breed was felt to be somewhat prestigious as Corgis were the favoured breed of the Royal Family and their Corgi dogs were often featured in the media. Thirdly, the name was short and snappy as was the popular Dinky name. The Corgi range was intended to be in direct competition to the popular Dinky Toys.

The Corgi Chipperfield range of toys was the branchild of Marcel R. Van Cleemput, Mettoy's chief designer. He was involved in every toy designed and produced by Corgi until its demise in 1983. It was whilst visiting Chipperfield's Circus at Midsummer Meadow in Northampton in 1959, that he had the idea of creating a series of toys based on Chipperfield's Circus. It should be pointed out that this is what they were - toys! - toys to be played with, and stringent tests were carried out on each new design to ensure that it would stand up to the rigours that any child could subject it to!

The relationship between Corgi and Chipperfields was to become a long and friendly association, in particular between Marcel Van Cleemput and the senior members of the Chipperfield family, Mr Dick and Mr John Chipperfield. This association resulted in a range of toys that would be the mainstay of Corgi Toys for many years, and in view of the numbers sold, ensure the name of Chipperfield was publicised and played with in many a home and many a playroom of that era! Sometime into the production of these toys, it was suggested by someone on the board of directors at Mettoy of creating a range of Billy Smart models. Perhaps out of loyalty to the Chipperfields, this idea never materialised.

So it was that in October 1960, the first Chipperfield toy was seen in toy shops across Britain. No. 1121 **Chipperfield's Circus Crane Truck.** Scale 1:48. Sold: 407,000 plus. Withdrawn 1969. It was based on the Mack NM6 tractor that was the prime mover of the large circuses at that time. It was not an exact copy of the Mack crane used by Chipperfield's Circus, which is a little surprising when one considers the lengths that Corgi went to on some toys to achieve the perfect copy of the real thing. However, cost was the main consideration and the Army International Tow Truck No. 1118, produced earlier in 1959, provided the bulk of the toy. The rear body and crane assembly was the only necessary addition. The crane jib was pressed metal, the Mettoy Company having much experience of this technique from their earlier tin-plate toys. It was the best selling Corgi Major of that year with 58,000 sales - not bad considering it was only released in October.

1961 saw the launch of the next toy: No. 1123 **Chipperfield's Circus Animal Cage**. Scale 1:48. Sold: 361,000. Withdrawn 1968. As ever concerned with authenticity, the bars consisted of metal wires around which the cage front surround had been cast. The mould for this had been designed on the same basis as the one for the No. 1111 Combine Harvester tynes. 20 reels of wire were fed through the mould with the aim of casting two cage fronts simultaneously. However their attempts proved unsuccessful as they were unable to fill the second frame. The zinc had to flow through the first frame before filling the second and due to the somewhat small section, and all the wires the metal had to pass over, it chilled before reaching the end of the second frame. Therefore the second frame had to be "blanked off" and they had to be satisfied with producing just one frame at a time. This was a very complex mould. The toy was originally produced with diecast sliding doors but these were to be changed to blue plastic in the following year. This toy was the second best selling Corgi Major of 1961 with 59,000 sales. Also in 1961 came the first circus Gift Set: GS12 Chipperfield Circus Set. Sold: 101,000. Withdrawn 1964. This comprised the 1121 Crane Truck and 1123 Animal Cage.

Moving on to 1962: No. 426 **Circus Booking Office**. Sold: 133,000. Withdrawn 1964. This was the No. 407 Mobile Shop, with a facelift, which included a revised printed metal insert, painted in Chipperfield colours. This year saw the second Gift Set produced: GS19 **Chipperfield's Circus Land-Rover with Elephant Cage on Trailer**. Sold: 473,000. Withdrawn 1968. The Land-Rover was the standard No. 406 version with metal hood, again in their colours. The trailer was the No. 101 platform trailer in red and blue. It was complete with plastic elephant and cage. Another Gift Set this year: GS23 Chipperfield's Circus Set. Sold: 75,000. Withdrawn 1967. This set consisted of Nos. 1121 Crane Truck, two 1123 Animal Cages, one with lions, the other with polar bears, No. 426 Booking Office, Land-Rover and trailer and elephant cage. This set was later produced in 1964 with a giraffe transporter instead of the Booking Office.

In October of this year came yet another model: No.1130 **Chipperfield's Circus Horse Transporter**. Scale: 1:47. Sold: 627,000. Withdrawn 1971. This was a totally new toy. It had three drop down hinged ramps and included six white horses. The cab to which it was articulated was the new design Bedford TX, with spring suspension and interior, plus wing mirrors. This cab would gradually replace the original and existing 5 type Bedford cab, which had served the range so well since 1957. At the end of 1962, the Chipperfield range had the best selling Gift Set GS19 with 82,000 sales, and three out of the top four best selling Corgi Majors. These were No. 1130 Horse Transporter with 58,000; No. 1121 Crane Truck with 48,000; and No. 1123 Animal Cage with 42,000.

1963 saw only one new item in March of that year: No. 607 **Circus Elephant and Cage** (kit). Sold: 43,000. Withdrawn 1967. This was identical to the cage in GS19 but a 'do it yourself' erecting job. GS19 was the third best selling gift set for this year with 61,000 sales. No. 1130 was the top selling Corgi Major with 106,000 sales.

June 1964 saw the only Chipperfield toy to carry the 'By Special Request' emblem on the box. No, Mr Dick Chipperfield didn't ask for this toy personally. It was simply a marketing gimmick used by the Mettoy Company! No. 503 **Giraffe Transporter**. Sold: 860,000. Withdrawn 1971. This was the new Bedford articulated cab unit with a three-sided open top box, and plastic hinged ramp. Two giraffes were included. This toy was the fourth best selling light commercial of this year with 200,000 sales. No. 1130 Horse Transporter was the second best selling Corgi Major with 108,000 sales. GS19 was the third best selling Gift Set with 73,000 sales.

The Parade Vehicle was dreamed up in 1965. No. 487 **Chipperfield's Circus Parade Land-Rover**. Scale: 1:46. Sold 304,000. Withdrawn 1969. This was the revamped No. 472 'Vote for Corgi' toy. Basically a change of colour, plus appropriate labels. The politician was replaced by a clown holding a microphone, and lady canvasser by a chimpanzee - most appropriate! The only best seller this year was the No. 1130 Horse Transporter in third place of the Corgi Majors with 96,000 sales.

It would be a further three years before another new circus toy would be seen, in October 1968. No. 1139 **Chipperfield's Circus Menagerie Transporter**. Scale: 1:48. Sold: 50,000. Withdrawn 1972. This consisted of the newly designed Scammell Handyman Mk. 3 prime mover cab unit. Its main feature was twin jewelled headlights. It had an eight wheeled diecast trailer with automatic coupling. On the trailer were three clear plastic animal cages suitably engraved with bars running top to bottom. A selection of lions, bears and tigers were included in the cages. For the third year there were no circus items among the best sellers.

Only five months later there followed another new toy in March 1969. No. 1144 **Chipperfield's Circus Crane Truck**. Scale: 1:48. Sold 48,000. Withdrawn 1972. This was an amalgamation of assemblies and parts from five previous toys. These included the cab and chassis of the Scammell Handyman Mk. 3 tractor unit, platform and deck castings of the Holmes Wrecker, the complete crane assembly of the circus crane truck, including its jib, one of the clear plastic cages from the Menagerie Transporter and, last but not least, the rhino from the Volkswagen East African Safari model. Painted red and blue and adorned with 'Come to the Circus' labels. No sales are available for 1969.

1970 saw the very last new Chipperfield toy to be produced. No. 511 **Chipperfield's Circus Performing Poodles**. Sold 104,000. Withdrawn 1971. This was easily recognisable as the No. 486 Chevrolet Kennel Service Wagon, in the Chipperfield colours and with a change of dog to poodles, three of which were moulded together in a row and fitted to a green plastic platform. This year also saw the last Gift Set to be put together, in April. GS21. Circus Set. Scale: 1:48. Sold 22,000. Withdrawn 1972. This consisted of the No. 1144 Crane Truck together with the trailer part only of the No. 1139 Menagerie Transporter and its three animal cages. The trailer was fitted with a bogie wheel carriage and tow bar at the front end. Also supplied was the elephant cage and elephant.

Of all the items that I have listed, in my opinion this Gift Set merits a special word, if only for its rarity. Very few people, including some of the leading toy dealers, were until recently aware of this Gift Set's existence. Many years ago, I was asked by a fellow circus modeller if I had ever seen the Chipperfield draw-bar trailer. At that time I was unaware of this item being made. With a bit of detective work and good fortune, I now have that trailer in my collection, though I have yet to see the Gift Set in its entirety.

As Marcel Van Cleemput himself said, "Where would Corgi have been without the circus?" Now children yearned for greater things. The age of the 'whizz wheel' and Corgi Rockets was here. There were more and more diecast companies producing toys to saturate an already diminishing market. The Mettoy Company was already on the slippery slope towards its demise. The attitude of people towards the circus was also changing for the worse. This indeed was the end of a 'golden era' for both toy manufacturers and the circus.

Now into the 90s, diecast toys have become models - to be cherished and displayed. They are very much sought after by collectors and the Chipperfield models feature very highly in this market place. As a collection of beautifully detailed models, they are a reminder of the great days of circus perhaps, and of my childhood, and of course are now an investment. **Nick Barnett**

First published in King Pole, March 1990.

Below: *the full range of original vehicles.*

Above: *the 94-95 range with Carl Moore's model.*

Corgi Classics - the 1994-95 range

Corgi, owned then by Mattel, launched a new generation of Chipperfield vehicles with the 1994-95 range of 12 sets, one released per month, with a full colour catalogue featuring Carl Moore's Chipperfield model circus for backdrop photographs.

In August 1995, Corgi management successfully completed a buyout from Mattel, returning the company to private ownership. No longer part of an international toy company, Corgi has more freedom to cater for the ever growing demand from collectors for high quality models and the flourishing company is a successful leader in an expanding market.

Each product comprised • The model or models. • Limited edition certificate: 12,500 of each produced • One of 12 replica posters • One of 12 collector cards.

The set of collector cards, six inches by four inches, showed Chipperfield acts through the years. These were designed to be stuck in a 28 page album.

The range comprised the following vehicles:

97915	Scammell Highwayman and two trailers
97303	Bedford O Artic truck
97886	Scammell Highwayman with crane
97957	ERF eight-wheel flatback
97896	AEC eight-wheel seating truck
96905	Bedford advance booking van
97092	Bedford O pantechnicon
97885	Scammell Highwayman, seating trailer and living wagon
97022	AEC Regal (coach) living wagon
97887	Bedford O Artic horse box
97888	Foden eight-wheel box truck and living wagon
97889	AEC four-wheel beast wagon and beast trailer

Below: *the Scammell Highwayman + two trailers.*

The colours are traditional Chipperfield red and blue, the exception being the AEC coach finished in matt brown with yellow doors, and the living wagons; one in blue, one in yellow. Chipperfield's Circus used this type of wagon for the family living trailers and the famous reception wagon. Posters of the 1950s-1960s period are reproduced and applied to the side of certain models. The only design from the original range is the artic horse box which is the same as was used first time round, now with a Bedford O series unit, but this time minus the horses!

Corgi Chipperfield Cameos
This set of ten cameos - 56901 Cameo Collectables - each with different Chipperfield livery - was launched in 1996. Limited edition: 11,000.

Ten Vintage Model Vehicles. Contents: 2 x Morris tankers • 2 x AEC vans • 2 x Morris trucks • 2 x Bedford buses • 2 x T Ford vans.

Corgi Classics - 1996 Gift Set
The 31703 Gift Set was launched for Christmas 1996. Limited edition: 12,500. Scale: 1/43 and 1/50. Contents: Land Rover • Morris Minor Pick-Up - Here come the clowns • Ford Thames Trader - Chipperfield's Royal Bengal Tigers • AEC Fire Engine - Chipperfield's Fire Department

Corgi Classics - 1997 Range
The 1997 range comprises animals and figures as well as vehicles. Launch dates: July to December 1997. Scale: 1/43 (Land Rover), 1/50 (heavy commercials).

07202 Land Rover public address with two clowns

17801 Scammell Constructor cannon and ringmaster

Below: *the original Raluy cannon in 1952-54.*

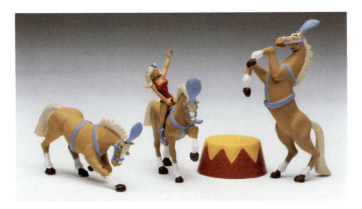

31901 Mary Chipperfield's liberty horses (3), rider + pedestal

14201 Foden S21, trailer with tank, Harry the hippo + Nile crocodile

Below: *Harry the hippo ridden by Angela in 1962.*

31902 Foden truck and trailer, Chipperfield's elephants (3), rider + pedestal

Below: *a Mack tractor and elephant trailer in 1950.*

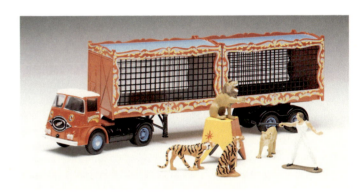

11201 ERF KV, trailer cages, 2 lions, 2 tigers, Richard Chipperfield, pedestal

Below: *the ornate cage for the leopard act in 1962.*

Corgi Classics Ltd.
Harcourt Way, Meridian Business Park,
Leicester LE3 2RL.
Phone: 0116 282 6622. Fax: 0116 282 6633.

Appendix 2
Chipperfield Transport

Opposite page. Top row: *Chipperfield's in Cambridge in 1964, photographed by Eric Nugus.*
Rows 2-4: *Chipperfield's Circus, around 1980, photographed by Malcolm Slater.*

Above: *a line of nine Macks in the early 50s.*

Above: *FWD SU COEs on the post-war circus.*

Above: *the Bedford petrol 'bowser' in 1955. Behind it is a bus adapted as a horse box.*

Above: *the Mack crane truck in 1960.*

Above: *the Thorneycroft baby elephant wagon - 1963.*

Above: *the family living wagons in 1959.*

Above: *zebras pass the Albion lion wagon and trailers on their way to the big top in 1964.*

Above: *the caravans of the advance publicity team in Lincoln in 1961.*

Above: *in 1964 - the converted bus which was the travelling home for the giraffes, with an enclosure on the other side, and the monkey trailer.*

Above: *Bedford advance publicity van in 1962.*

Opposite page: *Chipperfield's on the Knavesmire in York in June 1975, photographed by Malcolm Slater.* **Top row:** *AEC Matador crane truck; the Matador with two seating trailers.* **2nd row:** *a Scammell tractor unit; Atkinson truck and trailer carrying some of the lions.* **3rd row:** *Albion CX22 tractor;.the trailer that formed part of the front.* **4th row:** *Bedford unit + articulated living wagon; Bedford generator truck.* **5th row:** *the Scammell artic; and Bedford horse and camel transporter (this photo taken in Bradford in May 1980).*

Above: *an ERF pulling the staff bunk wagons arrives in Wibsey Park, Bradford, in May 1980.*

Malcolm Slater (75 Broome Close, Huntington, York YO3 9RH) is a fairground and circus photographer with a range of Chipperfield exterior photos.

Alan Pepper (93 Vernon Drive, Stanmore, Middlesex HA7 2BW) is building a detailed list of FWDs and Macks used by circuses and fairs, including Chipperfield's Circus.

Appendix 3
The Build Up

Above: *Chipperfield's Circus building up in Keighley in 1963. Photo: Derrick Londrigan.*
Below: *building up at the Knavesmire, York, on 15 June 1975. Photos by Malcolm Slater.*

Above left: *the fork-lift lifts the king poles onto the A frames so they can be pulled into a vertical position.*
Above right: *the four king poles are erect, with the beast wagons for the wild animals behind.*

Left: *hammering in the stakes for the big top.* **Right:** *off-loading the sections of canvas.*

Left: *carrying out the quarter poles.* **Right:** *each canvas section is laced together and attached to the bale rings around the king poles.*

Left: *the seating trailers used at this time were designed and built by Dave Freeman and Marnie Dock. They were pulled into the big top and winched out to form a section of tiered seating.* **Right:** *pulling out the big top and putting the side poles in position.*

Left: *while the big top was built up, the stable tents for the elephants and horses were erected.* **Right:** *ready for opening, with the pictorial front and pay box in front of the big top.*

Appendix 4
Chipperfield Showfronts

Chipperfield's was unique among the "Big Three" touring circuses in the 1950s and early 1960s in having painted showfronts, a reminder of their time on the fairgrounds where such fronts are commonplace. Bertram Mills' and Billy Smart's circuses both had coloured canvas foyer tents bearing the show's name.

The fronts were painted by W.H. (Bill) Smee, who was the official "Scenic Artist" on the show until his retirement in 1965. He was brought up in Shirley, Southampton, and trained as a scenic painter before the Second World War, moving to London to work in theatres in the West End. After peace in 1945, Bill was approached by the Chipperfields to paint their showfronts and he left his wife, Gweneth, and their young family behind in Totton to go on tour. He also became Pee-Wee the clown, this being his school nickname, and he was on the receiving end of hundreds of eggs per season when Tommy Fossett, clown Grimble, was on the show.

Bill Smee retired from Chipperfield's Circus when they were in South Africa in 1965 but he continued to paint their fronts in the late 60s and 70s. The box fronts were also painted by him, each one with the head of an animal on the circus, and his last such assignment was for Sally Chipperfield's Circus in 1978.

Top: *the front for the Big Show in 1953.* **Above:** *Bill Smee.* **Right:** *Anne Chipperfield and the 1956 front showing Raluy's car and the Cowboy Carousel.*

Appendix 5
Carl Moore's Chipperfield model

Above: *Carl Moore displays his model at rallies and exhibitions. Contact number: 01203 373953.*

Below: *Chris Guest, Corgi Classics Managing Director, with Carl at the Corgi Biggest Little Show in Donington in 1995.*

Chipperfield's has been one of the most popular circuses for modellers to recreate and the most ambitious model is that of Carl Moore of Nuneaton, Warwickshire, whose display won the International Model Circus Championship six times from 1983 to 1991, before he withdrew it from competition, as well as many other trophies.

Carl's model of Chipperfield's in 1953 and 1954 contains the 20 pole big top, an audience of 1000 in 200 ringside seats and ten sections of tiered seating, 24 spotlights and 212 miniature lights within the big top, the authentic front illuminated by 64 running lights, artistes and animals, 150 pieces of fencing, and over 120 vehicles, including the Corgi range and others that Carl has adapted himself. These have been painted in Chipperfield colours and each vehicle has its correct number plate.

Adding movement are a dozen electronically controlled animated acts, including recreations of acts from Chipperfield's such as Arturos on his 70 foot swaying pole, Sally Chipperfield's performing dogs, the clowns' comedy car and the Antares revolving aeroplane act.

Postscript

Above: *elephant painting by Bill Smee in 1955 - from Dick Chipperfield's autograph book.*

I was born in Christchurch in 1949 and spent my childhood in Poole, on the south coast of England. In those television-free days, visits to outside entertainments such as the cinema, pantomime or summer shows were infrequent enough to be events. Even rarer but more exciting was the circus and I paid my first visits to two of the Big Three, Billy Smart's in 1956 and Bertram Mills in 1957, plus smaller shows including Lord George Sanger's, before my first encounter with Chipperfield's. Each of the Big Three was a massive touring show by today's standards and each had a strong and distinctive character. Bertram Mills, "The Quality Show," was immaculate and old fashioned, a circus that had appealed successfully to the upper classes and had held a pre-eminent position in British circus since the 1920s. Of its two rivals, Billy Smart's Circus, headed by the extrovert showman, "the Guv'nor," the ex-fairground operator from west London, was spectacular and influenced by Ringlings in America, and Chipperfield's Circus was more colourful and featured a greater array of animals, while being less polished and a bit rougher round the edges.

My first visit to Chipperfield's was to Kings Park, Bournemouth, at Easter 1959 when I was a ten year old schoolboy. I started the day with a minor flu bug but this had gone by the time we returned home, such was Chipperfield's magic. The posters in local shops whetted one's appetite with the long list of animals and human attractions and the sense of anticipation was enhanced further by the sight of the large white canvas big top surrounded by the transport, painted bright red with pale blue lettering and white walled tyres, gigantic ex-Army tractors, lorries, trailers, and caravans and showman's style living wagons. The collection of animals in the menagerie surpassed those in the other circuses for variety - lions, polar, black and brown bears, chimps, Harry the hippo in his tank, George and Georgina the two giraffes in their enclosure by the converted double decker bus that was their home, camels and llamas in another enclosure, long canvas stables for the big group of elephants and the row of horses and ponies, some of whom were in a paddock outside. For the show itself, we sat in the tiered seats near the bandstand and artistes' entrance, revelling in a privileged position of being able to see the comings and goings of the acts behind the curtains as well as the action in the ring.

My enthusiasm developed through more visits and joining the Circus Fans' Association of Great Britain, buying new and second-hand books and taking the World's Fair weekly newspaper for circus news. When Chipperfield's Circus returned from South Africa and started travelling in Britain again in 1969, I went along, helping here and there, taking photographs and gradually getting to know members of the family, which led in turn to spending holidays

Above: *clown sketches by Dame Laura Knight - from Dick Chipperfield's autograph book.*

and weekends on the show, watching numerous performances, and to long lasting friendships. During the past 28 years, my visiting has extended around Europe, to America, Australia and South Africa, and now includes many diverse forms of the circus, from Ringling's three ring show and the Swiss National Circus Knie to Roncalli, Krone and Barum in Germany, from the Gruss circuses in France to the Big Apple Circus of New York, from wonderful buildings like Blackpool Tower, the Great Yarmouth Hippodrome and the Cirque d'Hiver in Paris to Russian, Chinese and Mongolian shows, to contemporary mould-breaking circuses, often with no animals at all and sometimes even disturbing, such as the anarchic Archaos and the fantasy world of theatre-circuses like Cirque du Soleil and Plume. There have been many changes in the world of circus but Chipperfield's Circus remains representative of the big, traditional, animal-based show that has been so popular in Britain and on its international tours and the Chipperfield family holds an important position in world circus, both historically, because of its longevity and the importance of some of its productions, and today. From the 1970s, there have been other circus presentations by the family - including Sally Chipperfield's Circus, Jimmy Chipperfield's Circus World, Chipperfield Brothers' Circus and Mary Chipperfield's Circus - but this book concentrates on the original show and its history.

In developing this book, I am very grateful to members of the Chipperfield family who have provided memories, photographs and other material. Dicky and Janet Chipperfield and Jim Clubb have given me access to their archives and Anne Tunnicliffe, Mary and Roger Cawley and Jimmy Stockley have provided material which has been very valuable, as have Sally and Jamie Clubb, Rosie Chipperfield and her sister Grace, Carol Coates, Maryann Shapter, Graham Thomas Chipperfield, Richard Chipperfield, Bobby Thompson, Alex Bridgewater, Doris Chipperfield, Louisa Pelly, Billy, Sheila, Tom and Caron Chipperfield. Thanks to them all for their help and encouragement.

Several people have provided valuable photos and memories of their years with the show, including Wynne Shearme, Elaine Yelding, Doreen Duggan, Ivor Rosaire, Karl Kossmayer, Alfie Gunner, Sally Ann Roncescu and Yuri Gridneff.

The Circus Friends Association holds the most comprehensive archive of historic British circus material and it has generously allowed its Chipperfield posters and programmes and its scrap books of cuttings to be used in this book as well as photos from the late Jack Niblett and Denn Curtis. My thanks to the Council of the CFA and its Archivist, Malcolm Clay. Fellow CFA members Sandy Davidson and David Harris have been extremely helpful in regularly sending material and photographs and CFA Librarian John Turner provided an invaluable list of references from his extensive database. Thanks also to Eddie Campbell, Don Stacey, Alan Southwood, the late Eric Nugus, Hal Fisher, Ken Wise, Derrick Londrigan, Richard McMinn, the late Hal Thomas, John Thompson and John Exton for their memories, comments and photographs.

For almost the whole of this century, the World's Fair weekly newspaper has provided news of Britain's fairs and circuses and I am grateful to Phil Clegg, the current editor, for permission to quote from some of the past items on Chipperfield's enterprises. These include articles from correspondents under such *noms-de-plume* as Kingsley and Adagio as well as the two long serving circus editors, the late Edward Graves and Don Stacey. The World's Fair is available from newsagents or from 2 Daltry Street, Oldham, Lancs. OL1 4BB.

In writing the early chapters, I was helped considerably with material on James William Chipperfield and his family by one of his descendants, George Testo of Middlesbrough who provided a wealth of photos and historic information. My thanks to Nick Barnett for his Corgi material, to Carl Moore for that on his model, to Malcolm Slater for transport and exterior photographs, to Derek Simpson, editor of Circus published by the Circus Association of Ireland, to Graham Downie, editor of The Fairground Mercury published by the Fairground Association, to Ned Williams of Uralia Press, to Tony Hopkins who presented Chipperfield's Circus from 1991 to 1996, to Vanessa Toulmin and the National Fairground Archive at the University of Sheffield, to Alan Pepper, Peter Wells and Adrian Towner on transport matters, and to Chris Guest, Angus McLeod and Adrienne Fuller at Corgi Classics.

David Jamieson
April 1997

Below: *W. McColl's 1949 Dundee sketches from Dick Chipperfield's autograph book.*

Index

Index of a limited number of names only. The first page where each selected name is mentioned is given, followed by the pages for some mentions or photographs only.

Alcaraz, the 112
Arnold, Tom 47
Austen, Brian 140, 143
Austins, Alby and Len 49, 50
Austin, Mike 117

Bale, Elvin 134
Bale, Trevor 54
Ballan, Silvana - see Silvana Stockley
Ballans, the 120, 121
Banks, Stewart and Jill 107
Barber, Louis 45, 47
Barrett, Norman 39, 93
Barry, Joe 52
Barry's Circus 19
Belfast 53, 57
Belle Vue Circus, Manchester 37, 110, 119, 125
Biasinis, the 61, 92, 117, 128
Bingley Hall, Birmingham 84, 89, 91, 93, 96, 97, 98, 117, 119, 129, 132
Biros, the 129
Blackpool Tower Circus 75, 122
Blumenfeld, Rudi 49
Bouglione circuses 122
Bouglione, Emilien 120
Boswell, Brian 107, 109
Boswell, Jane (née Stockley) 102, 108, 109
Boswell, Stanley 101, 103
Brady, Captain 102
Brick, Hans 31, 83
Bridgewater, Alex 20
Bronnetts, the 34
Bruni (wrestling bear) 34
Buick, Wyn 114, 115
Busch-Roland, Circus 121
Butson, Clem 47

Cairoli, Charlie 120
Campbell, Eddie 64, 81

Carlos, Frank 31, 49
Carmo's Circus 19, 57
Cavanagh, Mickey 41
Cawley, Mary (née Chipperfield) 26, 45, 75, 121, 122,
Cawley, Roger 148
Chako 86
Chapman, G.B. 26, 37
Chipperfield, Anne - see Anne Tunnicliffe
Chipperfield, Billy (Weymouth branch) 20, 110
Chipperfield, Charles 129
Chipperfield, David 148, 149
Chipperfield, Dick (1904-1988) 20, 26, 36, 45, 62, 136
Chipperfield, Dicky (1943-) 36, 86, 101, 105, 107, 110, 111, 113, 124, 128
Chipperfield, Doris (née Morche) 61
Chipperfield, Graham Thomas 129, 138, 144
Chipperfield, Henry 20
Chipperfield, James (born 1775) 10
Chipperfield, James Henry 18
Chipperfield, James Seaton Methuen (Jimmy) (1912-1990) 20, 38, 68, 80, 94, 108, 117, 137
Chipperfield, James William (1803-1866) 10
Chipperfield, James William (1824-1913) 11
Chipperfield, James William Francis (born 1847) 11, 14
Chipperfield, Janet (née Thomas) 112
Chipperfield, Jim (Irish branch) 19
Chipperfield, Jimmy (Weymouth branch) 20, 110
Chipperfield, John (West Midlands branch) 20
Chipperfield, John (1921-1978) 20, 51, 95, 106, 125, 126
Chipperfield, John Jnr. 116, 127, 129

Chipperfield, Marjorie - see Marjorie Stockley
Chipperfield, Mary Ann 20, 14
Chipperfield, Mary - see Mary Cawley
Chipperfield, Maude - see Maude Fossett
Chipperfield, Myrtle (née Slee) 36, 101, 143
Chipperfield, Richard (1875-1959) 14, 20, 67, 91
Chipperfield, Richard 119, 144, 149
Chipperfield, Rosie (née Purchase) 24, 28, 45
Chipperfield, Sally - see Sally Clubb
Chipperfield, Sheila (née Duggan) 59, 60, 67
Chipperfield, Sophia Sarah 11
Chipperfield, Suzanne 148, 149
Chipperfield, Tommy 112, 125
Chipperfield, William 10
Chipperfield Brothers Circus' 129
Chipperfield's Circus to 1929: 10-22; 1930s; 1946-1952: 41-67; 1953-1955: 68-81; 1956-1964: 82-100; in South Africa: 101-109; 1969 to 1979: 110-127; 1980s: 128-139; 1990s: 140-143
Chipperfield's Circus World, Jimmy 127, 129
Chipperfield's Circus, Sally 125, 129
Chipperfield's Menagerie 15-17
Christie, Ian 45
Cimarros, the 99
Cirque d'Hiver-Bouglione 115, 122
Clubb, James 114, 115, 116, 121, 123, 125, 132
Clubb, Jamie 123
Clubb, Sally (née Chipperfield) 36, 83, 116, 121, 123, 125, 132
Coady, Harry 39, 45
Coan, Harriet Amy 10
Coates, Carol (née Stockley) 106, 116

187

Corgi Toys and Corgi Classics 93, 170-175
Cottle, Gerry 130, 143
Courtney's Circus, Ireland 123, 125
Coventry Zoo 21, 107, 110
Cutanos, the 72

Darnell, Evelyn 111
Darnell, John 111
Davidson, Sandy 64
Dock, Les 93
Dock, Marnie 181
Domis, the 74
Dorchesters, the 74
Dredge, William Lofty 71, 95
Dresslers, the 54, 62
Dublin 57
Duffy's Circus 63, 121, 138
Duggan, Doreen 52, 60, 84, 85, 94, 110, 113, 114, 121
Duggan, Elaine - see Elaine Yelding
Duggan, Maureen - see Maureen Waite
Duggan, Sally Ann - see Sally Ann Roncescu
Duggan, Sheila - see Sheila Chipperfield
Duggan, Terry 68, 73, 85, 138

Emney, Fred 89, 90
Enos, Phil 128

Featherstone, Peter 137, 139, 143
Feld, Kenneth 144
Fiery Jack 47, 65
Fischer, Carl Jnr. 116
Fitzroy, Olivia 44
Fossett, Bob 110
Fossett, Jacko 120
Fossett, Maude (née Chipperfield) (1909-1994) 20, 22, 29, 85, 142
Fossett, Shirley 85, 87
Fossett, Tom 29, 85, 87
Fossett, Tommy (clown Grimble) 85, 111, 143
Fossett's Circus, Sir Robert 57, 110
Fossett's Circus (Ireland) 82
Freda 94, 97, 98, 99
Freeman, Dave 121, 181

French, Les 132
Gebel, Mark Oliver 144
Gebel, Sigrid 144
Gebel-Williams, Gunther 97, 144
Gentleman Jack 106
Granby Halls, Leicester 91
Graves, Edward 101
Gray, Rex 115, 120
Great Yarmouth Hippodrome 106, 111
Grice, Arthur 94, 106
Gridneffs, the 38, 44
Gruss, Cirque Arlette 144, 149
Gruss, Cirque Christiane 144
Gunner, Alfie 88, 105, 109

Harringay circuses 47, 52, 53, 57, 78
Hayes, Wynne - see Wynne Shearme
Hediger, Dr Heini 118
Hinde, John 54
Hong Kong 130, 134
Hopkins, Tony 140
Howes, Gordon 117, 121, 123, 125
Howes, Sidney 32, 84
Hubert 85, 105
Hudd, Roy 120
Hughes, Tony 144
Hylton, Jack 67

Indonesia 133, 136

Jacobi-Althoff, Circus 121
Japan 135
Jay, Peter 115
Jones, Elizabeth (1823-1856) 11
Jonsson, Harder 54, 67, 72

Katharyna 96
Keith, Charles 11
Kelvin Hall, Glasgow 39, 52
Kiley-Worthington, Dr Marthe 138
Knie, Circus 78, 118, 119
Knie, Frédy 78
Konyot, David 119
Korea, South 136
Kossmayer, Karl 48
Kossmayer, Wenzel 47, 48, 83
Kovar, Harry 31
Kuhne, Serge or Ernesto 57, 58

Larenty, Brenda 116
Larrigan, Marion 84
Liverpool Stadium 126
Living Skelton 12-13
Londrigan, Derrick 66
Lunas, Menyus 111

MacManus, Clara 111
MacManus, Evelyn - see Evelyn Darnell
MacManus, Ken 111
Merchant, Little Billy 49, 50, 120
Merk, Clem 38
Mills' Circus, Bertram 36, 57, 66, 75, 91, 93, 101, 106, 107
Mohawks, the 111, 120
Moore, Carl 183
Morche, Doris - see Doris Chipperfield
Miaz, Captain 57

New Zealand 136
Nutkins, Harry 49

O'Boyle, Vincent 102
Ohstianis, the 61

Pastry, Mr (Richard Hearne) 85, 97
Paulo, Clara - see Clara MacManus
Paulo, Harry 38
Pauwels, the 121
Peters, Marcel 110
Philippines, the 133, 136
Picture Post 44, 66
Poole's Caucasian Circus 39
Purcell, Frank 76
Purchase, Andrew 24
Purchase, Tommy 25, 26
Purchase's Menagerie 23
Purchase, Rosie - see Rosie Chipperfield

Rainbow Theatre 115
Raluy 60, 61, 83
Rancy, Cirque Sabine 110, 111
Reco (Herbert Wroe) 38
Ricardo Bros. Circus 30
Ringling Brothers and Barnum & Bailey Circus 97, 113, 144
Robert Brothers' Circus 72, 84, 110, 132, 140

Roncescu, Sally Ann (née Duggan) 116, 142
Rosaire, Carlos 92, 94
Rosaire, Carmen 92
Rosaire, Dennis 92
Rosaire, Ivor 52, 79, 80, 97
Rosaire, Joan 111
Royal Italian Circus 19
Royal Society for the Prevention of Cruelty to Animals 138

Sandow, Dick 39
Sandow, Dick Jnr. 85
Sandow, Peter 111, 143
Sanger, William 11
Saunders, Don 106
Scott, Circus 34
Shapter, Maryann 109
Shearme, Wynne (née Hayes) 48, 50, 56, 59
Shuster, Harry 101
Singapore 133, 134
Slee, Myrtle - see Myrtle Chipperfield
Sloan, Jackie 50, 54, 61
Smart's Circus, Billy 37, 80, 101, 110, 125, 143
Smee, Bill 85, 113, 182
Smith, Jack 86
Stacey, Don 71, 110
Steibner, Werner 112, 113, 115, 118
Stockley, Carol - see Carol Coates
Stockley, Jane - see Jane Boswell
Stockley, Jimmy (1914-1973) 39, 40, 88, 118
Stockley, Jimmy Jnr. 104, 106, 122
Stockley, Marjorie (née Chipperfield) (1916-1975) 20, 29, 39
Stockley, Maryann - see Maryann Shapter
Stockley, Silvana (née Ballan) 121, 122

Taiwan 134
Thailand 134
Thames Television 117, 119, 120, 121, 124
Thomas, Dave 121
Thomas, Hal 31

Thomas, Janet - see Janet Chipperfield
Thompson, Bobby 20, 42, 46, 82, 101
Tiller, Ambrose 53
Tipney, Robert - see Living Skeleton
Testo family 14
Togni, Circo Enis 117
Trufelli, Frank 19
Tunnicliffe, Anne (née Chipperfield) 36, 109, 127
Tunnicliffe, Mike 115

Waite, Cyril 76, 88
Waite, Maureen (née Duggan) 60, 63, 79
Weidmann, Eugen 77
Weight, Charles 132
Wesley, Harry 14
Wilkie, W.H. 57, 101
Williams, Circus 110
Williams, Harry 57
Williams, Jackie 73
Williams, J.H. 45, 69
Wise, Ken 31

Yelding, Elaine (née Duggan) 59, 60, 61, 74

If you're a circus enthusiast, join the Circus Friends Association! You and your family can get to know more about this amazing British entertainment which holds a unique place in our culture.

- Members receive the colourful magazine, **King Pole**, full of circus articles, news and photos, four times a year (March, June, September and December).
- The CFA operates the Circusline information service. By making a phone call, members can find out where they can see circus performances.
- A school information pack is available for topic work.
- The CFA Circus Awards are presented as a result of voting by CFA members who see a huge number of performances each year.
- Circus programmes, posters, books, models and other items are available through CFA Merchandising.
- There's a mammoth library of circus books to borrow and archives of circus memorabilia for British historical research.
- There are special rallies to circuses where you can meet the artistes and other members for a get-together after the show, and regular sales of circus memorabilia.
- CFA members can purchase the ACP/CFA Privilege Card, allowing them free admission to circuses which are members of the Association of Circus Proprietors.

For an application form and current subscription rates, send a stamped, self-addressed envelope to: The Membership Secretary, 20 Foot Wood Crescent, Shawclough, Rochdale, Lancs., OL 12 6PB, Great Britain.

CIRCUS BOOKS, PROGRAMMES & MODELS

The Merchandising Department of the Circus Friends Association of Great Britain has a range of circus items, usually including programmes, posters, postcards, models, books, badges, ties, the book **Introducing the Circus**, and issues of **King Pole**, the colourful circus magazine published by the CFA.

For a copy of the current list of items, please send a stamped, self-addressed envelope to: CFA Merchandising, 31 Crown Avenue, Pitsea, Basildon, Essex SS13 2BE, Great Britain.

ALSO AVAILABLE FROM
AARDVARK PUBLISHING

ANIMALS IN CIRCUSES & ZOOS: Chiron's World?
By Dr Marthe Kiley-Worthington. The fascinating book of the only major scientific study of animals in circuses - training, handling, husbandry, travel, veterinary care, physical and mental health - by one of the world's foremost animal behaviour experts.
Fully illustrated. Little Eco-Farms Publishing. ISBN 1 872904 02 5

THE GOLDEN AGE OF THE CIRCUS
By Howard Loxton. Circus consultant: David Jamieson. A circus history of 112 pages, profusely illustrated with a wealth of colour photos and historic posters.
ISBN 1 84013 020 2

BRITISH CIRCUS POSTERS 1930-1960
A Pictorial Celebration of Circus Artwork and Design. Over 160 posters and other items, over 80 in colour. Compiled by John Exton and Malcolm Clay for the Circus Friends Association.
ISBN 1 872904 08 4

MARY CHIPPERFIELD'S CIRCUS BOOK - 2nd Edition
By David Jamieson. With over 70 new photographs in colour and black and white.

NORMAN BARRETT - RINGMASTER - My Life in Showbusiness
As told to Geoff Stevens. The story of Britain's best known circus personality, covering his life with the family show, with Robert Brothers, Bertram Mills, the Circus World Championships, Belle Vue Manchester, and for over 25 years at Blackpool Tower Circus and at Peter Jay's Superdome Circus at Blackpool Pleasure Beach.
"The warmth of his personality, his love for circus and his love of people leap from the pages." Don Stacey, *World's Fair*.
192pp A4. Fully illustrated with over 100 photos. ISBN 1 872904 05 X

INTRODUCING THE CIRCUS - 2nd Edition
By David Jamieson. 24pp A4. Colour and black and white photos. ISBN 1 872904 01 7

CIRCUS POSTERS. Set of 8 A6 colour poster cards. Chipperfield, Billy Smart, Belle Vue, Sir Robert Fossett, Rosaire, Bertram Mills.

CLUBB-CHIPPERFIELD ANIMAL ACTS. Set of 6 A6 colour photo cards: lions with John Campolongo; mixed group with David and Tina Lowrie; mixed bears with John Illig; tigers with Louis Knie; mixed panthers with Emile Smith; Samoyed dogs with Miss Alexia.

For an order form, send an stamped, addressed envelope
or an international reply coupon to
Aardvark Publishing, Fir Tree Cottage, Little Hormead,
Buntingford, Herts. SG9 0LU, England.